Old Friends

BOOKS BY TRACY KIDDER

The Road to Yuba City

The Soul of a New Machine

House

Among Schoolchildren

Old Friends

OLD FRIENDS

Tracy Kidder

A Richard Todd Book

HOUGHTON MIFFLIN COMPANY

BOSTON · NEW YORK

1993

For information about permission to reproduce
selections from this book, write to Permissions,
Houghton Mifflin Company, 215 Park Avenue South,
New York, New York 10003

Library of Congress Cataloging-in-Publication Data
Kidder, Tracy
Old Friends / Tracy Kidder.
p.   cm.
"A Richard Todd book."
ISBN 0-395-59303-4
1. Aged — United States — Case studies.   2. Aged —
United States — Psychology — Case studies.   3. Nursing
homes — United States — Case studies.   I. Title
HQ 1064.U5K475   1993   93-22859
305.26´0973 — dc20   CIP

Printed in the United States of America

Book design by Robert Overholtzer

BP 10 9 8 7 6 5 4 3 2 1

AUTHOR'S NOTE

This is a work of nonfiction. I have changed some
names. The following are pseudonyms: Clara,
Dan, Fleur, Martha, and Norman.

 Printed on recycled paper

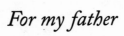
For my father

There is an ancient proverb:
Don't judge a life good or bad before it ends.

— SOPHOCLES, *Women of Trachis*

The Last Place

☙☙

I NSIDE LINDA MANOR, upstairs on Forest View, the lights in the corridors brighten. The living room windows begin to reflect the lights on the plastic Christmas tree, and the view through those windows is fading, the woods growing thicker, the birches glowing in the dusk. At the west end of Forest View's longer corridor, a white-haired woman in a plain housedress and sneakers leans against the heating register, a cane in her hands, and she gazes out at clouds. She is very forgetful and yet very nostalgic and, of all the people who live here, the most devoted to windows. "They come and go," she says of the clouds. "I guess that's to be expected. First they're dark and then they're light. First they're there and then they're gone." She makes a small laugh. She goes on gazing through the glass. "I don't know what all this business is about, living this way. I tried to figure it out, but I can't." The clouds hovering above the silhouette of the far ridge are sharply etched, clouds of the north wind, dark gray in the last light of a sky that is still too bright for stars.

The light seeps away. The windows at the ends of Forest View's corridors throw back watery images of carpeted corridors that could belong to a clean motel. It is night. Lou Freed comes out of his room, down on the north hall just past the elevators. Lou is small and plump in the middle, with fleecy white hair and thick, dark-framed glasses. Behind the lens, the lid of his left eye droops. His close-cropped mustache is a dash of white across his face. His forehead and cheeks are deeply furrowed. Lou wears a look of concentration as he comes out into the hall. He holds a cane in his right hand. Its black shaft is striped like a barber pole with yellowish tape. Lou applied the tape several years ago when his eyes began to fail and he couldn't cross a street very quickly anymore. He used to hold the cane aloft as he crossed, hoping it would catch the attention of drivers. He no longer has to worry about crossing streets, but he's left the tape in place since coming here, on the theory that it will help him to spot his cane if he should misplace it. He never does misplace it.

As he walks, Lou leans on his cane, but not heavily. Now and then he extends it forward, searching for possible obstructions. Lou walks with his legs spread well apart, his left arm swinging free and a little away from his torso while his right arm works the cane. He crosses the corridor perpendicularly and then turns south, following the carpet's border, traveling in a slow, sturdy gait, like an old sailor crossing a rolling deck, passing along a wall equipped with an oak handrail and adorned with cream-colored wallpaper and rose-colored moldings, passing several numbered bedroom doors of blond oak veneer and framed prints of flowers and puppies and English hunting scenes.

The nurses' station, enclosed with a Formica counter, is brightly lit as always. Lou stops at the corner of the station. He shifts his cane to his left hand and slides his right hand up the wall until it touches the edge of a four-gang light switch. His fingers are nimble. They move with a confident inquisitiveness, but they fumble slightly over the plate of the light switch. This isn't the switch that Lou wants. He finds the one he wants by finding this one first. His hand pauses here tonight, however. The plastic plate surrounding these four switches feels warm. In Lou's experience, this sometimes signifies a circuit overload. Nothing serious, but he'll have to remember to tell Bruce, the director of maintenance, tomorrow.

Lou's hand moves on across the wall, fingers fumbling again until they strike a two-gang switch. Then with a flick of the forefinger, joyous in its certainty, Lou throws both switches up, and in all the bedrooms of Forest View the night lights come on.

Night lights are important. They might save other residents from falling on the way to their bathrooms in the middle of the night. They might save Lou from such a fate. April, one of the aides, has forgotten to turn them on. Or else she's been too busy. When that happens, Lou does the job. He doesn't mind. It is a job.

"Hi, Lou." A nurse, a young woman in slacks — the nurses here don't wear uniforms — stands nearby, behind the medication cart, studying her records.

"Hi," Lou says. "Who's that?"

"Eileen," she says, adding, "Lou, did you get your iron to-day?"

Lou lifts his right arm and makes as if to flex his biceps. His arms are thin. The flesh sags from them. But some muscle rises. "Pretty soon I'll be sweating rust." Lou has a soft, gravelly voice.

The nurse chuckles. Lou smiles. Then he shifts his cane to his right hand, his face grows serious again, and he starts slowly back down the carpeted hallway toward his room. As Lou nears the doorway, he hears the sound of screeching tires. He enters to the sound of gunfire.

Within, the lights are out and the curtains drawn. Lou's roommate, Joe Torchio, lies on his back on the bed nearer the door, a bald-headed, round-faced, round-bellied man. In the changeable glow of his TV, Joe looks beached and bristly. Lou feels his way past Joe to the other side of the room, and in a while he begins to get ready for bed. The charge nurse knocks. Joe flicks his remote control at the TV, leaving it lit but mute, and the nurse enters, carrying pills.

Back in his eighties, Lou knew all the names and functions of his medicines. Now he takes too many to remember, though he still makes inquiries about new ones now and then. Joe has said he doesn't know what pills the nurses give him and he doesn't care. "If they want to kill me, go ahead," Joe likes to say, and Lou replies, "Joe, don't talk that way." But Lou says he isn't worried either, because the pills he takes all have arrows on them, to tell them where to go once they get inside. The nurse laughs: Lou and Joe may take a lot of pills, but they are among the most physically healthy of Linda Manor's residents.

Joe turns his head on his pillow and looks at Lou, who has climbed into his bed and under the covers. "We're the best!" Joe exclaims.

"God help the others if we're the best," Lou says. "Anyway, I can't read."

"I could read if I could see."

"I have half a brain, and you can't see," Joe says.

"And so betwixt us both, we licked the platter clean," Lou says. He smiles, the covers pulled up to his chin, and he sighs. "Ahh, dear. It's a great life, if you don't weaken."

Joe aims his remote control at the TV. The sounds of a car chase resume, and Lou drifts off to sleep.

At eleven, the night shift takes over on Forest View. They turn out the hallway lights, leaving the corridors in the glow of the cherry-colored exit signs, a red that grows increasingly lurid as the night wears on. The charge nurse and her two aides sit in the pool of light at the nurses' station over endless paperwork. The lights on the Christmas tree blink on and off in the living room across the way. Christmas carols play softly on the staff's communal tape recorder. It is the season of long New England nights, the year's midnight.

On Forest View, morning begins long before dawn. Around five o'clock, a voice comes out of the darkened west corridor. "Howdee! Howdee! Howdee! Hello to you, hello!" the voice sings.

A thin man on a cane limps out of the shadows. The man has wings of gray-white hair on either side of his bald dome and a gray mustache.

"Hi, Bob," says the night nurse. She looks up from her paperwork and smiles at him.

"Excellent!" Bob says to the nurse. Then he says, "Adios, amigo," and, cane in his left hand, his right arm held tight to his side, he limps on, with a purposefulness that makes his progress seem rapid, up to the living room doorway. Deftly, Bob lets his cane handle slip deep into his palm and snaps on the living room lights with his fingers. He surveys the room, twisting his mouth critically. Then he lays down his cane on the seat of an armchair and starts moving furniture around, pulling chairs here and there — one-handed and hobbling. Bob is a victim of left-brain stroke. He is seventy. "There," Bob says when he's assembled a semicircle of armchairs near the living room door. He sits down to wait, keeping an eye on the door.

Gradually the chairs around Bob begin to fill. First comes Clara, in slacks, orange sweater, and high heels, carrying a gigantic pocketbook. Without asking or being asked, she bends down and ties Bob's shoes, Bob saying, "Excellent! Beautiful! Thank you kindly." Then Eleanor comes in out of the shadowy corridor. She wears a red flannel floor-length robe and pink slippers. Her short, curled gray hair looks as neat as if she'd just come from the beauty shop downstairs. Her makeup is already in place. Eleanor enters in quick, dainty steps, with slight unsteadiness and yet with erectness of shoulders and chin. Eleanor is eighty. One can imagine her in younger days sweeping into a grander room and turning some heads, not so much with her looks as with sheer force of will. She sits down in a tall-backed upholstered wing chair, looks at Bob, and says, "So."

"For the birds," Bob says. He looks at Eleanor. "I wish I could talk now."

"You've said enough," Eleanor says. "What would you say if you *could* talk?"

"Forget it," Bob says. "For-get it."

Then Art appears in the doorway, a short, broad-chested man of eighty-four with a fine head of white hair and sad-looking watery eyes. Art has the Parkinson's shuffle. He walks as if wading through water up to his waist. But his voice is cheerful. It is also deep and sonorous. "Good morning, Mrs. Zip Zip Zip," Art says to Eleanor. She beams up at Art. Only Eleanor knows the song to which Art is alluding. He sang it for her not long ago. It dates back to World War I:

Good morning, Mr. Zip Zip Zip
With your hair cut just as short as mine
With your hair cut just as short as mine.
You're surely looking fine.
From ashes to ashes, dust to dust
If the camels don't get us, the fatimas must.
Good morning, Mr. Zip Zip Zip
With your hair cut just as short as
With your hair cut just as short as
With your hair cut just as short as mine.

"Excellent," Bob says, looking up at Art.

"We've got to change that word, don't we," Art says to Eleanor.

"What shall we have?" Eleanor asks. " 'Incredible'?"

Bob's eyes dart from Art to Eleanor. "Incredible!" Bob declares. He grins.

"That's pretty good," Art says.

"For a change," Eleanor says.

Bob jabs his index finger in Art's direction, then at the fourth armchair in the circle. Art sits down, and the circle by the door of the living room is complete. With shaky hands, Art pulls his electric razor from its case and begins to shave. First he asks Eleanor, "This won't disturb you too much now, will it?" To which Eleanor waves a deprecating hand. "No!"

Art's wife died here a couple of months ago. He has only recently begun to fraternize with other residents. To her select group of confidantes, made up mostly of nurses and aides — she refers to most other residents as "them" — Eleanor has begun to speak of Art as if he were her personal discovery. "A *bon vivant*," she'll say, pointing out the many coincidences of their lives. That they both got married around the same time and had their first children the same year, that her husband, too, was named Art, and that both she and this Art knew a passion for performance, Art through his singing and she through the theater. Eleanor's father was a flamboyant, itinerant producer of minstrel shows late in the last century and early in this one. Eleanor acted all her life in amateur and semiprofessional theatricals. Some months ago she assembled a theater group, the Linda Manor Players. Eleanor is the director. She has a production coming up.

Art packs his razor away in its leather case. Clara watches. Bob helps. "This takes two people," Art says to Eleanor. Art's hands shake, and Bob can use only his left. "There," says Bob at last. Art pulls a cracker out of his shirt pocket and hands it to Bob. Art laughs, Eleanor laughs, Bob laughs as he bites into the cracker, and Clara looks confused and starts laughing just as the others are finishing. It is a two-way conversation after that, in the small circle of armchairs, Clara listening quietly and Bob listening with agitation, his eyes jumping back and forth between Art and Eleanor.

"So," Eleanor says to Art. "How's your new medication working?"

"Not working," Art says. "I get tired very easily in my legs."

Eleanor tries a different subject. "How early did you start singing?"

"I was a boy soprano," Art says. "I could hit a high C like nobody's business. Then the change hit. Around twelve or thirteen. I became a baritone." Art smiles. The expression looks brave beneath his sad-looking eyes.

"I had a lot of fun, though," Art goes on. "In light operas. I sang at a numerous amount of weddings. And funerals." Abruptly his voice gets very soft. "I won't say any more. People would say I was bragging."

"Well," Eleanor says, "I'm going to listen to the weather report. It's almost six, isn't it?"

Bob looks at his wristwatch. "Oh boy." He gets up and limps fast out the door. It is time to turn on the corridor lights. Bob does that every morning. Then he returns to his seat in the living room. Eleanor, meanwhile, goes back to her room. She takes the diuretic Lasix for her heart when she first gets up, and it takes effect around six. But the weather report is not entirely a ladylike ruse. When she returns to the living room a few minutes later, with little steps — in her hybrid gait of daintiness, frailty, and vigor — Eleanor announces to the others, "All right. It is twenty-six degrees. It is going to snow in the Berkshires. It is going to sleet tonight. Tomorrow's going to be cloudy and cold."

Art and Eleanor resume their chat, turning to the subject of breakfast. "We never have donuts here," Eleanor says.

"I've been here since April and not once," Art agrees.

"Coffee cake twice," Eleanor says.

Bob speaks up vehemently. "Lousy! Lousy!"

"Louie gets the English muffin," Art says.

"Louie gets bagels," says Eleanor.

"Louie! Damn right!" Bob cries. He thrusts his left arm out, like a boxer jabbing, in obvious approval of Lou Freed and his breakfast.

They begin to discuss the behavior of other residents at meals. "Phil causes trouble," Eleanor says.

"That sonofabitch!" says Bob.

"And there's Dan," Art says.

"Oh, he can talk," Eleanor says.

"Nonstop," Art says. "But Winnie the Pooh, she can go from one topic to another. Boy, she can do that smoother than anybody I ever heard. I remember the first time I met her. I kept thinking, 'I'll get out of here sometime. There's got to be a break somewhere.' First chance, I got out of there. 'Twas rude. But I had to. If I hadn't, I'd still be there, I guess."

Eleanor smiles. Bob smiles, darting looks toward the doorway behind him. Out there, around the nurses' station, the night nurse and the aides hurry to and fro. Many call bells are beeping. The bustling in the corridors makes the living room seem cozier, like a cabin in a storm.

The first gray light has just appeared in the living room windows, black mirrors a moment ago, now opening on the view of the woods to the south. Art has announced the dawn, saying, in an ironic tone, "Darkness shall not prevail." And the four coffee klatchers have begun laughing again — including Clara, who has developed an ensuing case of the giggles, which has reignited the others' laughs — when the imposing figure of Phil rolls up in a wheelchair into the doorway. Phil has a huge head and huge ears, the head of an old lion. He wears the same institutional-green cardigan sweater as always. His silver hair is slicked back. His lower front teeth are missing; the effect is more disturbing than if he had no teeth at all. He looks dangerously irascible, but his hands are soft looking, white, and small, and his trousers bunch up at the waist, a common sight here, signifying diapers beneath.

The four have stopped laughing. Phil rolls himself in his wheelchair through the coffee klatch. The others move their feet out of the way. Phil rolls up to the center of the room and the table piled with magazines. Eleanor studies Phil and makes a face. "Now he'll complain about how old the magazines are," she murmurs.

Phil is, as it happens, lifting a copy of *Time,* wearing a dour expression. "October 1990. That's good. That's only two months old." He starts paging through it. "Old George, he's got troubles over there in Kuwait."

The four coffee klatchers resume their chat, ignoring Phil. But then Eleanor mentions the Forest View resident who broke her hip a few days ago and has not returned from the hospital. And Phil, still sitting in front of the table, joins their conversation. He says, "That's the thing. First they have the walker. Then they have one of these." Phil looks down at the arms of his wheelchair and pats them with his small white hands. "Then they go to the hospital. And that's the end of that."

Art turns around in his chair. "Look at you," he says to Phil. "You fell down the other day and nothing happened to you."

Phil seems not to hear this. He picks up another magazine, cocking his great, leonine head. "Yeah," he says. "Leonard

Bernstein, he died. Only seventy-one. I used to love to watch him jump around the podium. He was Koussevitzky's pet."

"Koussevitzky," repeats Art, without turning to look at Phil. Art seems deep in thought.

"I was surprised Forbes died so fast," Phil goes on, musingly, pleasantly. "Another actress died. She was really famous. I can't remember her name."

Eleanor now speaks up. "Well *I* saw Helen Hayes on TV the other day. She looked *wonderful*." Eleanor's voice quivers over the last word.

"She's somethin' else," Phil agrees. Then he adds, "She lost her daughter, lost her husband."

"Jessica Tandy is ninety," says Eleanor. "She's still going strong!"

For a moment no one speaks. Then Phil says, "Sergio Franchi, he's dead. He was only in his fifties, for cryin' out loud."

Eleanor makes a face. Art says over his shoulder to Phil, "He died three or four years ago, didn't he?" Art's voice insinuates the question, Why bring that up now?

"Yeah, I was surprised at that," says Phil, ignoring Art's tone. "Sergio Franchi. He had *some* voice. His sister was a singer. Country and western."

"She was?" Eleanor says, brightening up. "I didn't know that."

"Yeah," Phil says. "Then they got those two girls, a mother and daughter who sing country music. The mother's s'posed to be dyin' of cancer."

"This goes on like Tennyson's brook," murmurs Eleanor, but silence descends on the room. Bob, who is Phil's roommate, has not uttered a word since Phil's entrance, but has glared at Phil from time to time, making a chewing motion. Now Bob stands up, says, "Bye-bye," and limps out. Each of the remaining coffee klatchers gazes a separate way. They seem lost in a collective case of the long thoughts, distant memories at hand, and none of them happy. Phil stares at his lap, but he alone does not look sad. "I never saw Al Jolson in person," he says.

"The nearest I got to him was in the movies," says Art in a distant voice.

"Yeah, he went overseas in the Second World War and got sick," says Phil. "And that was the end of that."

This is not exactly an argument, but more like a contest. Given the subject, Phil is bound to win.

2

It seemed so new a place for people so old. Linda Manor had opened for business only a little more than a year ago. It stood in what had been a hay field, in a suburban-bucolic setting, on Route 9 a few miles west of downtown Northampton, Massachusetts. The developer named Linda Manor after one of his daughters. The building had balconies and balcony railings along its flat roofs and wide frieze boards under its eaves. Out front there was a portico, supported on four Doric columns, and two tall flagpoles, also a little fountain, like a child's wading pool. And everything, except for the brick walls, was painted white. The building looked not quite finished, like the parts of a giant wedding cake laid side to side.

The obligation of finding a nursing home for a sick, aged person usually falls to a daughter. On any given day in the region, a middle-aged woman would be looking around for an acceptable establishment. There were a few. But there were also places where the stench of urine got in one's clothes like tobacco smoke, where four, sometimes five, elderly people lay jammed in tiny rooms, where residents sat tied to wheelchairs and strapped to beds, where residents weren't allowed to bring with them any furniture of their own or to have private phones or to use the public pay phone without nurses listening in. One woman, on a recent tour of a nearby place, had been shown a room with a dead resident in it. Some nursing homes looked fancy and well kept but were all veneer. When Linda Manor's portico hove into view, it looked like one of those.

Large windows surrounded Linda Manor's lobby. Thick carpeting covered the floor. A huge brass chandelier had been hung from a coffered ceiling above a baby grand piano with a gleaming, black lacquered finish. Linda Manor's owner wished that residents were banned from his lobby. That wasn't an extraordinary practice at nursing homes. But the administrator refused. (She worked for the huge nonprofit medical corporation that leased Linda Manor, and she had full authority over the running of the place.)

What most people take for granted is unusual in nursing homes. Linda Manor had some unusually pleasant qualities. The staff wasn't the largest per resident in the area, but large by the prevailing standards and far larger than the state required. Every room in the building got natural light. There was a small greenhouse. Residents were allowed to bring their own furnishings and to have their own telephones. Most rooms contained two beds. A few were singles. And none of the residents was tied up. This policy of "no restraints" was rare in the world of nursing homes. The local newspaper carried a long story about it when Linda Manor first opened. The publicity helped to make the policy work. A good reputation meant lots of applications for beds. The management could afford to turn away the very violent and most floridly demented.

Some residents were brought from great distances, from places like Florida and California, to be near their families. Most came from western Massachusetts, and collectively they made up a fairly accurate cross section of the area's old people. A few were wealthy. About 30 percent paid the high private rate. Medicaid and Medicare paid the room and board for most. Some owned nothing when they arrived. One man did not even own a change of clothes; several of the staff rummaged through their husbands' closets and outfitted him.

Periodically, wheelchair vans or ambulances or private cars parked in front of the portico and new residents were escorted in, a few on their own feet, others in wheelchairs, some on gurneys. New residents arrived from hospitals mainly, and occasionally from other nursing homes. Some arrived directly from their own or their children's homes, and for them the transition tended to be hardest. Some newcomers left their relatives' cars only after coaxing. And, on the other hand, a few residents would say that they felt sad but relieved when they arrived. The eighty-five-year-old woman, for instance, who had lived alone in a two-story house, crawling up and down the stairs, bathing herself with talcum powder for fear of the tub, subsisting mostly on tea and toast.

A few people died within days of arriving — one on her very first day — and it was hard to resist a Victorian explanation, that they died of broken hearts. More often, though, the physical health of new residents stabilized or even improved, in some cases because they had received marginal care and feeding before. Some residents merely stopped here, to rest and receive a few months of therapy, on the way home from the hospital. One well-traveled, well-read woman declared, soon after arriving, that she never played bingo in her life and did not intend to start now. She stayed at Linda Manor for a year, read most of Proust, and then returned home. But hers was an exceptional case.

By this time, December 1990, Linda Manor was running at capacity — 121 beds, all full. Most of the residents were over 70 years old. The oldest had reached her 103rd year in remarkably good health. About two thirds were women, a figure in line with national actuarial figures. It went without saying that everyone had an illness. Most had several.

The building was organized, generally, by illness. The upstairs wing, Forest View, was home to the physically healthier residents, so-called Level III's. Among them were Lou and Joe and the nostalgic woman who often stood at the western windows and Eleanor and Phil and the other coffee klatchers and a man named Dan. He was only sixty-five, one of the youngest residents, but gaunt and pale. Most hours of the day found Dan lying on his bed upstairs, dressed in street clothes and wearing a thin, blue nose catheter, which was attached to an oxygen concentrator burbling next to his bed. Dan had a huge television set at the foot of his bed and a powerful, programmable speaker phone beside him, a phone fit for a fair-sized office. He had only to lean a little out from his pillow and punch a button, and all by itself his phone would dial up the office of the junior senator from Massachusetts. Lately, Dan had been calling that office regularly, to find out if any action had been taken on his complaint about his breakfast eggs, which the Linda Manor kitchen wouldn't prepare the way he liked them — runny. The kitchen said they couldn't oblige him because of the risk of salmonella, but Dan suspected they were just being contrary. The last time he called the senator's office, a voice over his speaker phone informed him that a letter on the matter of his eggs would soon be in the mail.

About half of Forest View's residents were able-minded. The management had mingled among them most of the residents who were demented but mobile and restless. Living upstairs made it harder for those people to find their way outside, where they might vanish in the woods or get hit by cars. There was a former inner-city schoolteacher who would sometimes rush down the corridors of Forest View, muttering threats to call the police if the children wouldn't behave, and a woman whom Phil had nicknamed Lady Godiva, because one night she ran nude and screeching through the halls, fleeing the aide who was trying to bathe her. That woman usually didn't run, but walked very gingerly upon the colorful, elaborately patterned carpet. In a place of damaged minds, a carpet full of complex shapes was a mistake. She balanced on the rectangular borders as if on the narrow ledges of a skyscraper under construction. Evidently, she saw an abyss in the carpet's deep blue background.

When the demented roamed the halls, Forest View could seem like an underworld of myth. There was Fleur, a tiny, spry ninety-two-year-old, her face quilted with wrinkles, who a dozen times a day would stand at the nurses' station counter and ask if someone wouldn't please call her mother. Clutching her pocketbook, Fleur would say that even though she liked this resort and her family had been coming here for years, it was time for her to go home now. There was Norman, who walked the hallways slowly, sometimes looking for an exit, sometimes looking for his wife. (When he mistook certain fellow residents for her, they got upset and yelled at him.) Zita was always out in the halls. Unperturbed by any of the sights and voices around her, moving at a steady pace, sometimes holding her hands cupped before her as if to receive a communion wafer, leaning slightly forward, her short gray hair swept back, her eyes half hooded, Zita paced the halls of Forest View from the time she arose until she went to bed. Sometimes she paused and, bending down, scratched at the flowers depicted in the carpet, trying to pick one.

Two thirds of Linda Manor's residents lived downstairs, on the nursing units called Meadowview and Sunrise. These units were, by and large, reserved for the very ill and the immobile, the so-called Level II's. Some never left their beds, and many didn't mix much, but some were gregarious, and none more than Winifred. She lived in a room just past the open fire doors of Sunrise. She endured great discomfort daily for the sake of sociability. In the morning she would lie in bed and stare unhappily toward her door as the Hoyer Lift, a contraption that looked like a miniature gallows on wheels, rolled toward her across the room, a nurse's aide pushing, another following.

Winifred wasn't tall, only five foot four the last time she was vertical. But she was big. She weighed over 200 pounds. Winifred was in her eighties. In her youth she had been one of the prettiest girls in Florence, Massachusetts.

The aides would truss her up in a black mesh sling and crank her out of bed. As she rose on the Hoyer Lift, Winifred groaned. She sobbed. "Oh, it bends and it breaks and it pinches." She wore a shocked and fearful look as she was rolled, dangling in midair, toward the bathroom. Eventually, the aides lowered her into her recliner. She'd sit there until it was time for her to be Hoyered into her wheelchair, so that she could sally forth to church services or resident meetings or any other local event — she went to all. After the aides wheeled the Hoyer out, Winifred sat weeping into her hands.

An epidemic of injured backs threatened to decimate Linda Manor's staff. A while ago, to prevent more injuries, the administration had ordered that Winifred and several others be lifted mechanically. It took its toll on her. Winifred had grown increasingly volatile, cheerful at one moment, weepy the next. Sometimes lately she shrieked at the nursing staff for small and imagined offenses. Behind all that lay her conviction that they had wronged her with the Hoyer Lift. To her, the hoisting signified defeat. She surmounted polio as a child and later a terrible car wreck, and she would not let herself think that she wouldn't walk again. But how could she, she'd cry, if they used the Hoyer? If they went on using it, she sobbed, her feet might never touch the ground again.

Soon, however, Winifred would cheer up, laid out in her recliner, her swollen feet elevated. "All my parts have been broken or bent." She'd laugh a high, cackling giggle. "Don't you think there ought to be some dump somewhere, like there are for used cars?" In a moment, she would turn to business. She was the preeminent fundraiser here. She intended to raise the money to buy Linda Manor a chairlift van, and she felt sure she would succeed. She had only to put her full mind to it.

In one of her many poems, Winifred had written:

> Youth fled, agility failed,
> With hoisted sails, high hopes afloat,
> I brace channels of stormy, ever-changing tide . . .
> Beauty not duty I left behind
> Back in the time when.

❖   ❖   ❖

Linda Manor's grounds were often empty. Their stillness lent a secretive quality to the sprawling, low-roofed building — set back from busy Route 9, surrounded by wintry woods and dormant grass, adorned with Greco-Roman columns, balconies and parapets, all as white as a nurse's starched uniform. As one stared at it, the place grew odder in the mind. The building looked so provisional. So new and yet containing so much of the past. Many residents remembered World War I as if it had ended yesterday. Some remembered firsthand accounts of the Civil War. They were like immigrants arriving in a new land with long lives behind them, obliged to inhabit a place that was bound to seem less real than the places they recalled. For most of those long-lived, ailing people, Linda Manor represented all the permanence that life still had to offer. It was their home for the duration, their last place on earth.

3

Lou and Joe had been placed together in the room upstairs beside the elevators ten months ago. People entering nursing homes have, for the most part, already lost control over their lives. Once inside, they usually don't even get to choose their roommates.

Lou had come to Linda Manor with his ailing wife, Jennie. They had been married for almost seventy years when Jennie died, in early March of 1990. In the weeks afterward, Lou walked the familiar corridors of Linda Manor on his cane. For hours at a time, he sat alone in the room he'd shared with Jennie on the Sunrise nursing unit. In the room, the two beds, which Lou had kept shoved together, stood apart.

Lou's daughter, Ruth, asked him to leave and live with her. But he said, "I couldn't do that to you, Ruth." If he lived at her house, he'd feel he was a burden, and he didn't want to feel that way. Besides, at her house, he'd inevitably spend a lot of time staring into space. So Lou thanked his daughter, but said he'd just as soon stay on at Linda Manor.

Jewish ritual prescribes a period of mourning that lasts for thirty days of outward abstinence from joy. This was easy for Lou to accomplish. He faced a new life, which consisted mainly of absences. He had thought of himself as his wife's main nurse and protector. Now he lacked his life's companion, and he lacked employment for the first time in eighty years. His daughter was very worried. She thought that Lou might find that there was nothing more for him to do in life except to await an end. And an end wasn't clearly in sight. Lou was ninety, but bodies keep their own time. Except for his eyes and occasional angina, Lou remained quite healthy.

Joe had left home for good in his early seventies, after a siege of operations. He had been disabled for many years, during which his wife had managed his care and feeding. His operations left him more disabled, his wife's own health was failing, and finally she could no longer take care of him at home. Joe lived as a convalescent patient for about four months at the veterans' hospital in Northampton, and then was moved to Linda Manor. When he arrived he was deemed a Level II and was placed on the Sunrise unit. When Joe began to walk again, he became a Level III, and was moved upstairs to Forest View. Joe had been the chief probation officer for the district court in Pittsfield, Massachusetts. He was a big man in his town. For thirty years he sat on the right hand of powerful judges, dispensing justice for a county. Now he lived in the care of strangers, exiled by illness from his family and his home. For hours at a time, shunning all scheduled activities, Joe lay alone in the room beside the Forest View elevators and watched TV, which he used to hate.

Both Lou and Joe became administrative problems. Joe had no savings, and nursing home bills had long since exhausted Lou's. The VA paid Joe's room and board, and Medicaid paid for Lou. Each man was occupying a two-person room, and the nursing home wasn't being paid to keep them in rooms of their own. Moreover, Lou did not belong on Sunrise — he was too healthy. Both men were wrongly situated. It was a truth, as Jane Austen might have said, that a single nursing home resident without the money for a private room must be in want of a roommate.

Lou traveled in Linda Manor as through a moonlit terrain. An irreversible ailment called vascular occlusion had extinguished his left eye. His right eye was afflicted with glaucoma, macular degeneration, and a cataract, but it saw enough light to help him get around. Out in the corridors he followed the carpet's blue and white border. Lou saw the border only as a lighter shade of gray than the rest of the carpet, but in his mind he made it pure white. He saw the outlines of people. He did not see faces. Lou could identify some fellow residents and members of the staff by their voices. By sight, he could recognize only the very tall or very fat or idiosyncratically mobile. He was left to imagine the rest of the appearances of the people who lived and worked around him, as he imagined color in the carpet's border.

The room upstairs on Forest View, to which the nursing home's administrator escorted Lou, was just the same as the room that Lou had occupied downstairs on Sunrise, but everything was opposite, like a mirror image. Moving up here, Lou would probably bump into things at first. Lou had never liked change for its own sake. He actively disliked the prospect of most changes now, he'd noticed. But he understood the situation. If he had to move up here, he'd just be extra careful for a while, until he memorized the landscape.

The administrator helped Lou find a chair. Joe was lying on his bed. Joe turned off his TV and the administrator made introductions: Joe, this is Lou Freed. Lou, this is Joe Torchio.

Lou looked across the room. The man over there was just a

hazy shape, made of shades of gray different from the surroundings, as if seen through several layers of gauze. Joe's voice, when he said hello, sounded rather gruff. "Who is this guy?" Lou thought.

The administrator chatted with them for a few minutes, doing most of the talking, then decided to leave the two men alone, to get acquainted, if they would.

A lot of men would say that their wives were their best friends, but Lou's wife really had been his. He hadn't lived in close quarters with another man since the Army, more than seventy years ago. "I don't know what it is to have a roommate," Lou thought. But he used to meet a lot of new people in his work. He reminded himself that he'd made many new acquaintances at meetings of the Power Maintenance Group of south New Jersey. This shouldn't be too hard.

"Where ya from, Joe?"

Joe came from Pittsfield.

Where was Pittsfield? Lou wondered.

Farther west. "Uh, wait a minute now. Ten, twenty, thirty, thirty miles away," said Joe. He explained that he had to count up to numbers sometimes. "Stroke. You know." He'd had a stroke in his early fifties. It had crippled his right side and still affected his speech.

How about Lou? Where did he come from?

Philadelphia, originally. Lou and his wife had moved to California when he was sixty.

Lou could have said a great deal more about both places, especially about Philadelphia. Lately, Lou had noticed himself forgetting items of the recent past, such as the date when he and Jennie had arrived here. Meanwhile, Philadelphia would arise in his mind, all at once and in its entirety. The old Philadelphia that no longer existed, of Irish cops walking beats and vaudeville houses and hawkers selling roasted chestnuts and "Balteemore crabs" on street corners. A couple of the nurses here seemed interested to hear all this described, but Lou knew that once he got started it was hard to stop, and when he got started, some people would suddenly have somewhere else they had to go.

Had Joe been in the service?

In the Navy, during World War II. Three years in the Pacific. How about Lou?

The Army, back in World War I. But Lou never got overseas. "The Kaiser heard I was coming, and he quit."

Where did Lou go to college?

He didn't. Lou finished eighth grade on a Thursday in 1914, and on Friday he started his first full-time job, sweeping floors in a factory for $3.50 a week. A fifty-two-hour week. And no coffee breaks. "They hadn't been invented then." How things changed.

Joe agreed with that. "Things change. Jesus Christ."

Lou had worked a lot of jobs, from assembly-line labor to managing a fountain pen factory to making models for an aerospace company. He liked to think back over the many different jobs he'd done, reviewing all the steps and motions and the thought required. It was almost as if he were performing them again. But this guy wouldn't be interested in the details.

How about Joe? Where did he go to school?

There were a lot of places. The Stockbridge School of Agriculture, for a year. "I studied, uh, breed and breeding, feed and feeding." Then Joe went to the University of Pennsylvania. Then Boston University, where he got a master's degree in sociology, then Boston College, where he got a law degree.

Lou had to stifle himself when he heard Joe mention the U of Penn. What a coincidence!

"Coming back to the U of Penn," said Lou. It so happened that Lou's son-in-law went there. And Joe probably knew Drexel Institute, which was pretty near the U of Penn — "Insteetute," Lou pronounced it, with his ingrained Philadelphia accent. Drexel Institute, Lou said, was where he did most of his studying of electricity.

Did Lou want to hear a good one? Joe arrived in Philadelphia such a country bumpkin that he spent his first several weeks at the U of Penn thinking he was at Penn State. Then he saw the announcement of a football game between the universities, and he wondered, "There are *two* of them?"

Joe lay on his bed, his shoulders shaking with laughter over that memory. He was a dark-eyed, swarthy man. His looks were unmistakably Mediterranean. "I didn't know the difference. Honest to God! Good God, huh?"

Lou chuckled. Joe's voice, in expostulation, reminded him of one he'd heard before. The blustery, booming voice of the Irish cop who used to walk the beat in Northern Liberties when Lou was a boy. Looking across the room, Lou imagined a face with blue eyes and ruddy cheeks on the foggy shape of Joe. It was the wrong face, of course, but a face nonetheless.

The maintenance men moved Lou's possessions upstairs the next day.

With help from maintenance and his daughter Ruth, Lou furnished his side of the room, the side near the window. Lou equipped his new resting place like an Egyptian tomb. He screwed a hook into his bedside dresser for his shoehorn. In a corner of the dresser's top drawer he had a partition constructed out of tape and cardboard. The enclosure contained Lou's nitroglycerine pills, so that he could find them at once without fumbling if he had angina in the night — he carried another bottle of nitro pills in his pants, always in the right-hand pocket, in case angina struck when he was out of the room. He put his little kit of scissors, pliers, and screwdrivers in that drawer. In a corner by the window he placed the four-legged walker that Jennie used before she went into a wheelchair. Lou hung his striped cane on the walker, also his blue machinist's apron, which he wore to meals because, in his near blindness, he sometimes spilled his food. He placed his push-button phone — it had oversize buttons — on top of his bedside dresser, and, on the wall behind, he had Ruth hang a piece of cardboard on which were printed large all of the phone numbers of Lou's surviving adult relatives.

Lou placed a straight-backed armchair in front of the window, facing in on the room, in a spot convenient to his tools, where the morning sun would warm his back. Lou covered the walls around him with old and recent family photos, which he could no longer see clearly even from up close, and also with a sampler that read *Shalom* in Hebrew. One of Lou's sisters had embroidered the sampler. She had misspelled the Hebrew, but Lou couldn't have cared less. She had also knitted the colorful afghan that Lou asked the aides to place on top of his bedspread when they made up his bed. All of those objects spoke of a life lived elsewhere, as if that life were incorporated in them.

The underpinnings of the room were functional and drab.

The floor was a pale gray linoleum tile, and the furniture was all institutional with photo-wood-grain finish. But Lou covered most of the surfaces around him: with cards and books, with his combination radio–tape deck, with various knick-knacks, including a small wooden box with the hand-lettered inscription "For The Man Who Has Nothing A Place To Put It." His and Jennie's framed wedding invitation, dated 1920, and pictures of Jennie and various great-grandchildren, which Lou had cut out and mounted on wooden backings, and a jar of peanut butter and a tin full of cookies and a few small potted plants — all stood on the windowsill behind Lou. He kept his photo albums in a stack beside his radio. Sometimes he asked Ruth or other visitors to read the captions beneath the photos in the albums. "So I can sit here and think back," he explained. The room seemed a small place for two people to do their living in, but with Lou's stuff installed it had a self-contained quality, sufficient unto itself of necessity, like a small boat at sea.

Joe's side of the room looked barren compared to Lou's. One time a visitor from Pittsfield brought Joe an old friend's obituary. Joe kept it for a day. Then Lou heard him crumple it up and saw him toss it in the wastebasket. Lou wondered why Joe didn't keep it.

Joe hadn't brought much with him to his new life — some clothes, a TV and VCR, an old oak cane with a shepherd's crook handle, and a worn anthology of American poetry, which he could no longer read. Joe used to love to read. But ever since his stroke, he couldn't get through more than a sentence before the words seemed to scatter in front of him like pigeons in a park. He could manage a part of the local paper, which a woman in the room next door tossed in to him when she was done with it. "Paper, Joe!" she'd call. Joe read the sports scores and a few comic strips. It usually took him three readings to get the jokes, he said.

Joe also had some photographs. The most striking hung above the TV across from his bed. It was a studio portrait of Joe and his wife on their wedding day. A pretty young woman looks serenely out at the camera, and beside her Joe is a trim, handsome young ensign, the same height as his wife, with round cheeks and black, curly hair. He wears the suggestion of a smile. Joe lay across from that picture, on the bed nearer the door, with his shoes off but otherwise fully dressed, with the head of the bed cranked up slightly, a pillow under his head and a pillow under his knees. One morning when the sun streamed in the window, Lou saw a glint from the hazy shape of Joe's head. Then Lou heard one of the aides tease Joe about his baldness. Yes, he'd lost his hair, Joe said. "And I don't care. I had it when I needed it, that's all."

Joe would get the fringing hair cropped close, to save money on haircuts. A portion of the southern slope of his belly lay exposed between his sweat pants and polo shirt. Between Joe in his wedding picture and Joe on his nursing home bed there was only a family resemblance. Joe might have been the young ensign's irascible grandfather.

As the weeks went by, Lou filled in other parts of his picture of Joe. He decided that Joe was "average size" — that is, about as tall as Lou, around five eight. Lou heard Joe say that he had to get his mustache trimmed, so Joe acquired facial hair. The more Lou learned about Joe's personality, though, the more Joe puzzled him.

Joe mentioned having trouble with his bowels, in a voice full of mock daintiness, saying, "I have a lot of trouble with my e-limination. I have a lot of trouble with my stools." Lou suggested prunes. For a while Joe was eating about a dozen prunes for breakfast, but almost nothing else. Joe said that, among other things, he had diabetes, and was afraid that if he gained more weight he'd end up having to take insulin by injection, and by God he'd rather die than do that. Joe's intent made sense to Lou, but once he understood the details of Joe's weight-control program, Lou began saying privately to Ruth, "Joe does some things that don't add up."

Joe would go out to lunch — members of his family took him out once a week — and he would come back and say, "Oh, dear God, I ate too much." He would heave himself onto his bed and add, "It was worth it." The next day he would weigh himself and fume at the results. "Jesus Christ! I gained a pound." He'd go on a diet for the rest of the week, eating little more than prunes for breakfast, which Lou thought must be insufficient for a diabetic. After breakfast they'd come back upstairs to the room. Lou would sit down in his chair by the window, and from across the room he'd hear a ripping sound. This meant that Joe was undoing the Velcro straps of his orthopedic shoes. A clattering would follow, the sound of the steel brace attached to Joe's right shoe hitting the floor. And then Joe's bed would creak, which signified that he was lying down again. He always lay down when he came back to the room, and he hardly ever budged from there between meals. And then he wondered why he had trouble with his weight.

Lou himself didn't get as much exercise as he thought he should. He used to take Jennie out for walks, pushing her wheelchair around the corridors. He didn't walk as often now. "I don't have the incentive," he said. But then, feeling slothful, Lou would get up from his chair, take his cane, and walk across the room and out the door. He'd cross the hall, touch the wall on the other side, and then return. Sometimes he'd do several laps before he resettled himself in his chair. And three mornings a week he went downstairs to the physical therapy room for the formal sessions of gentle exercise and stretching called Music and Motion — M&M's for short. All the exercises were performed while sitting down. It was a pretty good workout, Lou said, touting M&M's to Joe. It gave Lou all the exercise he could handle. Joe would benefit from M&M's. Maybe he just needed encouragement. So, on one M&M's morning, Lou said toward the shape of Joe, "Why don't you come down with me?"

But Joe said he didn't feel like it, and Lou resolved to hold his tongue. Lou's father-in-law used to say: "No one knows what goes on between the sheets." In other words, mind your own business. Lou believed in that advice, up to a point.

Two small sliding windows flanked the picture window behind Lou. He cracked one open to let in the first airs of May. The room was often filled now with the folksy voices of Boston Red Sox play-by-play announcers from Joe's TV, and with the louder sounds Joe made while watching — shouts of joy sometimes and, at least as often, strings of oaths as Joe thundered at the Red Sox manager, "Jesus Christ! Goddamn it, I told you not to put him in! Jesus Christ!"

Lou was amused. But he thought it only right to warn Joe that if his granddaughter should come in to visit just when Joe was cussing out the Sox, well, Joe knew how easily little children picked things up. And Joe agreed. He'd have to watch himself. It was just a game, Joe said. Just a game, but Jesus Christ, the Red Sox made him mad.

Lou could not imagine getting that emotionally involved in baseball, but this was not as strange as other tendencies of Joe's. A young nurse's aide came into the room to check their vitals. Lou listened to Joe question her about the intimate facts of her life. Was she married? Did she have any kids? She had two and another on the way? Three children were enough, Joe told her. "Tell your husband. Vasa-sectomy! Snip, snip, snip."

Joe was laughing when he said that, but he always grilled the staff. "You married? You living with someone? Why the hell don't you marry him?" One of the staff said she'd gotten a dog. "Did you worm it yet?" Joe wanted to know. And there were any number of nurses and aides — Lou couldn't say just how many, because he couldn't tell all of their voices apart — who, under Joe's questioning, revealed that they had trouble collecting alimony. Joe told them how to go after their ex-husbands. Sometimes he gave them names of people to call. But maybe that was Joe's lawyer training coming back, Lou thought. Joe had been a probation officer. Maybe he was trying to keep his hand in.

And then there was the matter of Joe on the telephone. He called home every evening. At the end, he said, "Okay, we'll see ya," and hung up.

Lou couldn't help overhearing. Joe's voice often sounded peremptory and gruff when he talked to his family over the phone. He rarely opened the conversation by asking them how they were, and he always hung up that way.

One evening Joe called his son and got his son's answering

machine. He growled into the phone at the answering machine, "This is your father. Jesus Christ!"

It sounded to Lou as if Joe had said, "This is your father, Jesus Christ." Lou had to make an effort to keep from laughing out loud. He wasn't sure how Joe would react if he told him how funny that sounded. It wasn't worth the risk. It might just make him angrier. If Joe got any angrier, Lou thought sometimes, he might keel over with another stroke.

For all of that, Joe was turning out to be good company. He had a sense of humor. He seemed to like hearing stories. Lou never felt that Joe's anger was aimed at him. "He gets angry, but he doesn't really mean it," Lou thought. He wasn't frightened of Joe, just puzzled.

Joe's son brought in tapes of movies. Late in the evening Joe would play them on his VCR. At first, Joe asked Lou if the movies disturbed him. Lou said he didn't mind them, and it surprised him to discover that this was true. He went to sleep a lot more easily to the sound of one of Joe's movies than to silence in the room, drifting off easily amid the mayhem.

Joe's taste in movies wasn't all bad. He had a tape of *Fiddler on the Roof,* which Lou loved to listen to. But he wouldn't have wasted his time on most of the movies Joe watched. "I don't know what he sees in them," Lou said out of Joe's hearing. "And they have all the *f* words in them. I'm not a prude, but I don't understand what Joe sees in most of those movies." But Joe seemed to enjoy them. Lou kept his comments mild.

"What's the movie for tonight, Joe?"

Joe looked at the latest tape his son had brought, and said, "*Marked for Death.*"

Lou chuckled.

The next morning Lou remarked, "The girl came in to make our beds. First she had to sweep the bodies off the floor."

From over on the other side of the room, Lou heard Joe laughing. Joe said he didn't know why his son brought him movies like that. But Joe went on watching them.

Night baseball games had begun. Now Lou went to sleep to the mingled sounds of play-by-play and his roommate's half-stifled cheers and curses. Almost daily, it seemed, Joe said, "I weighed myself. Jesus Christ, it's impossible! I don't eat!"

Lou could not resist offering a little advice, the solution seemed so near at hand. Lou said again, "Why don't you come down to M&M's with me?"

All right, Joe said. He'd try it.

Entering the room, Joe sometimes stopped to gaze out the picture window at the view of field and woods, now very leafy, very green. He'd been working outside on a hot day this time of year just before his stroke, almost twenty years ago. The small sliding windows on either side of the picture window were now closed against the heat. The windy sound of the ventilator, in air-conditioning mode, no longer competed constantly with the sounds from Joe's TV. Joe lay on his back, his TV off. Lou sat by the window. Joe was telling Lou about the missing big toe on his partially paralyzed right foot. The operations Joe underwent before coming here had included that toe's amputation. Joe said that after the surgeon cut off the toe, he asked what Joe wanted done with it. "I told him, 'Why don't you send it Chicago and have it bronzed? I'll put it on my mantelpiece.' For God's sake."

Lou smiled.

But, Joe said, he wished he'd told the surgeon to wrap up the severed toe and send it to a certain judge in Pittsfield, the judge who forced Joe into retirement about eight years ago.

Lou remembered the company that wouldn't give him a job because he was a Jew. Lou eventually got even. While running the pen factory, Lou said, he had the opportunity to tell one of that company's salesmen that he wouldn't do business with him. And that squared matters, as far as Lou was concerned. Lou could understand how a person might hold a grudge. But, Lou said, he couldn't think of any he held himself.

Some of the things Lou said surprised Joe. Some were hard to believe.

Lou said he dated only one girl, and he married her.

Joe said he dated many, and none ever dumped him.

Lou said that back during Prohibition he built a still for a relative, but he didn't drink any of its product, because that would have been illegal. Actually, Lou said, he got drunk only once in his life. "Did I tell you that story?" he asked Joe.

Lou sometimes repeated stories. But Lou was an old man, Joe told himself. He had already heard this story, but he didn't say anything, and Lou told again how on his birthday years ago he went to a nightclub called the Stable, in Philadelphia, and had about three beers. "I suddenly felt something I never felt before. I was spinning around. I excused myself and went across the street to a drugstore and got some Alka-Seltzer."

Joe guffawed. "Three beers. That isn't drunk! I used to *drink.* Good Gawd."

Lou said he'd never smoked. He believed in moderation.

Joe had smoked most of his life. He smiled at the ceiling. "Moderation I was never for."

Lou said that he grew up in tough, seamy parts of Philadelphia. "I sometimes wonder, growing up where I did, why I didn't get in more trouble."

But Joe had worked with people who got in trouble. Lou's stories made it obvious that Lou had never gotten into anything like trouble.

On Saturday mornings, the phone rang for Lou constantly. All of his relatives called. Joe turned down his TV so Lou could talk, which meant that Joe could not help overhearing. "I love you," Lou said into the phone every time before hanging up. Every time! Joe heartily disliked his own brother-in-law, and made no secret of it. Wasn't there anyone in Lou's family Lou didn't love? Was there anyone in the world this old man didn't like?

They got talking about their wives. Lou told of how, before her death, Jennie suffered from skin irritations. She was incontinent, and Lou figured out that the nurse's aides made up her bed all wrong for a person in her condition — with a plastic sheet beneath her bottom sheet instead of absorbent pads. Lou said he showed the aides how to do it right, and, his soft voice suddenly loud and severe, he told how he had struggled with the staff sometimes, to make sure they gave Jennie proper attention. The staff worked hard and most were good. Lou often praised them. But one time he found Jennie wet, and he set off every call bell in their room, and no one came. So he grabbed his cane and marched down to the Sunrise nurses' station. "I could see a little better then." On the other side of the counter, he saw the shapes of aides and nurses, all in a group, and the figure of a man standing in front of them, addressing them. The man had to be a doctor. Evidently the staff thought a doctor's words of wisdom more important than call bells. Evidently the doctor thought so, too. Lou slapped his hand hard on the counter and yelled at them. "Jennie needs attention. And she needs it *now!*" Lou's countenance was stern, recalling this. "And I got results."

More softly, Lou said, "I still wish I'd'a went with her. But I thank the good Lord I didn't have to leave her alone."

Joe listened, gazing intently at the ceiling. Joe listed his own wife's many ailments. "I wore her out. She couldn't take care of me anymore, that's all."

Lou said that he and Jennie never went to sleep without kissing first.

"Well, I did." said Joe. "Because we'd argue, and she wouldn't talk to me."

"I don't think I ever had an argument with Jennie," said Lou. He and his wife had disagreements, but never went to bed without settling them first, and kissing.

Joe sat up in bed and stared at Lou. "Jesus Christ! That's impossible!"

Lou was too much. It sometimes seemed as if he must have lived in an entirely different world from the one that Joe had known. And yet they had a certain amount of history in common. Lou's parents were immigrants, from Austria, and Joe's father was a shoemaker from Calabria. Joe, too, grew up in a largely immigrant neighborhood, on Pittsfield's Dewey Avenue. Lou grew up within walking distance of burlesque shows and whorehouses, while it was said of Joe's grammar school that the graduates became either judges or bank robbers. But all of Lou's father's business ventures failed, while Joe's father's business, Artistic Shoe Renovator, prospered modestly during the Depression, when many people got their shoes repaired instead of buying new ones. Joe's parents had been able to send him to college. As a consequence, Joe was much more widely read. There were deeper differences.

Lou said he loved the Horatio Alger rags-to-riches books as a boy, and later on, the poems of Robert Service. Joe had wider, less sunny tastes in literature. The kind of poem he didn't like was one he used to hear recited, and could still recite in part himself. " 'Grow old along with me! The best is yet to be,' " Joe chanted. "When I was thirty, forty, I thought it was all right. But now, bullshit, it's false." One of his favorite poems — it lay in the anthology that Joe had carried with him across the Pacific in the Navy — was Stephen Crane's "The Wayfarer."

> The wayfarer,
> Perceiving the pathway to truth,
> Was struck with astonishment.
> It was thickly grown with weeds.
> "Ha," he said,
> "I see that no one has passed here
> In a long time."
> Later he saw that each weed
> Was a singular knife.
> "Well," he mumbled at last,
> "Doubtless there are other roads."

Joe smiled wryly over that poem. "*Doubtless* there are other roads."

"I quit lying in my thirties," Joe said once. Then he amended that statement. "I quit lying about everything *except* drinking."

Lou told again about that time when he'd gotten drunk. "I

can remember the place. Place called the Stable. I never felt I missed something."

"Well," said Joe, "you missed something."

"I saw enough people that way that I never wanted to be that way myself," said Lou from his chair over by the window.

"I saw a lot of people get drunk and got drunk myself," Joe said, lying on his bed.

"I enjoyed life without getting drunk," Lou said.

Joe's voice softened. "It made it easier on the people you were close to."

To Joe, Lou's general outlook was strange, not alien, but something he himself had left behind long ago. Most cynical and pessimistic utterances seemed to leave Lou truly puzzled — puzzled as to why some people chose to think that way. One time when Ruth was visiting, she said that she had a Ph.D. in guilt, and Lou said, "I don't think I feel guilty about anything." And Joe thought to himself again, "Jesus Christ, that's impossible." If in the privacy of their room Joe made a little sport of a fellow resident, Lou might join in, but he would often end up saying, "Poor soul. We shouldn't laugh." And then, if one of those people got sick and was confined to bed, Lou would go and pay a visit. Perhaps Lou did dislike some people after all. He sometimes talked as if he did. "But," Joe thought, "it has to be a very mean man."

There was one exception. Lou seemed to have it in for the director of food service here, and as far as Joe could see, that man was nothing but pleasant, patient, and obliging. Among his mementos, Lou had a book of recipes for dishes he used to make. He said he did all the cooking at home after Jennie got sick. He would say that if he could see now, he'd go into the kitchen and show the food service director how to cook "something decent." Joe didn't think the food was all that bad. Maybe Lou saw the director of food service as a rival, who'd won the right to do what Lou felt he could do better only because the director was young and had his sight. Anyway, it gave Joe some comfort to see Lou step into a more easily comprehensible character now and then.

After his experiences with other roommates, during his time at the VA hospital and when he first came to Linda Manor, Joe had thought that he'd just as soon not have another roommate. He hadn't relished the idea of a ninety-year-old's moving in with him. Being only seventy-two himself and burdened with a textbook's worth of ailments, Joe had figured that by ninety there couldn't be much left of a person. But Joe now had to remind himself how old, really old, Lou was. The man sometimes seemed too virtuous to be true, but he clearly wasn't senile. "He's got all his buttons, by Jesus," Joe thought. He felt grateful for that. Lou said his sense of smell had vanished suddenly a couple of years ago. He applied deodorant liberally, he explained, lest he give offense unknowingly. A little thing, but not inconsequential for close-quartered living. And Lou, unlike Joe's other roommates, didn't do a lot of complaining. Lou's voice got teary when he talked about his wife sometimes, but teary over her and not himself— and that was an important difference to Joe. Occasionally Lou said, "If I had my sight, I'd still be doing something productive."

Several times already Lou said he'd asked the authorities to install a handrail in the weighing room downstairs, but to no avail. "If I could see, I could put the damn thing up in a couple of hours."

But, Lou added, there was a saying he guessed was true —

that if you could choose among everyone else's troubles, you'd end up choosing your own.

"You'd still be working if you could see," said Joe, looking pensively toward the ceiling.

The maples in the woods outside the window turned fiery. Baseball season ended. The Red Sox didn't win the pennant again. "Wait'll next year, that's all," Joe sighed.

Lou's son, Harold, flew in from California and visited for several days. Reminiscing with Harold about things they'd built together in their home workshops, Lou remembered making toy soldiers years ago for the children in the family. Thinking back over his old jobs and workbench projects, though pleasurable, made Lou's hands yearn for something in the here and now to do. So he asked Harold to look for those old toy-soldier molds when he got back to California. A few days later Harold called to say he'd found them. Lou asked him to send them to a family friend who worked in metal, and not long after that, a box full of toy soldiers arrived at Linda Manor in Lou's mail.

Joe, meanwhile, put the finishing touch on his weight-loss program. Lou had inspired the program, but the details were all Joe's. The weekly luncheon outing and occasional Linda Manor baked chicken dinner, at which Joe also overate. The mounting of the scale. The subsequent dieting. And the exercising, which now included not only M&M's but also daily rides on the exercise bike in the occupational therapy room.

When Joe was out of earshot, Lou said, sotto voce, to their favorite nurse's aide, "The dietary people should look at what Joe eats. It isn't healthy for a diabetic. And," he added, "don't tell Joe I said so."

Joe's rides on the exercise bike were also worrisome. Lou gathered that every time Joe rode, he pedaled farther and faster. Lou felt he ought to warn him. The man didn't seem to know where his own best interests lay. Lou couldn't help himself. "Joe, you're going at that bike too hard." But Joe simply denied it, and kept on riding farther.

When Joe left the room for his bike ride, Lou opened the cardboard box and took out a small shiny infantryman. He got a piece of sandpaper out of his top dresser drawer and set to work. Seated in his chair with his back to the window, in late autumn afternoon light, Lou sanded rough edges off one toy soldier after another. He paused now and then to stroke the toy soldiers with his fingers. He'd give some to his great-grandchildren. Maybe he'd try to sell some in the gift shop downstairs.

Lou lifted a hand from his work, extending the index finger. "Another thing I don't understand about Joe. He wears those sweat pants and he keeps heisting them up, and he has no pockets in them. When we go downstairs, he asks me to carry things for him. I don't mind, but I don't think I could get used to pants without pockets."

Lou's hands went back to his work. He'd sand awhile, then pause, stroking the toy soldiers, hoping to find more rough edges to sand.

❖ ❖ ❖

Both Lou and Joe packed overnight bags and went away for Thanksgiving, Lou to his daughter Ruth's house and Joe back to his former home in Pittsfield. Lou returned to Linda Manor feeling all worn out. For him, trips away had become exhausting. "I don't know what the problem is. Too many birthdays, I guess."

Joe limped back into the room on Forest View saying that there had been too much company back home. He'd had to retreat from it to his old den at times. Joe also weighed a few pounds more than when he'd left. This didn't surprise Lou, nor did the consequences. Joe went right back to the exercise bike, to work off Thanksgiving, and then, on an afternoon a few days later, after an especially vigorous ride, a blister erupted on the big toe of Joe's left foot, his good foot.

It was a little blue capsule with some red at the edges, the kind of blister that weekend carpenters raise on their thumbs. As soon as the nurse's aide saw it, she summoned the charge nurse, and the nurse put in a call to Joe's doctor, who made a special visit. He put Joe on an antibiotic.

Diabetes reduces circulation. Even Joe's relatively mild case made his toes, because of their distance from his heart, especially vulnerable to infection and the risk of gangrene. This blister, like a broken hip, could lead to graver complications. Out of Lou and Joe's hearing, a nurse remarked, "Joe could lose the toe." Whether Joe's body or his spirits could withstand another blow like that was an open question. Lou didn't entertain dire thoughts like those, but he knew the blister must be serious if it had caused a doctor to make a special visit here. And a parade of aides and nurses kept coming in to have a look at Joe's toe. After listening to the commotion for a time, Lou got up, fetched his cane from the walker in the corner, and, saying to Joe that he guessed he'd take a walk, he made his way to the elevator and rode downstairs. He walked down the long central corridor, turned left into the administrative hallway, and stopped at the second door on the left, the door of his favorite nursing supervisor. She had been very helpful and adept in Jennie's last days. Lou knocked on the door with the handle of his cane. "Kathleen?"

"Yes, Lou?"

"Kathleen, I'd like you to take a look at Joe's toe."

Kathleen discussed the blister with Lou and said she'd come and look at it. Lou thanked her, then made his way, by cane and handrail and carpet border, back upstairs to his chair.

Kathleen had told Lou that Joe's blister would almost certainly heal, and Lou believed her. The nursing care was good in here. If a person came down with something curable, a lot of the staff acted as if they'd been given a present. But why take chances? Joe shouldn't go downstairs for meals for a while, Lou decided. Lou told Joe he should take it easy, stay upstairs, and keep his foot elevated.

But Joe wouldn't hear of it. "The hell with it," he said.

It was a morning a few days after the blister had appeared. Lou sat by the window, warming his back in the morning sun, and said to Joe, "*Eingeshpart*. Stubborn." Joe lay as usual on his bed, but with his wounded foot bared and propped up on a pillow. "That's what you were on that bicycle, Joe."

A privacy curtain hung from tracks in the ceiling. Joe had pulled the curtain a foot or so out from the wall, to shield his eyes from the morning sun. Now he sat up in bed and pulled back the curtain so he could confront Lou directly. "No, I wasn't!"

"Yes. I told you you were overdoing it."

Joe lay back and grunted at the ceiling.

Lou smiled. His eyes were squinted shut behind his thick glasses. The low December sun suffused his white hair. "You guys don't listen to me. After all, Joe, stop and think about it. I'm old enough to be your father."

"I know it!" Joe laughed, not making much sound but jiggling his bed. Then his right arm went into a jackhammer-like shaking. With his left hand, Joe grasped the wrist of the shivering arm and pulled it over onto his stomach, and it stopped moving.

Lou murmured, "My son'll be here in January."

4

Since Lou's arrival, Joe was getting out a little more. He now went to bingo three times a week. Lou went to most scheduled activities *except* bingo. He had his Saturday morning phone calls. On Sundays they both looked forward to a TV show that carried them off to other parts of the country — Joe watching and Lou listening. Tuesday morning they both went to Literary Hour, when Ruth, who was a retired high school English teacher, read aloud to residents in the activity room. Many visitors called on them. Members of Joe's family came weekly, and from time to time his friends from Pittsfield. And almost every morning, seven days a week, Ruth arrived.

She entered through the lobby, dressed in her parka. The first resident she saw was usually Bob. Bob had turned an armchair so that it faced the inner front door. He sat there for hours at a time, keeping watch. Visitors would offer him weather reports, doing pantomimes of shivering as they came in, and saying, "*Brrr!*"

"Cold out there!" Bob would reply. December brought north

winds, which sometimes blew the outer door back open behind the visitors without their knowing it. Then, as they came into the lobby through the second set of doors, they would find themselves confronted, not by the cheerful mustachioed man, proferring a hand for shaking and saying, "Beautiful. Excellent. Thank you kindly," but by a strange, fearful sight: Bob on the edge of his doorkeeping chair, quivering with what certainly looked like wrath, jabbing his cane in the air at them, and mumbling something emphatic. The visitors stopped in their tracks, alarmed. What had they done? Bob jabbed his cane toward them, then toward the doors. Eventually, most got the point, went back out, and pulled the outer door shut.

But Ruth always got a cheerful welcome. When from his chair Bob saw through the bay window her thin, elegant, silver-haired figure coming toward the door, he'd say, "Oh boy. Beautiful. Here she comes *now*." Entering, Ruth received Bob's Howdee!, also his left-handed handshake and a "Cold out *there!*" Ruth sometimes felt in need of such a greeting.

She had a great incentive to like Linda Manor. Not many people can bear to feel their parent's nursing home is bad. But Ruth knew this was a decent place. She knew most of the staff by now, and liked them. A faint odor like buttered toast, with the butter a little off, lingered in parts of the building. Ruth sometimes caught the sharp whiff of urine when passing by some bedroom doors, but Linda Manor on the whole was remarkably odorless. As for its sights and sounds, Ruth had long since grown accustomed to them, and they did not frighten her as they did some first-time and infrequent visitors. It was not the place itself but the visions of the life to come that got her down. The visible decline of residents who came to her Literary Hour — that woman who seemed so sprightly last week on her cane, appearing this week in a wheel-chair, bravely trying to smile — and the glimpses Ruth had of the nearly comatose laid out in their bedrooms, and of the demented wandering the halls. Once when she was on her way out, a nice-looking resident approached her and asked if she wouldn't please give him a ride home. She left in tears that day, feeling sorry both for the man and for the fact that her own father now resided among people who seemed consigned to live no kind of life at all.

"Guilt's my middle name," Ruth said. It was entirely self-inflicted. Lou often reminded her that he'd rather live here than at her house, where inevitably he'd be alone and bored a lot of the time. He was always telling her that she didn't have to come every day, always urging her to go away on trips with her husband, Bob. But now, when she and her husband were both retired and in good health and had the money to travel, she couldn't tear herself away. She tried it once. She took a trip to England with her husband and felt miserable the whole time. She made herself busier these days, taking courses and doing charitable work, than when she was teaching. As she understood her reasons, she had to feel that what she did instead of taking care of Lou at home was arduous and important enough to justify his being here. Maybe if he had turned into a querulous old man and insisted that she visit him every day, it would have been possible for Ruth not to do so, or at least to feel that she was being dutiful enough. Lou's cheerfulness and consideration intensified her "guilt spasms." But they also made her visits pleasant. She enjoyed her father's company, more now perhaps than ever before, now that she had so much of it.

Ruth came in order to visit Lou, but gradually she realized that she also came to visit Joe. On Saturday mornings Lou's phone began ringing at around ten o'clock. "It's either Aunt Esther or Aunt Ruth. Wanta take bets?" Ruth said to Joe one Saturday morning when the phone rang.

"Esther," said Joe from his bed. The foot with the blistered toe was bared and rested on a pillow, looking oddly separate from Joe, like a part removed for repairs.

"Hi, Esther," said Lou into the phone.

"See?" Joe said to Ruth.

While Lou talked on the phone, Ruth and Joe talked to each other. Joe said he'd seen some news on TV about an advance in the prevention of strokes. "I wondered if they had something if you already had one. No, huh?" Joe laughed a little.

At such moments Ruth felt keenly aware of the difference between her father's age and Joe's. It was one thing to be in your nineties and in a nursing home, but Joe was only six years older than Ruth and her husband. Imagining herself in Joe's place, Ruth imagined herself very bitter. The first time she mentioned her husband's love of downhill skiing, Ruth felt like slapping her hand over her mouth. Joe, she thought, might well feel jealous. She thought *she* would, in his place. But Joe said, "It's good that a man of sixty-five can do that." And he seemed to mean it.

On her morning visits, Ruth often told stories. One of her favorites was about a Jewish mother of her acquaintance who told her son, as he was leaving for his honeymoon, "Don't forget to wear your rubbers." At the wedding, when someone asked this woman's son if he wanted a drink, the mother said, "No, he's not thirsty."

"My mother said the same thing!" cried Joe from his bed. "'No, he's not thirsty.' We go into, uh, store. 'Say thank you to the man, Joey.' And I was forty years old, for Christ's sake!" Joe levitated off his bed in laughter. "Oh, God. Jewish sons and Italian mothers, it's all the same."

Another time Ruth arrived to find Lou and Joe fulminating about an item on that morning's TV news. America was sending food to Russia while, Lou and Joe angrily protested, people here went hungry. "*We're* starving," Joe said, meaning that some Americans were.

"Forgive me for saying so," Ruth said to Joe, "but you don't look it."

Joe laughed and laughed.

On Sundays Ruth used to bring the *New York Times* crossword puzzle. She thought that Lou and Joe would enjoy struggling through it with her. "Joe, give me a Red Sox catcher whose name begins with *P.* "

Joe stammered. "Uh, uh. Ah, the hell with it. I got half a brain, you know."

"It functions, that's all that matters," said Lou.

Finally, Joe told Ruth, speaking of the crossword, "Don't get me started on that goddarn thing." After that, Ruth stopped bringing it.

When she first met Joe, she thought he must be a little crude, the way he lay on his bedspread, scratching his stomach, watching TV. Then one day Ruth sat down in her usual place, in a chair across from the foot of Lou's bed, and she mentioned that she'd just read a review of a new novel that sounded interesting — a novel by Joyce Carol Oates called *Because It Is Bitter, and Because It Is My Heart.* And the blustery man, who had to count up to numbers, said, "Stephen Crane. That comes from, uh, poem by Stephen Crane."

Joe directed Ruth to his poetry anthology. He had Ruth read the poem in question.

> In the desert
> I saw a creature, naked, bestial,
> Who, squatting upon the ground,
> Held his heart in his hands,
> And ate of it.
> I said, "Is it good, friend?"
> "It is bitter — bitter," he answered;
> "But I like it
> Because it is bitter,
> And because it is my heart."

"Oh-ho," Joe said. "That's good." He had Ruth read his favorite poem of Crane's, "The Wayfarer." As Ruth read the last line — "Doubtless there are other roads" — Joe's face grew flushed. He grinned at her from his bed. "Ah-hah! That's good."

"That's what we call irony," Ruth said.

"Yeah, but it's good," Joe said.

The whole transaction astonished and delighted Ruth, the former English teacher. That, she thought, was the moment when she really began to know Joe.

Joe wasn't just well read; he clearly had a taste for bitter irony, in life as well as literature. In some ways, Ruth realized, she resembled her gentle-minded father less than she resembled Joe.

Ruth usually stayed for a couple of hours, and left before lunch.

On her way out, she stopped to button up her coat and say goodbye to Bob in his sentry chair.

Bob looked up at her. "It's a bitch."

"No, it's not," Ruth exclaimed. "It's a beautiful world."

Bob looked at her, his brow knitted. "It's too bad."

"Yes, it is," Ruth said.

"Beautiful," said Bob.

5

At seven o'clock in the morning, Joe awakened to the sound of a cane rapping on the door, followed by Bob's voice. "All right?"

Joe was still half mired in sleep. "All right!" he called back testily.

"Okay," said Bob's voice from the doorway. "Bye-bye."

Lou sat across the room in his skivvies, slowly pulling on his pants. "You know, Joe, I've been thinking. With Bob, we don't need an alarm clock."

Joe wasn't sure he wanted one at these moments when he struggled up from sleep. Once again, Joe considered telling Bob to stay away from his door at this hour. But as Lou often said, these self-appointed duties made Bob happy, or at least they kept him busy. And Bob had a special claim on Joe's sympathy. For a time after his own stroke, Joe could say only three things: "Jesus Christ," "balls," and "goddamn." He meant to say other words as well, but only those came out. Gradually, Joe had regained most of his powers of speech. But Bob had not, in spite of therapy.

When at a loss for words, Bob would often say, in a plaintive voice, "I wish I could talk now." He would add, in an angry voice, "It's a bitch, I'm tellin' ya. It's a *bitch.*" Bob could repeat new words, but most didn't seem to stick. He retained a vocabulary of only about three dozen words and phrases. With them, he mustered a range of expression that was quite amazing. His greetings, for example. For curt hellos, at all times of the day or night, Bob would say, "Howareyouthismorning," the phrase all one word, like a priest's mumbled devotions. For quick but more enthusiastic hellos, he sometimes used "Beautiful" or "Excellent." His truly cheery greetings, like the ones he delivered to Ruth, resembled songs: "Hi oh dee oh dee oh to you. Howdee! Howdee! Howdee! Hello to you hello!"

Bob worked as a factory machinist most of his life. Right up until his stroke, he spent his spare time restoring antique horse-drawn sleighs and buggies. Bob had two fat albums filled with photographs of his work. He showed them eagerly to any staff and fellow residents who were interested. "Buggy. Buggy," Bob said, pointing at the photos. Those who viewed them didn't have to pretend to be impressed. The sleighs and buggies looked brand-new, with lacquered finishes and delicate scroll-work painted on them.

"These are beautiful, Bob."

"You're damn right. I'm tellin' ya. I wish I could talk now." Bob would turn the page and point at another example of his handiwork. "Excellent. Excellent. Buggy. Buggy." He would turn to a picture of a neatly lettered sign, standing outside what had been his workshop. "Bob's Restoration Company," read the sign.

Bob's wife had told Lou and Joe that if someone dared to move a tool so much as an inch out of place in his workshop, Bob would know at once, and often there'd be trouble. So Bob's exacting ideas about order preceded his entry into Linda Manor. But creating and maintaining that order around him was virtually Bob's sole occupation now. Here at Linda Manor, an activities aide sometimes held pottery sessions. Bob, who had been right-handed, painted bowls left-handed. He no longer had many chances for doing something well.

Right now Bob would be limping quickly through the long central corridor downstairs and into the activity room, still empty at this morning hour, to begin rearranging furniture. Once in a while the cleaning staff left the upright piano a little out of place — on the wrong side of the parakeet cage, for instance. On such occasions, Bob would jab his cane at the piano, saying, "Ree-diculous!" Bob couldn't move the piano by himself. Muttering, "Sonofabitch. Ree-diculous," he'd get to work on things he could move. No rearrangements mattered as much as the assemblage of chairs Bob made in the wide doorway that connected the activity room and the dining room. Bob would place five chairs in two rows, like theater seats, facing in on the dining room. The two chairs in the back row were reserved for Art and Art's roommate, Ted. The front-row left-hand seat was for Joe, the right-hand one for Lou, and the middle seat was Bob's, and woe to the resident who tried to sit in any of those five chairs while waiting for the meal.

Eleanor tried to do so once, some months ago, when she was still new here. Bob jabbed his cane at her. "Get out! Get out! Black bastard! Get out!" Eleanor, whose skin without makeup was alabaster white, hadn't sat in one of those chairs since. Eleanor now called Bob the Inspector General, after a play by that name. One morning back around that same time, Bob threw a fit in front of the lab technician who periodically came in to take blood samples from residents — Eleanor had nick-named her affectionately the Vampire Lady. The technician was adept at taking blood painlessly and was a popular figure among residents. Bob liked the Vampire Lady, too. "She's a damn good girl, I'm tellin' ya." But that morning she arrived some fifteen minutes late, and delayed Bob's pre-breakfast preparations. "Bob went into just a spastic rage in front of her," Eleanor remembered.

In honor of that episode, the Vampire Lady gave Bob an additional title: Mayor of Linda Manor.

When Bob had the five chairs arranged, he'd say, "Okay, that's enough." He'd be sitting in his chair now, waiting all alone while the activity and dining rooms filled with sunlight.

Bob started setting up those five chairs in the dining room doorway a month or two ago. Since then, before every meal, Joe and Bob and Lou would sit there in the front row, Art and Ted behind them, and the five would watch and kibitz as the dietary aides moved around the dining room, setting the tables. Lou called their little group the Nudniks. And Lou also named their pre-meal kibitzing sessions. "Stupidvising," he called them. But Lou couldn't really participate. He couldn't watch the dietary aides. Most of the time he probably had no idea which aides the other Nudniks were talking to. When Joe realized this, he decided to learn the name of every dietary aide. It wasn't, on reflection, something he'd have done in his former life. Joe rarely bothered back then with the names of casual acquaintances. "I wasn't interested. Now I'm interested, that's all." The loss of tangible gift-giving power lay heavily on Joe. He couldn't often find a remedy, so when he did, it seemed significant to him, however small the gift. Now that he had all the aides' names down, he'd call them out for Lou during Stupidvising.

Lou was ready for the journey down for breakfast, dressed in his blue machinist's apron. Joe told him to go on ahead. Gingerly, Joe eased his damaged left foot into his shoe. The blister didn't hurt much, just enough to remind Joe of its presence. What a ridiculous aggravation, a blister the size of a nickel. Back when he had his health, he'd have hardly noticed it.

Joe's shoes were black, his right one blunt-toed with a steel brace attached to its heel. One-handed and deftly, Joe strapped the brace to his calf. Shod at last, Joe picked up his cane and, rising a little more unsteadily than usual, headed downstairs. He did his stepping forward with his good left leg, leaning heavily on his cane while that leg was in the air. Then he paused to bring the right leg up to where the left leg stood. His walk was an inchworm-like series of movements, slow and deliberate, a forced adaptation that revealed what a complex activity normal walking is. Joe's left hand worked the cane. His left arm still carried a fair portion of its once formidable muscle. His right arm hung limply, like meat on a hook.

As Joe turned into the activity room door, Bob's voice rang out, "Here he comes *now!* " There they sat, Bob and the other Nudniks in the Stupidvising chairs. All was in readiness for the morning's ritual.

Sometimes Joe found it hard to believe that he was about to join in this silliness. A lot of life was silly, though. This wasn't a great deal different from spending Saturdays playing hearts at the Legion bar in Pittsfield. Of course, you could take that two ways. The present could look better, or the past could look worse. But these pre-breakfast high jinks made him laugh. That was the important thing. It didn't really matter that he was often laughing at himself for taking part. "Jesus Christ, if I couldn't laugh, I'd go nuts in here," Joe often said.

Joe stopped a few feet from the Stupidvising chairs, took a deep breath, which lifted him fully erect, and sang out toward Bob, "Howdee! Howdee! Howdee!"

"Howdee! Howdee! Howdee!" Bob answered.

"That's gonna be on his tombstone," Joe said, smiling at Art.

Joe sat down — heavily, in one motion of surrender to gravity — then looked at Bob. "Everything under control?" Joe asked.

"Beautiful! Excellent!" said Bob, offering Joe his hand for shaking. They shook left-handed, their afflictions meeting. Looking at Bob with an appraising eye, Joe lifted the tip of his own cane in the air. "He's the Mayor of Linda Manor. And *the In*-spector General."

Bob grinned. "You're damn right!"

"He's one of the few mayors that, uh, that doesn't take bribes," Joe said. "Right?"

"That's right!" Bob reached over and slapped Joe's leg. "You hot shit."

"Hot stuff, Bob," Lou said softly. "Hot *stuff*." Lou had started this campaign a while back, as another effort to protect Joe's granddaughter and his own great-grandchildren from vulgarity.

Bob looked at Lou. "Hot stuff," said Bob, the still unaccustomed phrase mumbly in his mouth. "Thank you kindly."

Then the main event began. Across the dining room,

through the swinging kitchen door came a pretty young dietary aide wearing an apron. Joe turned. "Lin-dah!" Joe called in a loud falsetto. Other aides emerged. "Sue-zeee!" Joe called in his falsetto. "Mare-eee!"

The aides called back greetings. Joe glanced at Lou. Lou was smiling. Good.

The aide named Mary walked over to the group of men and slapped high, low, and medium fives with each of them.

"Thank you kindly," Bob said to Mary. "She's a damn good girl, I'm tellin' ya," Bob said to Joe as Mary went back to work.

"Yes, she is," Joe replied.

A crowd of gray and white and bald heads, seated in wheelchairs and leaning on walkers and canes, had now collected in a disordered line at the dining room doorway, alongside the five Stupidvising chairs. This was always a slightly painful sight for Joe. He agreed with Lou: people their age shouldn't have to stand and wait. At last a nurse's aide arrived and called out "Okay!" from the dining room, and the breakfast-bound crowd started moving. "Let's go, let's go," said Bob. Joe watched as Bob got up and limped headlong into the dining room, weaving around wheelchairs, barging past old women on walkers. Joe shook his head at the sight.

Joe looked forward to breakfast, the best meal served here in his and Lou's opinion. He was hungry now, as always. But before he could eat, Joe had to interpret for Bob. The dietary aide waiting on them this morning was fairly new. She wondered if Bob wanted his eggs scrambled this morning.

"Yes," Bob declared.

Joe looked up at the aide. "No. Wait a minute. He wants them, uh, poached."

"You're damn right," Bob said to the aide. To Joe, Bob said, "Thank you kindly."

This was no time to have Bob get riled up over his eggs, but Joe would have interpreted for Bob anyway. "Because I was in the same position, that's all," Joe had explained to Lou. "Guys with a stroke say yes when they mean no, see."

The aides took their orders and had just begun to emerge through the swinging doors with trays of food, and Joe was looking hungrily at the tray coming toward him, when from a table off to Joe's left came the sound of a woman's voice bellowing, "This is crap right here!" It was Rosa. This was going to be one of those mornings. Smiling, Joe turned in his chair to watch.

Rosa, a fellow Forest View resident, was a dwarfish woman, usually dressed in sweat pants that looked about to fall down. She was a poet. The other day, encountering Rosa upstairs, Joe asked her to recite, and she declaimed rapid-fire:

> Here's to Hitler, the sonofabitch.
> May he die of the seven year's itch.
> May his pecker be hit with a seven-pound hammer
> And his asshole will whistle "The Star-Spangled Banner."

As a rule, Joe confined his own swearing to invocations of the deity, with a "bullshit" or a "sonofabitch" thrown in now and then. He didn't much care for dirty jokes, but he made an exception for Rosa's. Turned in his chair, forgetting breakfast for the moment, Joe watched as an aide tried to reason with her.

"*Rosa*, it's a pear."

"I don't want it," Rosa declared.

Joe looked around the table. His comrades were all smiling. "And in this corner, we have . . ." intoned Lou. Joe's shoulders shook with laughter.

In a moment the tiny figure of Rosa waddled furiously by, leaving the dining room in a huff, a nurse's aide hurrying after her.

"Goodbye, Rosa," Joe called.

Joe turned to Lou. "Yesterday she walked out of lunch, she walked out of dinner. And they, uh, grounded her." Joe's shoulders shook again.

6

Once the theater gets in the blood, it never leaves. Eleanor was living proof at eighty. She sat in her armchair in her room on Forest View's west wing. She gazed out her window at the wintry landscape, making mental notes about the coming dress rehearsal. "I should have had a property person. Well, here's Eva's wig and Simon Legree's whip. Supposedly the piano tuner will help lower the pitch. They're all going to be terribly nervous with their families here. The lights and the PA system make *me* terribly nervous. But that's typical of the day before a performance."

Some things had gone perfectly today. Eleanor finally got, after weeks of requests, a baked Idaho potato for lunch. Her blood sugar was good at 7 A.M., and was probably better now because of the potato. On top of that, some young woman she'd never seen before, someone visiting a relative here, had given

Eleanor a hat. "Oh, what a lovely beret," Eleanor said to the stranger as they were passing each other in the hall, and just like that, the young woman took off her hat and presented it to Eleanor. Not that Eleanor really cared about clothes, but she knew a fine thing when she saw it. She liked the way it looked on her in the mirror. "A beret for the *bon vivant*," she said. And as for the rehearsal, well, *c'est la vie*. Eleanor sighed toward the pine trees outside her window. "Well, if we haven't done anything else, we've created a little adrenaline in these people." She meant her fellow residents.

"Hi-*lo!*" said an extremely cheerful voice from the doorway. Eleanor's roommate, Elgie, a large smiling woman in a dress, came in, pushing the wheels of her wheelchair while padding along with her feet — the caterpillar walk.

Eleanor glanced at her. "You can come in now. I'm going."

The remark didn't seem to faze Elgie. "Well, I hope the dress rehearsal goes lovely."

"It won't," Eleanor said.

Elgie laughed heartily, a high-pitched laugh with a master-of-ceremonies quality about it.

Eleanor stiffened at the sound. "They never do," she said.

"That's what I've heard," Elgie said.

Eleanor got up, picked up her cane, her script, a bonnet, a small riding crop, and a brown wig, and headed for the door with her small quick dainty steps. Elgie's voice trailed after her, saying, "Goodbye and good luck to you. God bless you all."

Eleanor had decided to call the coming production a cabaret. In fact, it was mainly an old-fashioned minstrel show — without blackface, lest she offend racial sensitivities. Eleanor had assembled most of the materials herself, culling skits and music from the faded pages of her father's old repertoire.

One of Eleanor's most vivid childhood memories was of traveling around upstate New York early in the century, with her young mother and middle-aged impresario father, as he put on his gypsy theatrical shows. Her father would go from one small town to another, bearing large black trunks full of props. He'd recruit local talent and direct them in a minstrel show. He wrote the skits, music, and lyrics. Part of the production would take place outdoors, when he'd lead a parade of the actors down the main street, half the town strutting along behind him and most of the rest watching from the sidewalks, in those days long before television. The company would promenade to the strains of a march Eleanor's father had written, called "The Minstrel Street Parade." The chorus went like this:

> Ta ta ta tum
> On they come
> Look at 'em mash
> Hear the drums crash
> Comedians in line
> Some of old time
> 'Tis the minstrel street parade.

Her father got paid out of the receipts from the indoor performances, usually staged under the auspices of the town's dominant church. He always claimed it as the church of his faith, becoming a Methodist in a Methodist town, for example, though he was actually Episcopalian. Eleanor wrote a short book about her father — she had it published privately. "In 1915 we were still in the north country and I performed in my first minstrel show," she wrote. Among other acts, she sang a song called "Only a Waif."

A sad-eyed, raggedly dressed little girl of five singing "Only a waif out in the street asking a penny from all." I would sing my song and then walk down the aisles, supreme tragedy, as I pretended to beg for a penny from people in the audience. Of course, I never took any money although the patrons would willingly have put the coins in my outstretched hands while tears streamed down their cheeks. Although only five, I can remember it even now, the odd satisfying sensation of making people feel sad because of my tragic appeal.

Reminiscing about that time, back when she was allowed to be one of the party, Eleanor said, "We trouped around the countryside, and then I went back to being a little schoolgirl in Glens Falls." She never got over that early experience. Deep down, she'd been restless ever since.

Eleanor relocated to Linda Manor nearly a year ago under most unusual circumstances. She checked herself in. What's more, she did so without prodding from family or friends and without the compulsion of grave illness. Eleanor lived previously in a retirement home for women, a venerable Northampton institution housed in a mansion not far from Smith College. Time had worn the old building to an elegant shabbiness. Each inhabitant still had her own silver napkin ring, and a sign on the old-fashioned elevator warned against using it during electrical storms.

The retirement home was clean. Although she had to share a bathroom with several other women, Eleanor had her own cozy private bedroom. Since she'd left, many people had asked her why she'd wanted to trade that life of relative independence and privacy for confinement in a nursing home. Eleanor's answers had by now a well-rehearsed quality. Her rest-home room had become insufferably hot in the summers, she'd say. She'd recall that one day her diabetes had flared up dangerously, adding that her own mother had died that way, in a diabetic coma. Although the rest home kept a nurse on duty around the clock, Eleanor would say that she felt she needed more nursing care, or soon would. And besides, there were no men at the rest home — well, there had been one, but he didn't count — and she'd found most of her fellow female residents too prim and proper. "They're all ladies," she'd say. "They never wear pants. They never say anything *risqué.*" But then again, people who had known Eleanor over the years said that she always came up with good reasons for making a change in her life or for leaving a place.

Eleanor's son wasn't surprised when she called him to say that she was leaving the rest home for Linda Manor. He figured she'd exhausted the rest home's theatrical possibilities, both the figurative and literal ones. In fact, Eleanor had already put on seven plays at the rest home, and had begun to find the resources for casting there much too limited. "There were only ten people I could work with." She visited Linda Manor, on a social call, the summer after it opened and liked the looks of the place. "There's so much I could do here," she said.

Relatives almost always assume the considerable burden of managing a move such as Eleanor's. But her two daughters lived far away, and, Eleanor insisted, she preferred not to trouble her son, who lived in Pittsfield. She also allowed that she had never been a very "family-oriented" person, adding that theater people rarely are. She made her decision to move, and then asked for her children's approval.

Eleanor didn't have much money. She had to enroll in Medicaid. The regulations said that if she did not prepay her funeral expenses, the state would take the money. So Eleanor was obliged to prepare her own funeral shortly after she arrived at Linda Manor. The mortician called on her there. It took three hours to get everything picked out, the newspapers in which she wanted her obituary to appear, the accoutrements of the ceremony, the urn for her ashes. Every day for three weeks afterward, she felt like weeping. "And I'm not a weeper," she said, adding, of her funeral, "I think I'm more afraid of going through with it now that I've paid for it." She would like five more years. And in five more years, she figured, she would wish for another five.

Linda Manor wasn't all that Eleanor had hoped. She disliked the food generally, and detested her roommate Elgie. She often spoke yearningly of Forest View's three private rooms, each occupied by a person paying the private rate. She'd never be able to pay for one of those rooms herself, but, Eleanor reasoned, she was doing a great deal for the nursing home in the way of arranging and managing activities for residents. She felt herself really to be more like one of the staff than a resident. So perhaps some arrangement could be made when one of the private rooms' occupants expired. Any of them might go at any time, Eleanor thought. Meanwhile, she was keeping busy. Speaking about one of the women in the room next door to hers on Forest View, Eleanor said, "She has *no* memory, and she doesn't have Alzheimer's. Maybe it's from having nothing to think about. *I* have found you've got to make a goal for yourself, even if you're living in a little corner of a little room." She swept a hand outward, gesturing at her half of the small room, furnished with an antique writing desk, a few family photographs, an armchair, a TV, a stack of books from a local library.

For months her chief occupation had been the Linda Manor Players and the cabaret. It had been a mountain of work. She'd assembled about thirty amateur singers, dancers, and actors. She couldn't find enough residents to fill all the standup parts, so she recruited members of the staff, also the nursing home hairdresser and the hairdresser's husband. And like her father before her, she turned to the churches and shanghaied an Episcopal minister and several members of a local Baptist church into the company.

Eleanor had to make painful concessions. The actors would read their parts. "If I'd insisted on memorizing, I couldn't have gotten a corporal's guard." It wasn't easy staging a play when you didn't have a stage and half of your cast was in wheelchairs and the other half was always too busy to make rehearsals. Although she scolded and cajoled, she hadn't managed to get everyone together at any one of the rehearsals — not until the dress rehearsal, which, she didn't mind saying, was pretty ragged. She also had to fire the first piano player she engaged. Several times lately she'd threatened to cancel the whole thing. "I should never have tried to do something this ambitious," Eleanor said, back upstairs in her room. But there was a lot of color in her face, not all of it from the rouge on her cheeks. She was smiling.

❖   ❖   ❖

"You say I inveigled you into Eleanor's play," Lou said from his chair by the window.

67

"You got me into . . ." Joe began to say, his voice on the verge of a bellow.

"Joe, the word you like to use, I don't like to use it. Bullshit. *I* got inveigled just by suggesting a few jokes to her."

They'd been having this same discussion for a few weeks now. "I did many stupid things," Joe said. "But this play of Ellen-er's . . ."

"Oh, you'll do all right," Lou said. "You signed the contract and you gotta live up to it."

"Listen." Joe rose up in bed, pulling back the privacy curtain to face Lou. "I did high school plays and I did all right. But this script, for Christ's sake, it stinks, huh?"

"Oh, it doesn't stink," Lou said, adding, "I don't have a script. I'm playing it by ear."

In the evening they made their way downstairs, dressed in their costumes — Lou in a large, floppy, snap-brim hat, Joe with a cloth band tied around his head. From the elevator landing all the way down on Sunrise, one could hear the babble of the gathering theater crowd.

As the cast assembled in the activity room, Bob looked around at their costumes, the floppy hats, the black gloves, the several fancy dresses, and said, "Oh boy, oh boy. Excellent."

"I don't want to hear that word," said Eleanor. "Not tonight."

Bob sat in the chorus, grinning at everything, along with Phil and several women in wheelchairs. The major singers and players sat in front of the chorus, in a row of folding chairs across the dining room doorway, in about the same position that Bob and Lou and Joe occupied for pre-meal Stupidvising. This spot now became the stage. The actors faced the dining room, where their audience sat.

At one end of the front row of actors sat Lou and Joe. Joe looked amused and a little embarrassed. Eleanor sat at the other end of the front row, beside the piano and the drummer, who was a nurse's son. The rest of that row were Eleanor's able-bodied, younger ringers: Linda Manor's director of activities, her assistant, an administrative assistant in charge of scheduling, two youngish Baptist friends of Eleanor's, the Baptist minister, who wore a dark suit and would serve as "Mr. Interlocutor," and a nursing supervisor whose pretty soprano equaled in volume the combined voices of the rest of the company and, it must be said, saved most of the musical parts of the show. The company rose, and with sweet and sour notes the cabaret began.

> On a bright and pleasant morning in the springtime
> When the birds are sweetly singing in the shade,
> There is nothing half so thrilling to the senses
> As to see a minstrel troupe do their parade.
> Ta ta ta tum,
> On they come . . .

The company sat down. Rising, Mr. Interlocutor gestured at the row of actors, saying to the audience, "Ladies and gentlemen, the funmakers of the evening." The audience clapped loudly.

The audience overflowed the dining room. In the back were a number of the actors' relatives — children, grandchildren, a great-grandchild or two, many of them standing, some sitting on the windowsills. The residents in the audience, mainly in wheelchairs, sat at the round dining tables. Most seemed more interested in the hors d'oeuvres than in the show.

Up on the stage — the open patch of gray linoleum floor where the stage should have been — Mr. Interlocutor said to Mr. Charcoal, "Your brother is an author, I believe."

"Oh, yes. Pinky am an author. Is you read his last book?"

"No. What is it?"

"It's pigs. De social life of pigs. It *sho'* am a *swill* book."

One of the residents in the audience said to another, "Well, at least they have a sense of humor." Behind them, though, the younger contingent laughed and laughed. As the show went on, the female residents at one table in the audience discussed the finger foods. Why did the kitchen serve them food you needed teeth to eat? And where were the napkins? But the rest of the audience drowned out most of that conversation. The audience laughed at all the right moments and applauded at the end of every song, dialogue, and skit.

Joe, playing Simon Legree in Eleanor's father's egregious "Uncle Tom's Nabin," fumbled his lines, trying to read his script. Eleanor prompted him, hissing from stage left, and Joe found his voice. "I'll have his blood!" Joe roared, flicking a riding crop over Uncle Tom, Linda Manor's chief of maintenance, who lay snoring on the floor. The third actor in this bit, a retired school principal in a wheelchair with a painful-looking hump, declared, her mordant voice improving the line: "You can't. He's anemic."

Eleanor donned a bonnet, tied its strings under her chin, and remained seated beside the drummer for her solo. "My mother sang this song in my father's revue when I was two and a half years old, but I'm no singer, so I will speak it," she told the audience, and then slipped into character, hunching her shoulders, clasping her hands together, pulling them to her chest, and saying, "I'm an old maid, an old maid. That's what the people say. Although . . ." She paused, her hands coming forward, palms facing up. "Although I'm very fond of men, they never come my way . . ."

Eleanor was the smoothest of the performers, clearly a trained actress acting. But Winifred, in the role of a nagging, weeping wife to a bankrupt ne'er-do-well, was utterly convincing, a natural talent now exposed. Everyone knew Winifred, and she got a big hand when her able-bodied partner in the skit wheeled her out before the audience. Winifred wore a bouffant, curly brown wig, like a headdress, and a satin print dress with perhaps two pounds of costume jewelry around her neck. Her wheelchair had leg extenders on which her swollen feet and legs rested, pointing straight out at the audience. Winifred was huge all over and in outline nearly shapeless, but for all of that she looked regal, like a queen in a peculiar dream. Her voice was very strong. It seemed a pity that she didn't have more lines.

Lou came on near the end of the show, rising and walking slowly on his cane to center stage. Lou didn't use any of Eleanor's father's material. He did three old vaudeville turns remembered from his youth. They were two-man acts. Lou did both voices. "On the way out I met an old friend of mine who just came back from a course in school where he learned all about nature. I said, 'You did? What is nature?' 'Well, I'll tell ya. You plant a sweet potato and it grows, that's nature.' 'Oh, nature is a sweet potato? Ah, you didn't learn nothin'. Tell the people everything you learned.' 'I'll tell them everything we *both* learned. It won't take any longer.' "

"Ladies and gentlemen," Lou said at last, "we'll be here

tonight, tomorrow night, and probably Saturday night. Provided police and weather conditions permit." The audience laughed uncertainly. "That's all, folks," Lou added, and everybody cheered.

Soon Mr. Interlocutor was saying, "Ladies and gentlemen, the finale by the entire company," and, led by the nursing supervisor's fine, strong soprano, they began, "Ta ta ta tum, on they come . . ." The front row of actors was supposed to stand to sing.

Lou stood up. Beside him, Joe inched himself to the edge of his low metal chair, planted his cane, and started to rise. Many days had passed since he had gone to M&M's or ridden the bike, because of his blister. Joe's arm trembled. He rose a little, and then settled back. He tried again. His arm shook as it tried to push him up.

Lou turned and reached down to help, but by then the song was almost over, and Joe waved him away.

7

Christmas carolers were abroad, and they were drawn to nursing homes like missionaries to the South Seas. Some groups gave semiformal concerts in the activity room. Many residents attended. They enjoyed the singing, especially when they were asked to sing along and when children came. The sight of children brought sudden infusions of color into the faces of almost every resident. The hearts of even the listlessly demented seemed to pump harder. But residents sometimes had no choice except to listen, since some groups serenaded in the corridors of the nursing units. All things grow oppressive if repeated enough. It seemed as if every religious and civic group had to come in and sing carols. Some residents, Eleanor particularly, began groaning at the news of yet another group's coming. But the carolers meant well, and it was Christmas season.

A nursing home proceeds to many different clocks. Illnesses and injuries hold people to different schedules from the world outside them. Time in Lou and Joe's room became the time of the blister on Joe's toe. It was marked by the judicious looks and noncommittal words of the nurses, and by Joe's growing weariness with the question, "How's the blister, Joe?" "It's, uh . . . Oh, the hell with it," he said, waving the question away.

Joe still could not return to M&M's or ride the exercise bike. But he couldn't resist weighing himself each morning. "Good God, I gained a pound," Joe said, lying on his back on his bed. "I think it was the Jell-O last night."

"I don't think so," Lou said from his chair by the window. He added, "When you were bicycling like mad, you weren't losing weight."

"I wasn't bicycling like mad," Joe said. But his voice wasn't vehement. He didn't even sit up in bed to argue this point anymore. What was the sense of arguing? Lou was right, and Joe might as well admit it.

"Yes, you were," said Lou. "I told you you were going at it too hard. Like do or die."

Joe gazed up at the ceiling. "That's right. *Eingeshpart.* Well, I paid for it. Two weeks and it won't heal."

Joe missed the bike. "It made my leg feel *strong,* you know."

But everyone here had problems of one sort or another, most much worse than this. The blister would pass, Joe told himself. Days ran into each other. Life in the room wasn't all that different, really. To be at Linda Manor at all was to be laid up. Joe was just a little more laid up for now.

He and Lou could not control most of the substance of their life in here, but they had imposed a style on it. The way, for instance, that he and Lou had come, in the past months, to deal with matters of the bathroom. Joe had to go there what seemed to him like a ridiculous number of times each day and night. He and Lou referred to the bathroom as "the library." The mock gentility of the term amused Joe. The point was to make a joke out of anything you could around here, whether it was weakened bowels or Bob's antics. Up in the room after breakfast, Joe would say to Lou, "I gotta go to the library. I have to do my, uh, uh, prune evacuation."

This room was now their home. As in any household, people entering were expected to follow local rules. The nursing staff was overwhelmingly female. Lou and Joe referred to all of them as girls, and indeed, next to them, even the middle-aged did look like girls. The staff had all, of course, been quite willing to talk frankly about matters of Lou's and Joe's biology. Too frankly for Lou. Too frankly for Joe, once Lou had made the point. The aides, "the girls," used to come to the doorway cradling open in their arms the large, ledger-like Forest View "BM Book," and they'd call loudly in, "Did either of you gentlemen have a bowel movement today?" It was Lou, some months ago now, who responded to this question by inviting in the girls who asked it, and then telling them gently, "All you have to say is, 'Did you or didn't you?' " The way Lou did that job impressed Joe. Lou did it so diplomatically, so much more diplomatically than Joe would have. Lou, as he liked to say, had trained all the girls by now. Joe took care of reinforcement.

It was a morning in December, in the third week of Joe's blister. Joe had the television news on. He and Lou were listening to the dispatches from the Middle East. It looked increasingly as though there would be war in Iraq. Joe watched intently, fuming now and then about the stupidity of war. He wasn't waiting for the aide with the BM Book, but he had a question ready for her. When the aide came to the door, she asked, "For my book. Did you?"

"Yes." Joe tilted his head toward Lou. "And so did he." Then, a little smile blossoming, Joe looked at the aide and asked, "And what about you?"

"None of your business!" The aide looked embarrassed. She laughed.

"Well, you ask me," Joe said.

"But I get paid for it."

"*Good* bye," Joe said pleasantly, and went back to watching the news.

Across the room, Lou was bending over in his chair, getting out his shot glass and bottle from his bedside dresser. Joe sat up in bed to watch. "Good God. That isn't drinking. One shot glass. Tee-hee."

Lou raised the glass. "*L'chaim.* Cheers, Joe." The room filled with the sweet smell of cheap brandy. The war news had concluded. Joe shut off the television and lay back on his bed. Now they'd talk. Lou was always ready to talk, and never at a loss for subjects.

Did they offer service-connected life insurance in World

War II, as they had in World War I? Lou wondered. He wished he'd bought that insurance back in 1917.

"Mine'll bury me," Joe said. "It costs you pennies a month, for God's sake."

"When I was first married, my wife didn't believe in insurance. She was afraid if you got it, you'd die." Lou shifted in his chair. He said, "One thing my wife and I discussed when she was still in her right senses, we didn't want to be a burden on our children. In fact, before we came here we purchased a burial plot." Joe heard Lou's voice turn thin. He glanced at Lou. Lou's chin was raised, his head back, his eyes closed. "She didn't want to be a burden on the family, and it's turned out that way." Lou sniffled, just once. He rolled his shoulders slightly, readjusting himself in his chair, his face recomposing itself.

Joe stared at the ceiling. He didn't speak. What could he say? He ran his good hand downward over his face and, his face thus cleared, made a chewing motion.

"Well," Joe said, "*I'm* gonna be cremated. Take up less space. Christ almighty. When the spirit leaves you . . ." Joe threw his left arm high in the air and said, "Whoop!" His spirit dispatched, Joe went on, "And I'm going to heaven, and it's going to be run by a woman."

Lou still had his eyes closed, but Joe had him smiling now. "Your vision."

"Yes, my vision," Joe said. "Through that window. God came down and said, 'I'm a woman,' and I said, 'Good!' "

"Dan," Lou said. "Dan sees little green men out *his* window." Their fellow Forest View resident Dan was very garrulous. He once told Lou and Joe that he thought he'd seen a UFO outside his window.

76

Outside, a story below their east-facing window, a grassy hillside led upward to an evergreen and hardwood forest. Some residents insisted that they once saw a bear crossing the field. Joe hadn't seen it. He didn't spend a lot of time gazing out. It looked cold outside, the grass brown, the oaks and maples and birches bare. It was very warm in the room. Joe raised his left arm, like a maestro conducting from bed, and he declared that he hoped his house back in Pittsfield was still in the family when he died. He hoped there would be an ice storm that day. "I want my ashes spread on the sidewalk. So nobody will slip."

"What if it's summer?" Lou said.

"Then I'll have them put on the garden. Sure. For God's sake."

Lou mentioned the story they heard on TV, of the funeral director who cut his expenses by cremating several people at once.

"What the hell difference does it make?" Joe said.

"It doesn't make any difference," Lou said. "But if you want the remains of your loved one, you don't want six or seven other people mixed in."

Joe laughed. He glanced at Lou, who lifted a hand from the arm of his chair and made a gun with the forefinger, saying, "Talking about ashes and stuff."

Joe knew what was coming, in a general way. "Yup," Joe murmured toward the ceiling. He gazed up, his bared toe aloft on its pillow. He let himself relax into his bed. He wondered which story Lou would tell now, and if it was one already told. Sometimes Lou told new ones, or added new elements to old ones.

"Speaking of ashes and stuff," Lou said. "As a youngster in Philadelphia, we had quite a few oyster saloons, they used to call them. They were only open in the *r* months. The shells were ground up and sold to chicken farms. Then they started using them on the roads." And there were the arcades, theaters, and vaudeville and burlesque houses on 8th Street: the Gayety, Forepaugh's, Lubin's Nickelodeon, the Bijou where Lou saw the first talking pictures, and the nearby sporting houses where Lou never went, though he sometimes earned a nickel by giving sailors the directions. A hawker used to set an open suitcase on a tripod on Summer Street, between Vine and Race, and pull out a postcard of a half-naked woman, moving it from side to side in front of Lou and his two schoolboy friends. All three boys wore knickers and snap-brim caps. The hawker practiced his pitch on them, and when adults appeared he would say, not unkindly, "Beat it, kids." As Lou and his pals walked away, they'd hear the hawker saying to his customers in a singsong voice, "I'll be here tonight, tomorrow night, and probably Saturday night. Provided police and weather conditions permit."

Lou's tongue did not quite form *th*, so "these" came out as "dese," but with a much softer *d* than in Brooklyn. His gravelly voice, not a basso profundo but from a deep place, rolled smoothly on, like the sound of a lone propeller plane in a quiet country sky. Joe could drift away on it. Lou's voice carried on for what seemed like both a long time and no time at all. "Yup," Joe said occasionally.

"Ahh, dear," Lou sighed. "The things you remember. What time is it?" He peered at his wristwatch, holding it up to within about an inch of his right eye, like a jeweler examining a precious stone. "Time to go down for lunch, Joe."

Months ago now, Lou had affixed, to the upper-right-hand casing of their doorway, a tiny *mezuzah* — the talisman found in many observant Jewish homes, to remind the inhabitants to walk in the ways of God. On his way out of the room for lunch, Lou paused in the doorway, reached up, and touched the little *mezuzah*. Then, after he crossed the threshold, Lou called back, "Joe, close the door."

Lou feared that if they left their door ajar when they went out, one of Forest View's demented residents might ransack their room. That made sense to Joe, but Lou seemed to think he had to remind Joe to close the door every time they went out. Every time.

"Jesus Christ," Joe muttered to himself, "if I don't close it, he'll kill me."

Joe followed Lou toward the door. Lou always touched his *mezuzah*. "Lou figures that the Tribe will go to heaven," Joe thought. "Well, for Christ's sakes, they got no more chance than anybody. The Chinese die, they're going to heaven?" Lou and the door. Lou and his *mezuzah*. But you never can tell. At the threshold, Joe reached up and touched the *mezuzah*, too. Then he closed the door.

❖　❖　❖

Joe's doctor changed Joe's antibiotic. Probably that did the trick, or maybe time deserved the credit. In any case, Joe awoke one morning near the end of December and for a moment he couldn't even see the blister. So Joe was cleared for a return to M&M's and stationary biking. But when Lou asked, "You coming down to M&M's?" Joe said he didn't feel like it today.

With Joe it was all or nothing, Lou thought. "He's his own

worst enemy." In the afternoon, contemplating the shape of Joe, lying over there, Lou had an idea. He got up and fetched his cane. "Joe, I'm going out for a walk." But that didn't work. Either Joe didn't get the hint or he chose not to.

Lou understood the problem. You get old and you get rusty. You go without exercise for a while, and you don't feel like exercising anymore. But persistence had worked on Joe before. He'd just keep asking the question until Joe got sick of it. "Joe, why don't you come down to M&M's with me tomorrow?"

"All right," Joe said finally. He didn't sound too happy about it, but he would be, Lou thought.

A little later, Lou went off alone downstairs. Just to take a walk, he told Joe. Actually, Lou went to the physical therapy room, searching for the voice of Carol, the physical therapy aide who ran M&M's and supervised Joe's biking.

The next morning all was just as it had been before Joe's blister. Joe limped into the physical therapy room and took his usual seat, an armchair next to Lou's. Carol welcomed Joe back. She told him she had attached some foam rubber pads to the pedals of the bike. That way Joe could ride it in his stocking feet, lessening the chance of another blister.

"It was an extra thing for you to do," Joe said to Carol. "Thank you."

"Well, I just wanted you to be able to use the bike again," Carol said. She paused, then added, "But maybe not quite so violently."

As she said these words, Carol glanced at Lou.

Joe's eyes followed Carol's to Lou. Lou was making an effort to look completely nonchalant. It showed. Joe smiled.

Lou could sense Joe's eyes on him. Lou rolled his shoulders, as if getting ready for the workout. Beside him, he heard Joe's voice, directed his way. "I'm not *eingeshpart!* "

8

The New Year's Eve celebration started at 2 P.M., in order to accommodate the nursing home's routines and the residents' bedtimes. A four-man combo, with drums, saxophone, accordion, and bass guitar, set up their music stands in the wide doorway to the dining room. Crepe paper streamers stretched in webs among the chandeliers, and party favors lay with every table setting. At Linda Manor's parties, there was always the appearance of a broad dichotomy between bustle and passivity — aides and managers dressed in party hats waiting on the tables, blowing party horns and clacking party noisemakers, singing brassily along to the music, while many residents sat quietly with open mouths, or smiling, or looking grumpy. Now and then a nurse slipped in among the crowd, with pill cup in one hand and water cup in the other, and knelt down before a resident.

The combo was entirely white-haired. All four of the musicians looked about as old as many residents of Forest View. But age creates great biological disparities, far greater than differences at birth. Facing in on a room full of parked wheelchairs and walkers, of backs bent by osteoporosis, of ankles swollen by renal insufficiency and heart disease, while here and there residents sat with vacant-looking faces holding stuffed animals in their laps, the elderly musicians in their ties and jackets seemed very vigorous.

The combo warmed up with a few polkas. "I guess you know that song was made very popular by Bobby Vinton, 'The Melody of Love Polka,' " said the vocalist-emcee. Soon they switched to old dance-hall numbers. "Let me call you sweetheart," crooned the vocalist.

Except for the bedridden, the partygoers represented most of the conditions of old age lived within these walls. There were a number on hand with vigorous minds and ruined bodies, such as Winifred, arrayed in her wheelchair, singing along. And there were almost as many in the opposite condition, such as gray-haired Zita, who wandered aimlessly around the dining room. She walked with a spryness that Winifred and Bob and Lou and Joe could recapture only in their memories and dreams.

Art, Lou, and Joe all sat apart from the other residents. They sat in chairs in the activity room behind the combo, instead of in the dining room, not talking to one another and, anyone could see, not listening intently to this music either, but riding away on it.

Art skipped high school to go to work. He continued his education informally while working as a janitor at Smith College in Northampton, the town where he was born, raised, married, and, here on its outskirts, would likely die. Art had liked crossword puzzles. When he got stuck, he'd visit professors in their offices and ask for help, which was how he acquired his impressive vocabulary. He started singing as a boy soprano in his Catholic church's choir. Later, while he was working as a custodian at Smith, his boss overheard him singing to himself during a lunch break, and he got Art free voice lessons. Art remembered going up to Hampton Beach with his wife one summer evening, to a concert at the band shell there. An organist played and encouraged the crowd to sing. Art and his wife sat near the back. "I was singin' away. At intermission the organist comes up to me and says, 'Are you a pro?' I says, 'No, semipro.' I couldn't understand it, all these people singing and he comes up to me. My wife says, 'That's the funniest thing.'" Locally, Art's voice was in demand for decades. He sang on the local radio station on Easter Sunday, 1940. He was once recorded singing the prologue to *Pagliacci* — out of the scratchy old recording his voice emerged like a deep bell lined with velvet. He had several teachers over the years. One had felt that Art could make it as a singer in New York, but Art did not believe it, and he never tried. Sometimes he still wondered if he should have.

Since his wife's death, he had suffered from memories. He recalled the time when he and his wife were young and newly married and she dropped a frying pan and he yelled at her. "If she could come back to life now, she could drop a hundred of them and I wouldn't give a darn." Few conscious minds exert full control of memory. Art remembered his nearly sixty years of marriage as very happy overall, but the stories that he now recalled most vividly and wanted most to tell were of that dropped frying pan and of his sixty-year-long disagreement with his wife about demonstrativeness. His wife would say she wished he'd tell her that he loved her, and he would protest that he preferred to do the sorts of things that proved it. She would say she understood, but that any woman wants to hear the words, and Art would answer, "It doesn't run in my family to be like that." He started telling his wife he loved her several times each day, in their room on Sunrise, during the weeks before she died. "But she never said a word. Not 'Yes, dear, I forgive you.' I would've liked that. It seemed it hurt her all her life." Probably she could not answer him then, if she even heard him, but he wasn't sure.

Nothing about his wife's death had gone as Art wished in retrospect. He was watching baseball on TV in their room when she died, without a sound. "Well, the Red Sox are losing again," he remembered saying over his shoulder to her. "I wish I'd've known," he would say. "Because I'd've had her die in my arms."

Eleanor, who liked being punctual, had gotten to the New Year's party before Art. She was sitting in the dining room among some other women, listening to the combo, feeling bored.

"Even though these men here have all these physical problems, it's so nice to be in a place that *has* men. They add a little something," Eleanor said. A week ago, on Christmas Day, standing with Art at the nurses' station on Forest View, Eleanor came right out and told him, "You don't know what a difference it's made to have you here."

Art said, "I think *she* would approve."

Art had already told her about his wife, so Eleanor knew who "she" was. Eleanor leaned over and gave Art a kiss, a Christmas kiss on the cheek. And Art said, "I *know* she would approve of that."

Eleanor often found herself thinking about Art these days. "He's a *very* sensitive person, I think. We've talked about things that older people don't generally talk about. He knows all the words to the old songs, and I know them all. He tells me when the *good* shows are on TV. He's still a good-looking man. He is the *nicest* man. He and Art" — she meant Art, her husband — "would have gotten on just fine. He knows every lyric, every song. He's such a nice man. His leg's been hurting him lately. But I can get him out of his moods."

Eleanor didn't see Art come into the New Year's Eve party, but after the first song, she spotted him out in the activity room, sitting alone, a little distance from Lou and Joe. So Eleanor threaded her way out past the tables and wheelchairs, and pulled up a chair next to Art's. One of the dietary aides brought Eleanor a paper crown with "Happy New Year" emblazoned on the front. Eleanor put in on.

Art was feeling blue. Eleanor could tell. She understood Art, she liked to say. No one around here understood Art as she did. She felt a little blue herself.

How does one grow old so fast? It seemed like only a little while ago when Eleanor was entertaining suitors in the parlor of her parents' house, and the alarm clock descended the stairwell, dangling from a string in front of her and her boyfriend. Lowering the alarm clock was her father's way of informing Eleanor's boyfriends that it was time for them to leave. Eleanor wasn't one to let herself wallow in nostalgia or regrets, but she felt edgy when she looked back on the affair she'd had years ago with a colleague of her husband's. It had begun because of a play, *Brief Encounters*. They had been costars. Love affairs, she thought, were occupational hazards for an actress. "I always fall in love with the person I play opposite," Eleanor said. "But this one lasted so long. Art knew about it. Everybody did. Even the kids. I don't know as I regret it. I'm a little ashamed of it. This man used to call me late at night. He wanted me to meet him at the university. He wanted me to go away with him. He'd say,

'Someday I'll do something *wonder*ful for you.' Eventually his wife came home and that was . . . it. The only thing I ever thought was, 'Well, it isn't quite me.' I think it filled a void at that time, of my father coming back to live with us, and Art not making much money, and having kids."

Dressed in her paper crown, Eleanor leaned over toward this Art and said above the music, "Not going to sing today?"

"No," Art answered.

"Well," Eleanor said, "I guess I'll go upstairs."

"I'll go with you," Art said.

When they got outside the activity room door, Eleanor took Art's arm. Behind them, the combo had just struck up "Show Me the Way to Go Home," which would have seemed a bit ironic and dreary to Eleanor a moment ago, but now seemed too good to be true. She started to sing the song and Art joined in, his fine, trained baritone growing in authority. They walked along, singing. The combo's music receded behind them. Art shuffled along and at the right moments doffed an imaginary top hat. Eleanor with her little steps easily kept pace. She held on to the crook of Art's arm and swung her cane in the air before her like a drum major's baton. Maintaining this arrangement, singing on, they boarded one of the elevators, ascended singing, got off and slowly promenaded, singing even louder, down the corridor. They finished up the sad old song standing arm in arm in front of the Forest View nurses' station. The nurse on duty applauded. Then Art got his usual midafternoon pills and repaired to his room, alone.

"Oh, I *like* him," Eleanor said, both her voice and body quivering, as if vibrations in the floor were being transmitted through her cane. "I *like* him." To Eleanor it seemed a fine ending to a melancholy day, and a good beginning to her eighty-first New Year.

❖   ❖   ❖

Downstairs the party was still going strong. During a lull in the music someone in the dining room said loudly, "These songs make me cry." Lou got up from his chair at once and groped his way to the door. Joe followed at a little distance, then stopped and watched as Lou walked down the administrative corridor. He was heading for the lobby. Joe wouldn't follow him.

He knew that Lou was thinking about his wife. Lou would probably go to the lobby and cry quietly, or if one of the staff stopped to talk to him, Lou might tell her about his wife's death and, his voice thin and wailing, say, "I held her hand right up until the end. That's the way we started, and that's the way we ended up." And afterward, Lou would probably say to his listener, "I think that little talk did me some good." Together in their room, Lou and Joe had discussed the issue of men crying. They agreed there was no shame in it. But Lou did not often cry in front of Joe. Perhaps that was because his crying was apt to make Joe cry, too. Lou clearly felt no shame in crying in front of anyone — in crying, that is, about his wife and not about his own condition. But Joe, no matter what he said, clearly did not like to cry in front of another man or to display affection toward another publicly.

The so-called labile tendency that sometimes accompanies strokes had lingered eighteen years in Joe. It made him feel like weeping over inconsequential things, such as the sight of a young tree growing. Even the news of an ugly gas station's being torn down could make him cry, Joe said. His fits were brief but powerful looking. He'd sob silently, often without tears, his mouth open and his shoulders shaking — a momentary, dry-heaving kind of sob. Then he'd run his good hand downward over his face and reappear unruffled, sometimes smiling, as if from the powder room. The combo's old dance-hall songs were strong stimuli, and Joe had wanted to get out of the activity room before he was overwhelmed. Joe couldn't prevent weepiness, but he'd get out of public places if he could when the fit was on him — just as he would make sure to wipe the numbed right side of his mouth periodically, in case spittle that he couldn't feel had collected there.

Joe belonged to the generation whose young men felt compelled, even desperate, to join the military and serve in World War II. He himself had searched for a military doctor who would overlook his congenital high blood pressure. He found such a doctor, and then discovered war to be less glorious than advertised. But Joe absorbed his generation's ideal of manly virtue, and more than ever now he tried to live up to it. He would say that he admired Hemingway for committing suicide, because suicide took courage. And if one chose to live on, one must weather one's own fate bravely, or at least without complaint. Joe saw examples of such virtue all around him here. At least once a week he and Lou would hear a loud thump through the wall, the sound of a woman who lived next door taking a fall, and Joe would say, "Oh, dear God. Mary." He or Lou used to go out and tell one of the staff that she had fallen, but then Mary asked them not to. Mary said she was afraid that if the staff knew how often she fell, she'd be "sent downstairs." So now Joe listened to the thump unhappily and said, "Mary, she never complains."

Joe said, "Art. He has, uh, Parkinson's. He's losing, uh, eye. He walks a little, he gets tired. And he never complains." Joe often made these expressions of admiration for the stoics around him when he himself was feeling pain — phantom pain in his missing toe, chronic pain in his knees or shoulder — or after some common sight, such as a resident drooling, reminded him that he'd ended up in a nursing home. At such times, Joe might recite the litany of his own wife's ailments.

Joe was also surrounded by counter-examples of stoical virtue, the "goddamn fools," as he would say, who complained about their lot and did everything they could to make their families feel guilty.

And then there was Lou. "Lou's hemorrhoids are bothering him. He has angina. His back's bothering him. He's legally blind. And he *never* complains. Good God, huh?"

The music wafted out of the activity room. This was Lou's first New Year without his wife. Joe watched him move slowly toward the lobby. "It's sad. Sad," said Joe. He limped toward the elevators. Joe got winded more quickly now than before his blister. Now when he walked from the dining room to the elevators, he had to stop on the way and rest. When he made this short walk in the company of an able-bodied visitor or one of the nurses whom he advised on matters of alimony, Joe timed these halts with the conversation. He made it seem as if he stopped and leaned awhile on his cane simply in order to emphasize a point. Joe rode up to Forest View alone.

New Year's Eve: at moments like these, when fragments of time coalesced and Joe realized where he'd been and how he'd gotten here, he'd sometimes say, "*Route* Nine. I never thought

I'd end up on Route Nine." The saying went way back. In Joe's house outside Pittsfield, or across from the courthouse in the Legion bar, there was a standing joke. If somebody did something peculiar or said something nutty, the others would point fingers at their heads and cry, "*Route* Nine!" That two-lane state highway winds east from Pittsfield to Northampton. It is a bucolic drive of thirty miles through the Berkshires. It also used to be the route along which mental patients rode, from Pittsfield to the tall gothic buildings and locked wards of the once gigantic Northampton State Hospital. To send people there was to "Route Nine 'em."

Joe remembered the journey east away from Pittsfield to the VA Medical Center in Northampton, the ride with which this new life of his began. He rode in the back of a VA van. His son rode with him. The rest of his family followed in a car. Joe sat in a wheelchair, looking out the windows. On the outskirts of Pittsfield, the van turned onto the famous two-lane highway, and Joe turned to his son and smiled wryly. "*Route* Nine!" he said. He didn't talk much the rest of the way. As the van passed through a town a few miles from Northampton where Joe's daughter lived, he caught a glimpse of his infant granddaughter. The babysitter just happened to be taking the child out for a walk in a stroller. Everyone involved in Joe's relocation agreed that the timing of that walk was a minor miracle. Joe beamed as he looked through the window at the receding figure of his granddaughter. Small and blond with the Torchio curls in her hair.

Joe didn't complain to his family when he was wheeled into his room at the VA. He tried to make himself seem cheerful. He was glad to be able to remember that. It was the right way to behave, and it was the least he could do for his family. Maybe it amounted to a little recompense.

Joe remembered disappointments from his years as chief probation officer. Disappointments came with the job. Trying to straighten out other people's lives, dealing every day with the county's routine, seamy social chaos — it could put a strain on sympathy. On the other hand, the job cultivated the habit of being needed, and it wasn't as though he hadn't helped a lot of people. The women with small children whose husbands weren't paying their alimony, for example. His office had the second-best record in the state for making those men pay up. And he often made it possible for the delinquent husbands to do so, by *not* putting them in jail. There were a lot of kids who came to him in custody, in their first big trouble. He was the first probation officer in the state to institute a program of work release instead of jail for them. And a lot of those kids straightened themselves out. In the early days, he and the first judge he worked for made some mistakes. People being hauled into court for the crime of cohabitation — that seemed pretty silly now. He and the judge should have released them on the spot. But Joe rid the courtroom of the "cage" in which the various accused used to await their hearings before the judge. He gave a lot of drunks a break. The police chief didn't approve. "Joe, Joe, Let 'Em Go Torchio," the police chief called him. The chief said he was going to stop giving Joe's office the arrest reports on drunks if Joe was simply going to free a lot of them. "Then I'll release them all," Joe retorted. Joe's son had worked awhile as a corrections officer in the county jail. He'd told Joe that, while working there, he ran into quite a few old reprobates who said, "I know your father. Yeah, he put me in jail back in '58. He's a good guy." His son said he wasn't sure if those testimonials qualified as compliments. Joe was greatly amused.

It is strange to remember an active life while lying on a bed in a nursing home. Joe's recollections of his former life seemed at moments now as stupefyingly improbable as a TV action-adventure. Once a large young man disagreed so strongly with the probationary terms Joe set for him that he pulled a knife on him. Joe, half the young thug's size, climbed over the top of his desk and took the knife away. Twenty years ago, only a couple of years before the stroke that divided up his life, a local lawyer, arguing with Joe about a real estate deal, called him a liar over the phone. Joe dropped the receiver, ran out his door and across several blocks — in his shirtsleeves, in the dead of winter — and up the stairs to that lawyer's office. The lawyer knew that he had made a mistake. He knew Joe. He had erected a barricade of chairs around his desk, and stood inside it when Joe arrived. Joe was too winded to get at the lawyer right away, and by the time he'd caught his breath, a policeman had appeared. Joe had a lot of clout with the local police force. There was no question of his being arrested. Afterward, in fact, the policeman said, "I tried to give you some time to hit him."

"I used to box intramurally," Joe remembered. He smiled. "Sometimes in bars." He didn't drink during working hours, but he spent many evenings in the Legion bar. After his stroke, his Legion pals sent him a giant card with the queen of spades on the front in memory of their Saturday games of hearts. It was an odd feeling to realize that most of the men who signed that card were dead now. A lot of friends had died.

Father John. Joe grew up with him, and John became a Catholic priest. Father John was one of Joe's most faithful visitors after Joe had his stroke. He would come over to the house, and they'd sit down at the kitchen table, and Joe's wife would put a bottle down between them. The bottle wouldn't last long. They'd argue theology. Joe remembered asking Father John if he believed what the pope had said about Mary ascending to heaven in her clothes.

"Yes, I have the faith," said Father John.

"Well, by Jesus, *I* don't," said Joe.

Then Father John contracted Lou Gehrig's disease, an excruciating fatal illness. Joe remembered visiting him on his deathbed, at a rectory in eastern Massachusetts. Father John smiled up at him. He said, "Christ suffered on the cross for three days."

Joe answered, "He didn't suffer as much as you!"

Joe was a devout Catholic as a boy. He lost his faith around the age of seventeen. "I just didn't believe the story anymore. Immaculate Conception, I used to believe that. God is in three persons. That's a mystery that we can't understand, right? I'm an agnostic leaning toward atheism. *But . . .*" Here Joe would raise his good arm and declare, "There's something that started the goddamn world!" The fault must lie in him for lacking religious faith, Joe thought, because so many other people had it. But his professional and personal experiences of life made the idea of a just God, mindful of the fall of sparrows, laughable.

It was around this time of year, long ago, when the doctor had said there was no hope for his first son. The boy died at the age of seven from leukemia. He used to apologize to his mother and Joe for the messes of blood his illness caused. And then their first daughter was born retarded. It took about a year before the fact was known. Joe and his wife eventually raised two healthy children. It was a relief to know that, but he never really got over what happened to his first son and daughter. He merely grew accustomed to the facts. "I was no good for ten years. I just went through the motions." But it would be dishonest to say he drank because of that.

Then the stroke hit. He was only fifty-four. He remembered falling out of bed and hearing his wife on the telephone, summoning help. Joe wasn't worried right away. He figured that whatever it was, he'd come out of it. Therapists and his wife and his best friend worked on him, and gradually his speech returned and he learned to walk again, after a fashion. And with a great deal of help from his wife and his assistants, he went back to work. He had a lot to thank those people for, especially his wife. About ten years later he was forced to retire. For a few more years he lived at home, in semi-isolation, keeping mainly to a small den that smelled of chimney smoke. He kept on drinking in retirement.

One day Joe announced, to a family friend who was visiting, that he would never drink again. Joe remembered his friend saying that he'd bet his house against it. Joe knew himself to be the sort of person who liked to do a difficult thing just to prove that he could do it. He'd always been that way — learning in grade school to recite the alphabet backwards just because a classmate said he couldn't do it. There wasn't anything mysterious about his wanting to quit drinking. "I got sick of it, that's all." Joe quit a few years before he underwent those several operations and had to leave home for good. It was almost five years now since he'd tasted liquor.

Joe limped into the empty room upstairs. Daylight still filled the window. He took off his shoes and lay down on his bed. He gazed at the ceiling. He was glad he had quit drinking. He wished he had quit sooner. But maybe not much sooner, to be honest. He had usually enjoyed himself. Drinking had enhanced his life, he thought. But it had not enhanced his family's, and now he really did wish that he had quit sooner.

To his family and friends, Joe still issued orders, but he kept from them a great deal of what he felt. He had resolved never to complain to them, if he could help it. A person in a nursing home has a lot of time to contemplate the shortness of what's left and to summon up regrets. "See, my wife was nurse, nurse's aide, physical therapist, and everything for me for fifteen years. And I got mad at her. She served steak. I said for Christ's sake, I'm sick of goddamn steak and every other goddamn thing. I didn't realize, and now I'm trying to make it up to her. Honest to God. And I drank too much. Honest to God."

In Joe's plan, he'd make what amends he could by making his close friends and family feel that he was happy at Linda Manor. "Perfect place," he'd say to them. In the privacy of his own thoughts, Joe gave a slightly different accounting.

He remembered his four months at the VA as vividly as a nightmare from which he had just awakened. The ward, on an upper floor deep inside the hospital building, was clean but old and drab. The staff were competent and pleasant, but they were practically the only people around who could carry on a rational conversation. They put Joe to bed in a five-man room.

On one side of him lay an all but comatose man. Joe saw a feeding tube protruding from that man's stomach, and tried not to look that way again. The patients lying in the other beds around him moaned and babbled and cried out, and the one man in the room who *could* talk complained incessantly, cursing the staff and Joe. Often alone with no one but the busy staff to talk to, Joe couldn't shake the feeling that he did not belong there, among the comatose and demented. Even at its best, life on that ward seemed to Joe like a case of false imprisonment. He considered suicide, but rejected the idea, and then wondered if he was a coward for doing so.

For about a week after he got to the VA, Joe writhed inwardly. "Then I turned over." Joe rotated his good hand as if opening a doorknob. "I decided to adjust." He remembered his first sight of Linda Manor. After the VA, it looked fresh and airy. But it was still a nursing home. He arrived in a wheelchair. When they pushed him into his room on Sunrise, his new roommate glared at him from bed and greeted Joe by saying, "They call me Miserable Merle."

The man's tone sounded threatening, and Joe wasn't going to let it pass. "I'm just as miserable as you, you sonofabitch," Joe told him. Joe got along all right with him after that, but the man was truly miserable and he complained a lot.

Joe remembered one young nurse's aide on Sunrise, the only aide around here he really didn't like. She was gone now. "You're quite bossy, aren't you," Joe remembered telling her. "Well, you don't boss *me*." Most of the time in here it seemed as if he were obliged to say please and thank you constantly. It still seemed that way. But maybe that was just because he'd said those words too seldom in his life before.

When he came to Linda Manor, he hadn't taken more than a few steps toward walking again, not since the surgeon had cut off his toe. Walking had been difficult ever since his stroke. Without the toe, he couldn't seem to get his balance. He wasn't going to bother to try. But the staff insisted that he transfer from his wheelchair to a regular chair in the dining room. He had to wait his turn for an aide to help him. He endured the procedure for a couple of weeks or so. Then one day, while he was in the midst of being lifted, turned, and deposited in a dining room chair, it occurred to him that learning to walk again couldn't be more aggravating than doing this three times a day. "The hell with it," he thought. Inspired by irritation, he relearned the art of walking. It didn't take very long. "It wasn't hard. It wasn't easy." Good thing he'd done it, though, or he might not have been moved upstairs and gotten Lou as a roommate.

Things were much better now than they had been. Lou was a vast improvement over his other roommates. And Linda Manor was a great improvement over the VA. But it was still the last place he ever thought he'd end up living in. "Perfect place," he'd tell his friends and family. To himself, he said, "It's as good a place as you can get without home. But who would choose this if you had any other choice, that's all."

Lying in the room on Forest View, Joe thought back to other New Year's Eves. "Before I got crippled, I used to, uh . . . *tie one on*. On New Year's Eve. Oh, Jesus!" It used to be midmorning tomorrow when he got in from celebrating. He laughed. He gazed at the ceiling. "But . . . that's gone forever. Just as well, or I'd be dead now."

Winter

❧

DORA SAT in a rocking chair beside her window on Meadowview. She was short and stocky. She had round, ruddy cheeks and brilliant white hair, hairdresser-curled, the coiffure slightly flattened in back, a common fate of coiffures here because of frequent reclining. Dora held a hardbound diary in her lap, opened to today's page — a day in early January. She smiled as she lifted her pen. Dora almost always smiled.

Every morning Dora wrote in her diary. Every entry began with Dora's own weather report. A few days ago, sitting here in her rocker, her diary in her lap, she glanced out her window and wrote, quite accurately, "Snowing here this A.M." It wasn't that Dora didn't see what others saw, but she saw beyond what distracted them. Nine days out of ten, in fair weather or foul, she looked out her window and wrote, "Beautiful morning here." Today the sky hung low and gray outside Dora's window. Visitors crossing the parking lot, passing through Dora's view, hunched their shoulders under heavy coats and with gloved hands pressed their collars to their ears. "Beautiful morning here," wrote Dora.

❖   ❖   ❖

On her way through the lobby, Ruth ran into an old acquaintance named Jean Duncan. Ruth had taught Jean's daughters in high school, and asked after them. They were doing fine, but Jean's husband, Earl, was not. He had just arrived at Linda Manor, he was very sick with heart trouble, and he was feeling pretty low. Maybe Ruth's father would visit Earl, Jean suggested. Earl needed a friend on the premises. His room was on Sunrise. Ruth passed the message along.

Lou set out for Sunrise. Earl seemed a lot less depressed than advertised, Lou thought. In fact, Earl said he'd be going home soon. He asked Lou to call on him again. A few mornings later, after fortifying himself for the journey with his usual shot of brandy, Lou headed off to perform what he called his *mitzvah*, his good deed for the day.

Lou could have made it from his door to the elevators on memory alone. He had only to keep a lookout for wheelchairs, or the tall stainless steel lunch cart sometimes in the way, or fellow residents. A shape, a lighter shade of gray than the surrounding grayness, was moving in his direction on a near collision course. The shape swayed from side to side like a metronome, a familiar movement. "Hi, Ted."

The elevator doors made two tall, bright rectangles before Lou. He reached with an open hand for the elevator button, missed by an inch or so, then found its raised surface and pressed with his thumb. He stepped back one step, looked up, and waited for the bells to ring and for the arrow to light above the left or right door. A sudden, nearly blinding glare made Lou squint. The elevator had opened — the interior walls were of a bright color. Moving quickly, standing outside, Lou reached around inside the elevator, found the stop switch by feel, and flicked it up. Now he could take his time, to test the footing with his cane, in case the elevator had landed with its floor not quite even with the floor outside.

"Going down?" said Lou to the shape of Ted. Lou smiled at his own joke, there being, of course, no other way to go. Bending over, and with a little more pin-the-tail-on-the-donkey fumbling, he flicked off the stop switch and pressed the left-hand button below it, bowing low to get his good eye close, so he could make sure that the correct button was lit. Then he straightened up and listened to the machinery with a practiced ear — he used to take care of elevator maintenance at the pen factory. Everything sounded okay. He smiled again at the shape of Ted. Lou's mood was sunny. "Well, like they say," he said as the elevator started to move, "life has ups and downs."

Lou had a picture of Sunrise in his mind, from the months he'd spent there with his wife. Sunrise's layout was identical to Forest View's. The only differences to Lou were the incessant, eerie, slurred cries of a certain Sunrise resident — "He'p me, he'p me out, wanna go back to bed" — and a number of gray shapes, brighter than the wall behind them, that Lou knew to be the heads of the people in wheelchairs parked along the wall opposite the Sunrise nurses' station.

Lou made his way around the counter and bore to the west, following the left-hand border of the carpet and counting doorways. The doors were light rectangles against a gray wall if closed, and brighter rectangles if open. He stopped at a brighter rectangle, the last on the left. He knocked with the handle of his cane on the open door and took a step inside. "Earl? It's Lou."

There were two beds in the room. Earl sat on the edge of the bed nearer the door. He wore a nightshirt. His gray hair was mussed and sticking up in back, like a cowlick. A blue oxygen catheter was looped over his ears and descended over his cheeks and across his upper lip like a long, slender handlebar mustache. His jawbones were prominent. His wrists were knobby. He was painfully thin. "I'm sorry, Lou," said Earl. He spoke rapidly, with a hint of nervous haste, the haste of a man short of breath. "I'm sorry, Lou. I haven't been able to sleep at all. My bowels. I've got one of these on."

Looking at the small, white-haired Lou, who stood leaning on a cane several feet away, and with a grimace, Earl pulled up his nightshirt, revealing a disposable diaper wrapped around thin thighs.

"I can't see. What is it?" asked Lou.

"It's one of these . . ." Earl started to say. "Like a child's bib. Not a bib . . ." Earl's voice trailed off. "I'm going to try to go back to sleep, Lou. I'm sorry."

"No need to apologize. I'll see ya later," said Lou. "Take it easy."

"I will," Earl said emphatically, swinging his legs back into bed.

Earl was obviously a newcomer. Among most of the men at Linda Manor, "Take it easy" called for an answer like, "At my age, you don't have any choice." Lou said the words for Earl, "You don't have any choice," and he chuckled. Lou meant to express solidarity. His chuckle was strained, though.

He headed back down the corridors. A member of the staff, falling in step with Lou, told him, "Earl might be dying now."

Lou pursed his lips. He looked grim. "That's what happens," he said.

Riding up on the elevator, Lou smiled. He was thinking about Joe's promise to take all of the Nudniks out to dinner with his bingo winnings. Lou had told Joe, "Okay, you buy the crackers, I'll buy the peanut butter." Joe had won a whole dollar at Linda Manor bingo yesterday. Lou's smile faded when he got back to the room.

Joe was still out. Lou hung his striped cane on the rung of his wife's old walker in the corner, and stood for a while facing the picture window. Sometimes in the late afternoons he thought he saw a rose-colored band of light out there on the grassy hillside below, a vision apparent only to him. He thought it might be a reflection of the sunset over the roof of the building. His eye doctor thought it a probable example of visual imagination.

Mitzvahs didn't always turn out well. This one had left him thinking about Jennie. He was picturing her as she'd lain in their room on Sunrise, during that time that Lou called "towards the end," when she'd weighed all of eighty pounds and the staff could pick her up as if she were a child. Facing the window, his deeply lined face slightly frowning, Lou said again, "That's what happens."

Earl rallied, not for the first time. A few days after Lou visited, Earl was sitting up on the edge of his bed, making notes about his family's history. This was an item on the list of affairs he had to put in order. While working on it, Earl escaped from here, back to 1910.

A young woman stands on a corner of Cabot Street, in the shadows of the tall, dark factories of Holyoke, Massachusetts. A little boy stands beside her. She cradles a baby in one arm. She is waving her free hand and looking toward a window high up in the brick façade of the Crocker-McElwain paper mill, which looks like a castle. The figure of a man stands in that window, waving back at her. In those days, the streets of Holyoke's lower wards held crowds of men around dawn and sunset, but they are probably quite empty at this midafternoon hour. Earl wasn't sure about the season or what the woman, his mother, wore. She must have looked at least a bit disheveled. She had just arrived by boat and train from Scotland. Her husband, waving from the window high above the street, had fled hard times in Glasgow, where he'd been a professional soccer player and stonecutter. He went on ahead of his family the better part of a year before, to work in the paper mill. A friend of his brought his wife up from the train station to this street corner, for this distant reunion. The factory gates shut early in the morning and did not open again until quitting time — not for a mill worker, not even to welcome his wife to America or to lay eyes on his new son for the first time.

That was the story as Earl heard it from his parents — at

least, as much of the story as Earl remembered hearing. Earl planned to get his notes in order, then make a tape recording of the history of the Duncan clan. He intended the recording for his descendants.

A vainer man than Earl would have replayed the story of his mother's arrival and emphasized the hardships of his childhood, in order to add luster to his own accomplishments. But Earl, who had always shunned unpleasantness, placed most of his memories in sunshine. He grew up in Holyoke, during that now impoverished city's industrial heyday. As a teenager he worked full day shifts at the Farr Alpaca mill and attended the Holyoke Evening High School. He was elected president of his night school class. He started caddying at the age of eight and early on discovered an ancestral talent for golf. Earl never went to college, but golf proved as useful as a diploma once he got into banking. "A lot of wealthy men wanted to play golf with me," he explained.

Earl retired, as a bank vice president, at the age of sixty-five. He had by then compiled a long record of public service. After retirement, he added to it. He served at one time or another as president, secretary, treasurer, director, trustee, or plain fundraiser for a great number of civic, professional, and charitable organizations. He'd been president and director of the Holyoke Rotary, a director of the local Red Cross, a member of the board of the local Chamber of Commerce, a treasurer of the Tuberculosis Society, a chairman of the United Cerebral Palsy and the American Heart Association fundraising campaigns, a treasurer, trustee, and senior warden of St. Paul's Episcopal Church in Holyoke, a member of the Bishop's Council, a president and district governor of two banking organizations. The list went on and on. He even served on a committee dedicated to saving a beautiful old merry-go-round. It was the *vita* of a man too gregarious and generous to say no.

Earl's first wife had died by the time he retired. In his sixties he married Jean, who was thirteen years younger than he, and began a second life made of public service, golf, family, and travel. Earl had mild high blood pressure and mild diabetes mellitus, and, in his early seventies, he was operated on for prostate cancer. But those ailments all appeared to be in check. He felt wonderful and young until, on a day in July in his seventy-ninth year, the day after playing in a golf tournament, he went to Cooley Dickinson Hospital in Northampton for his routine, quarterly cancer checkup. He had a deep, dull pain in his chest. He felt nauseous. He told the receptionist he didn't feel up to having a check-up and was on his way out the door when he decided he'd better find out what was wrong with him. Earl later said — no doubt correctly — that he probably would have died if he hadn't turned back. In almost no time at all, he was whisked into the hospital's cardiac care unit and hooked up to various monitoring devices, which diagnosed a rapidly progressing, left ventricular myocardial infarction, a common kind of heart attack.

The staff administered the standard intervention, but it failed. Starved of oxygenated blood, a large portion of the muscular left wall of Earl's heart died.

By feeding an array of drugs into his bloodstream, the doctors brought Earl to a stable condition, and eventually they sent him home. A few weeks later, though, he was rushed back to the hospital. This pattern held through the summer, fall, and early winter. Earl would spend a week or two in the hospital on the verge of death — from heart arrhythmias, from cardiac arrest, from congestive heart failure, from intramural thrombus (an aneurism formed in the left wall of his heart), and, mainly because his heart had become an inadequate pump, from fulminant pneumonia and kidney failure. Again and again the cardiac unit staff brought him back, with oxygen therapy, with a pacemaker, with drugs that lessen, in various ways, the work that the heart has to do. Again and again Earl rallied, and his doctors sent him home with a virtual pharmacopoeia — digoxin, Capoten, Lasix, Quinaglute, Zaroxolyn, Coumadin, potassium chloride, sublingual nitroglycerin. At home in Northampton, Jean ministered to him. Visiting nurses helped out. For a while he'd seem to improve, but it was never more than a few weeks before he was being driven back to the hospital, gasping for air.

Only a decade or so before, Earl would probably have died shortly after his heart attack. The steady advance of cardiac pharmacology deserved much of the credit, perhaps also the blame, for his having survived these last six months. But even some medical people, whose professional training should have cured them of metaphysical thoughts, expressed surprise at Earl's durability.

Practically the only adversity from the past that Earl freely acknowledged now, while making his notes on family history as he languished at Linda Manor, was his loss in a golf club championship back in 1933. He'd all but won, got overconfident, and lost the match. Several years later, he found himself in the opposite position. "I said to myself, 'Don't give up.'" He came from far behind to win that second match. "Life is that way," he said. "If I hadn't been defeated earlier, I probably wouldn't have won later." Earl derived this moral from that memory: Don't give up.

"Is this man a cat?" a nurse remarked over Earl during one of his five return trips to the cardiac care unit. Jean said, "There's something tough in there." For his part, Earl did not deny that the last six months had been a torment, but he didn't like to dwell on them. Of that time he'd usually say, "I've been tied up since July," and leave it at that.

Earl's side of the room on Sunrise was barren except for institutional furnishings. He hadn't brought any of his own stuff here, because he didn't intend to stay long. However, on the small, standard-issue bulletin board that hung beside every bed at Linda Manor, Earl pinned a photograph of himself as he had been six months ago. In the picture, Earl, standing between two golfing buddies, has full round cheeks with a healthy-looking glow in them. Many residents had pictures of their younger selves on their walls, such as Joe's picture of himself on his wedding day. In those pictures, one could read by comparison the great, slow changes of time and illness and yet still see a resemblance between the resident then and now. But it was hard to see any resemblance at all between Earl in that photograph in his golfing clothes and Earl just six months later in the nursing home bed. When the photo was taken Earl weighed about 165 pounds. He now weighed about 105. He didn't look a great deal older. He had shrunk. And his once ruddy cheeks had turned gray, nearly the color of his hair.

Earl recalled his heart attack in the way unlucky soldiers recall their battle wounds, as an event that still defied belief. He remembered saying to himself, "What's going on here? I've never really been sick." True, he'd had cancer, but it hadn't turned out to be nearly as serious as this, and he'd always thought that cancer was far more dreadful than a heart attack. He could not make out how this had happened to him. Not that the biology behind his transformation puzzled Earl. He'd heard enough doctors' explanations and implicitly believed in their descriptions of what had gone awry down there in his chest. But that this could have been his destiny, to wind up gasping for breath in a place like this, without his ever having had the slightest premonition, that lay beyond understanding.

Earl would look at the photo on his bedside bulletin board and say, "That was me just six months ago." He hadn't had time to get used to the face he saw in the mirror of the nursing home bathroom. He imagined it temporary. In his mind he repossessed his former, healthy body, in spite of what he knew.

After Earl's most recent and most serious bout with the complications of living with a half-dead heart, his family doctor recommended that he go to a nursing home, at least for a while. The doctor felt Earl needed twenty-four-hour care of a sort that would be hard to arrange at home.

For Earl, entering Linda Manor was nightmarish. He didn't mind the routine full-body check that the nurses performed the day he arrived or the crinkly feel of the plastic bed cover under his sheets. He was used to hospital beds and procedures. In fact, he wished Linda Manor felt more like a hospital and less like a place designed for long stays. What frightened him most was the lineup of residents across from the Sunrise nurses' station, old men and women sitting there with their mouths open and heads lolling to one side. They clearly had arrived at the end of the line. He didn't belong here among them, did he?

A few days after Earl arrived, one of the evening nurses wrote in his chart:

> Disturbed that wife couldn't come in this p.m. Has called her 4 times begging to be removed from here, says he feels "trapped."

Earl hadn't ordered his own phone. He didn't plan to stay long enough to justify the expense. His first days he made so many trips, padding along behind his wheelchair, half out of breath, down the long central corridor to the pay phone, that for a time the Sunrise staff thought he must be demented. He was not. Earl was calling almost everyone he knew, just to hear familiar voices.

Earl felt so desperate to call yet another old friend and tell him where he was that sometimes, in his first days here, he'd push his wheelchair out to the Sunrise nurses' station and beg permission to use the phone there. He had to wait, surrounded by distressing sights and sounds. Sunrise's long corridor lies a little closer to the woods than Meadowview's. And just across the asphalt drive outside, there is an earthen berm, which makes some parts of Sunrise feel partway underground. It gets a lot of sun, but it seems one shade darker than Meadowview or elevated Forest View. And there was always that lineup along the wall across from the nurses' station. One ninety-year-old man often sat there, by the water fountain, sometimes calling out while stamping his feet: "Seventy-seven turkeys. May his soul rest in peace. God save the King. Seventy-one five. Please Lord, let the country prosper. Amen." Deep in reverie, he believed himself to be simultaneously at a turkey shoot and playing the organ in church. A woman who always wore a turban sat at the other end of the Sunrise lineup, issuing orders to passersby. She believed this was a hotel and that she owned it. Often she sat there conversing with the parakeet in the cage to her left. The bird inside could speak that woman's name and would now and then utter a long and drawn out "Yee-ahsss" in an accent just like hers. And often a man without any legs was sitting there, calling out, "He'p me! He'p me out! Wanna go back to bed!" When Earl first heard that man's voice, it went right through him.

Earl was waiting there for the phone one day, in that place he thought of as Bedlam, feeling more lonely than ever before in his life, when a woman in a wheelchair approached, an aide pushing her. She was large, brown-haired, toothless, dressed in a silky gown, with hugely swollen legs. Earl was almost afraid to look at her, but then she spoke. "I have a phone. You can make a call on it anytime you want. You just come in my room anytime," she said.

Thus Earl met Winifred. Earl soon got his own phone — "Boy, am I glad to see you," he exclaimed when the service man appeared in his doorway. He never did use Winifred's phone, but her gesture comforted him a little. Rational, even generous people survived, after all, in some of these ruined bodies around him. Earl's roommate, a stroke victim, seemed weird at first, wheelchair-bound and given to fits of weeping and periods of incoherent talk. But after a few days of sharing a room with him, Earl discovered a person he liked underneath that unfortunate man's symptoms.

Lou visited. Earl liked Lou. And Earl met some congenial people in the dining room. He began taking mild exercise with the physical therapists. He told everyone he met that he'd be leaving in a week or two. He still had hopes of a recovery, not a full one perhaps, but he imagined that he might play golf and travel again. He decided that he had to know if his hopes were realistic. About a week after his arrival at Linda Manor, Earl's family doctor visited him in his room. Jean was there, but waited outside in the corridor while the doctor examined him. When Jean left the room, Earl asked his question. He thought he was prepared for the worst, and he hoped, of course, for good news.

"Listen, Doc, I'm not a kid anymore. I want to know where I stand."

Earl's doctor had heard this question many times in his career. He was in his sixties and had made a specialty of geriatric medicine. He liked dealing with elderly patients partly because they usually permitted candor from him. Over the last six months of crises, Earl had told him several times that he worried about whether Jean would be able to manage her own financial affairs without him. This worry had special force, since Jean's first husband had died in a car accident, and for a long time afterward she had found herself utterly lost among bills and checkbooks. So the family doctor thought he owed Earl an honest answer. He wasn't God, he said, but he doubted that Earl would be alive in six months. And, he added, a fatal event could occur suddenly, at any time.

How soon at the earliest? Earl wanted to know.

The doctor didn't want to say.

Earl pressed him for an answer. "I'm not a kid anymore."

Finally the doctor gave in. Maybe a week, he said.

"That's what I wanted to know," said Earl bravely.

Some months later, recalling the day when he delivered that

bad news, Earl's doctor remarked, "People usually want to know. They don't usually want to hear it."

3

In the activity room, the aide was calling today's last game of bingo. No other event drew such a large crowd. Two dozen residents sat at dining tables, each equipped with a single card and a stack of bingo chips decorated with images of cartoon teddy bears and cats and ladybugs and bees and bunny rabbits. Rita, the activities department aide, called out the letter-number combinations through the tinny sound system. "B-two. B-two."

One of the women at the table next to Joe's said, "Beef stew again."

Joe smiled.

He sat at the same table as always, with Art, as always, seated to his left. Art's eyes were failing. Sometimes he had trouble placing his bingo chips correctly. He wouldn't let just anyone help him. He'd turn to Joe. Today a third man sat at Joe's table, the resident of Sunrise who had no legs. He sat across from Joe, on his stumps, in a wheelchair. On the way to and from the elevators, Joe had often heard his eerie cries. But Joe had heard and seen worse here, and at the VA. And the legless man had surprised Joe today. Joe saw that he wasn't very old, and he could carry on a conversation. He hadn't done any yelling. It might be possible to like this guy, Joe thought.

Joe listened to the voices from the tables around him, chuckling now and then at the comments he heard. This last game stretched on and on without a winner. A woman at the next table said, "Somebody's gonna yell pretty soon." Her voice was tense with excitement.

"I-sixteen," called the aide through the metallic sound system.

"Bing-*go*," Joe said. He smiled, an inward-looking smile.

"Oh, Joe again," said the aide through the microphone, in mock consternation.

"He's always got it," piped up Eleanor's roommate Elgie from the next table.

"See, it pays to be cute," said the aide.

"Oh, Jeez," Joe said as the aide placed a dollar bill beside his card.

"That won't buy a beer," said Art, looking at the dollar bill.

Joe chuckled, pocketing the dollar. He winked at the legless man, but the legless man's eyes didn't seem to see Joe now. His eyes looked far away.

Across the room the aide was packing up the bingo equipment. Residents were moving, by cane, walker, and wheelchair, slowly toward the door. Joe was chatting with Art. Suddenly the legless man began to shout. "He'p me, he'p me out!" He was yelling right in Joe's face. Actually, he was yelling for help toward the doorway, and Joe happened to be in the way.

"Oh, boy. Jesus Christ," Joe groaned, turning his face away. What pain the man must be in now! An aide hurried up and wheeled the legless man out. The cries died away. Joe looked at Art and said, "Without your legs . . . you know."

"He's got a voice like a bull," Art said.

Joe looked at Art. Then Joe started to smile, his shoulders bouncing a little, and in a moment his face returned to normal.

Around here, a person could count on incidents like that to remind him where he was. "Nice place to be, huh?" Joe would sometimes say. There was too much sadness concentrated here, Joe thought at these moments.

A couple of tables away Winifred was chatting with another resident. Winifred was doing all of the talking.

"We could use her tongue for an antenna," Art muttered.

Joe smiled. Then he limped off on his cane toward the lobby.

A chilly sunlight filled the lobby's many windows. The piano, at the center of the room, gleamed darkly. This was Joe's eighteenth winter since the stroke. To the left of the front doors, Bob's armchair was pulled out from the wall and turned to face the traffic. Joe sat down in it. Bending forward, he unstrapped his orthopedic shoes and took them off, and began surveying his world.

There was only one other person in the lobby just now, a very old woman, thin and gnarled with shoulders humped high as if she wore football shoulder pads. She sat on a sofa across the room. She'd been a schoolteacher. She was ninety-five. Joe didn't know her well, but she had all her buttons, he'd decided. They chatted a little from either side of the lobby.

"Who's your roommate now, Joe?"

"Lou Freeze." Joe looked out the bay window toward the south visitors' parking lot. "He gets mad at Phil. Oh, God."

"You roomed with Merle for a while."

"Yeah. Miserable Merle. I got along with him all right," Joe said. "What time is it?"

The former schoolteacher studied her wristwatch. "Two minutes of. You wouldn't hang a man for two minutes."

"No, I wouldn't," Joe said. He smiled, looking toward the window. "You know, nine or ten, I played bingo. And I didn't play again until I got here." Joe's smile grew. Suddenly, clutching his belly with his good hand, he hooted, "It's a stupid goddamn game!"

What a marvelous joke that was. Joe Torchio playing bingo in a nursing home. And enjoying it!

A few minutes later the former schoolteacher dozed off, her head falling onto her shoulder. And then the front door opened and a couple of visitors, an elderly man and woman, came in. They paused in front of Joe.

"It's cold out there today," said the woman.

"I wouldn't know," Joe said. He laughed.

Joe Torchio didn't even know what it was like outside. This was a fine joke, too.

The couple moved on. The man, gray-haired and stooped, smiled at Joe as he passed. Joe turned and watched him walk away. That guy was *old*. "I know I look that old and gray and everything," said Joe, "but I don't *feel* that old."

He smiled at himself again. While sitting here, Joe often found his mind making loops in time. The other day, deep in thought, he glanced up and saw the back of a gray-haired woman passing by, and he was on the verge of calling out, "Hey, Ma!" before he caught himself.

Joe gazed out the bay window, looking for birds. There were none in sight. He had a view of brown grass and parking lot. Out there the state flag on the tall flagpole flapped in the wind. The door opened again, and a young woman in a parka came in. She was a nurse who sometimes worked on Forest

View. Her son had cerebral palsy. Little by little she'd told Joe all about her boy and her problems in getting help for him. Joe had told her to bring her boy in, and she had done so on one of her days off. Joe had sat on his bed chatting with the boy, and then pulled up his trouser leg and showed the boy his brace. "He has a helper, too," the child had said to his mother the nurse. The boy's face had lit up. "He has a helper, too."

"Hi, Joe," said the young nurse.

"How *are* ya?" asked Joe.

She stopped, but didn't seem to want to. "Don't ask, Joe," she said.

"Come on. How's your kid?"

"He's all right." She seemed on the verge of tears or fury. She clearly didn't want to chat now.

"I'll talk to you upstairs," Joe said, and she nodded and passed inward.

The lobby was quiet. Joe looked out the windows. "These nurses and aides, they all have troubles. That's why they're so nice."

In a moment, Art shuffled in and sat down on the sofa next to Joe. Art had recently started traveling by cane. His was made of metal but had a shepherd's crook handle like Joe's. Once seated, Art hooked the handle around his neck and pulled gently down on the shaft of his cane. He did this to relieve the stiffness in his neck.

"Did you tell your doctor you only walk a little way and you get tired?" Joe asked.

"Yeah."

"That's because you're not walking enough!" said Joe.

The other day, down here in the lobby, Joe said something in which Art misheard an insult. Art stood up, his hands shaking with anger. Joe was surprised, but at once he started speaking to Art in a soothing voice, excusing himself finally by saying, "I have half a brain, you know." Which made Art laugh.

Joe liked Art. Art usually said something that amused Joe during these lobby sittings — the time, for instance, when a youngish visitor asked Art how old he was and Art said, "Eighty-four," and the young visitor said, "Eighty-four isn't really old," and Art replied, "It is if you're eighty-four." Art still ranked high on Joe's list of local stoics. "By Jesus, he's tough," Joe would say. Art was quiet, private, and undemonstrative around most people here. When he couldn't manage to be all those things, he tended to seek out Joe. That had happened just recently. Art had sat down next to Joe and told him this story:

Up in his room Art had spoken to his wife's photograph, a custom of his. "How you doin' today? Are you up and around? When you were living, you'd say I'd never tell you I loved you. That's true. You had to goad me." Then Art lay down on his bed for a nap and closed his eyes for a moment. When he opened them, he saw his wife, restored to the world, sitting in his recliner at the foot of his bed. She was trying to tell him something, he thought. Art closed his eyes and opened them again, and she was gone. Had she been trying to tell him what death was like? Where had she gone? He told himself, "It can't have been to a very bad place if she was up and around like that."

Tears had streaked Art's cheeks as he'd told all this to Joe. He apologized to Joe for being "a crybaby." But Art had wanted to know what Joe thought. Could Art really have seen his wife?

It was a tough question for an agnostic leaning toward atheism. "If you believe it," Joe said finally, "it's probably true." That had seemed to cheer Art up.

Joe's shoes lay in a heap by his stockinged feet. Art was looking into the middle distance, his cane hooked around his neck. Joe was practicing the word "podiatrist." "Po-die-uh . . . Po-die-uh-trist," Joe mumured to himself. He almost had it down. He still couldn't find the word "diabetes" half the time. He'd end up having to ask Lou for help. "Lou, what do I have starts with *d* ?" Lou would tell him. Joe would repeat it: "Di-ah-beetiss." Why was it he couldn't say "diabetes"? Joe wondered. Because he didn't want to admit that he had it?

"Po-die-trist. Po-die-*uh*-trist," Joe was murmuring, when from the direction of the administrative corridor came the familiar call: "Howdee! Howdee! Howdee!"

Bob stumped rapidly across the carpet, saying, "Hello, hello, hello to you, hello. Hello to you. Howdee! Howdee! Howdee! No way, no way."

Joe turned to Art and said, "He's cuckoo."

"He's cuckoo all right," Art said.

Bob limped up. "Howdee! Howdee! Howdee!"

"Howdee! Howdee! Howdee!" answered Joe, outdoing Bob in volume, then in a softer voice, "How *are* ya?"

"Excellent. Thank you kindly." Then Bob realized that Joe was in his sentry chair. Bob eyed Joe and scowled. This was sport. One time Bob found Joe in his chair and, in high dudgeon, shook his cane right under Joe's chin, while Joe tried in vain to keep from laughing. When the positions were reversed and Joe found Bob in the sentry chair, Joe would smile and say to Bob, "Why don't you go to the bathroom?"

"No way, no way."

"I'm going to wait for your bladder to fill up," Joe would say, and Bob would start looking agitated, partly from amusement maybe and partly, it seemed, out of a real worry that Joe would get the chair somehow. Today, though, Bob made no complaint. He just pulled another chair out from the wall and sat down facing Joe, who said, "I still have my hair." Joe sprinkled hair over his bald dome with his fingers, then bent over so that Bob could examine the top of his head.

Bob reached out and tapped Joe's head. Joe sat back and laughed.

"You hot shit," Bob said.

"Hot stuff," Joe said.

"Long time ago, boy," said Bob.

Lou arrived and sat down on the sofa next to Art. The four men watched the traffic and chatted. And then a very thin man, who was not a resident, wheeled his wife out to the lobby. The couple sat down on the other side of the piano, near the old schoolteacher, who shook herself awake from her nap. This happened every afternoon. The couple would sit over there. Sometimes they'd argue a little with each other. Then, when he got ready to leave, the husband would wheel his wife to the north-facing bay window, and she'd sit there and watch his car drive away, waving and weeping. The scene had saddened Joe once, but no longer. It was the same scene every day, and he'd realized that the weeping woman was probably deranged and also quite wily. Her husband was a quiet man. She was loud and full of recriminations. "I don't think there's anything so wrong with my brain," she'd shouted at him one time in here. "I went to a doctor and had my brain tested and I came out higher than anyone has since 1818. So don't tell me my brain has been damaged." Sometimes she'd start in on her husband as soon as they arrived in the lobby.

"You didn't even wave to me yesterday."

"Yes, I did."

The ninety-five-year-old schoolteacher, fully awakened, spoke up. "Yes, he did."

Over on the other side of the lobby, Lou said to Joe and the others, "She's something."

"She's not something," Joe said. "She's a pain in the ass."

Across the lobby, the husband was trying to leave. He told his wife he'd see her tomorrow. The woman started crying. "Well I hope you stay longer than you're staying today," she wailed. The man settled back in his seat. He was going to stay a while longer, evidently.

Over on their side of the piano, Joe smiled and Bob grinned at Joe. Bob usually listened in intently on the couple's daily lobby drama. "Oh, Jesus," said Bob, grinning with a furtive quiver of pleasure. And Lou said, "It's a shame."

There was a fair amount of traffic today. A young-looking man, carrying a small black bag and dressed in a suit, came in the front door. Joe watched the man as he passed quickly by. Joe figured him for a doctor. He had the doctor look. "Intense. They go to their patient. Intense. Goddamn fool."

Then Martha appeared, a spry woman with sparse gray hair. When Joe first encountered Martha months ago, he placed her in the has-all-her-buttons category. Martha had come here with her husband. Joe used to see her pushing her husband around in his wheelchair, Martha calling cheery greetings to everyone, as sane as anyone in here as far as Joe could see. But in fact Martha suffered from one of the irreversible diseases that cause dementia — probably Alzheimer's, the doctors said. And after her husband's death, she began to make frequent departures, pausing in the lobby to tell Joe or Bob that she was going home. Sometimes Martha would say that her husband was coming to pick her up, and sometimes that she planned to walk home. Once in a while she'd ask if anyone knew the directions. "It isn't far, is it?" Martha would go out, walk around the building, and come back in on her own. Sometimes, though, she walked into the woods and got some distance down an old logging road before a nurse or an aide caught up with her. Sometimes she headed right down the long driveway toward Route 9. On those occasions, Bob, in his capacity as doorkeeper, would get up and limp to the receptionist's window, informing the receptionist with elaborate gestures of his cane that Martha was heading for danger.

Today, Martha wore her cloth winter coat. She had her pocketbook slung over one arm. She stopped in front of the men and said, "I'm going home. Maybe I won't come back, seeing you don't love me anymore." She laughed gaily. "Bye-bye," she sang.

"Bye," Joe said.

"Bye-bye now," Bob said. As she went out, Bob turned and watched through the window, as vigilant as a blue heron. But this time Martha merely circled the building and returned a few minutes later. "My husband is living," she said to the men. She seemed to study their faces with nervous eyes. Soon Martha headed back inside.

Over on the other side of the lobby the weeping woman's husband had wheeled her to the bay window. This time he really was leaving. "That's my car," he told her, pointing out.

"Now she'll cry," Joe murmured.

Joe was right.

"I never get a chance to go out with you anymore," she wailed to her husband.

"Yes, you did," he replied. "I took you out to lunch Sunday." He started for the door.

"It was a lousy lunch!" she yelled after him. Then, weeping quietly, she turned back to the window and began to wave.

That scene had by now the quality of ceremony. It signified that another afternoon neared an end. Lou said, well, he guessed it was time to go upstairs and get some pre-dinner pills. Joe told Lou he'd see him upstairs. Joe would sit here a little longer and chat with Art, while Bob listened in. In the lobby, shadows lengthened. Joe talked baseball for a while. Baseball talk warmed up the landscape for Joe.

Art said he agreed with Joe, that Ted Williams had been a greater player than DiMaggio. Art liked Pepper Martin, too. "You should've seen that guy. I saw Dizzy Dean pitch. I liked to hear him announce, too. 'And he *slud* into third.' "

"I remember when he hurt his toe," Joe said.

"His best performance was 1934," Art said. "He won thirty games and lost four. But Pepper Martin, he was a live wire, boy. He put everything into it. Gotta give him that. Well, that was Pepper Martin."

Though Art did not complain of pain, it was a rare afternoon in the lobby when he did not speak of boredom. "It's very boring, this kind of life. If I didn't have that bingo on Tuesday nights, I'd go nuts." Art played bingo every Tuesday evening at a local Catholic church.

"Oh, hell," said Joe, "I watch TV."

"I can't very well," Art said. "Ted watches those darn soap operas and I can't watch that stuff."

Joe looked to the right. Two women had come out and now stood near the front door. They buttoned up their winter coats. They were rather young by the standards of this place, and late-middle-aged by those of the wider world. Occasional or first-time visitors, Joe thought.

"Oooooh, look at the wind out there," said one of these women, looking over and down at Joe and Art and Bob. "You guys are lucky to be in a nice warm place like this."

Art was gazing out the windows. Joe stared at the women. They shivered in anticipation, for the old men's benefit. Then they went out the door.

"Never a lack of people to tell you how good you have it in here," Joe said to Art as the door closed.

"I'm in the dark a little bit," Art said.

"Everybody who comes in and goes out tells you how good you have it in here," Joe repeated.

"I'll tell the next one, 'You can swap places with me anytime you want,' " Art said. He smiled.

"Well," Joe said, "make the best of it." Leaning down, Joe strapped on his shoes. He rose in his laborious way, inching himself to the edge of his chair, planting his cane, then lifting himself, his good arm trembling all over as it caught the weight of his body through the cane.

"Laugh instead of cry, that's all," Joe said to Art. Joe chuckled, his shoulders bouncing, as if to demonstrate. "I mean it!" He laughed again.

126

Bob got up quickly and stumped over to the chair that Joe had vacated at last. "Excellent," said Bob, settling himself and peering toward the windows. "Beautiful."

"*Good* bye," Joe said in that tone of voice he often affected, a tone full of self-mockery.

4

Sunlight stretched across the gray linoleum floor of Earl's room. Earl lay on his bedspread in clothes he could have played golf in, except for the slippers he wore and the oxygen catheter. His slippers were made of brown leather, appropriate to a banker in his boudoir. Jean sat beside him, a handsome, stocky woman in her sixties with broad red cheeks, dressed in tweeds. Earl's clothes hung loosely around him. But his voice had a quick, bird-like energy. "If I'm gonna die, I want to die at home or in a hospital. Not here."

Jean rose from her chair and straightened the collar of Earl's turtleneck. He submitted without protest as she smoothed down his gray hair, which had been sticking up in back. "Like a rooster's," she said.

"I don't want to kick the bucket here," Earl went on, looking up at her.

"I don't want you to kick the bucket *there* either."

"The doctor said one *week* to six months," Earl said.

"But you're a tough old cookie."

"I've escaped five other times." Earl stared at the wall across from his bed.

"It's a dirty trick."

"Boy, it is. Here I was seventy-eight and feeling like a fifty-year-old."

"And then, kafooey, you lose all this stuff overnight, practically. You think if you live a good life, keep active and healthy . . ."

Earl smiled at her. "We traveled all over the place."

She smiled back from her chair beside him. "But you're a spark plug. I have plenty of good ideas, but you *move* on them. We did more stuff because of that."

"I'd like to get home." Earl looked away, then back at her, and the matter-of-fact, manly quality he put in his voice did not entirely conceal the plaintiveness implied as he said, "I hope it's gonna be this weekend."

"Well, don't push it, honey." Jean looked down at her lap. "Please don't push it. I'd like to have just a calm weekend before you come home."

"Well, okay," Earl said briskly. His voice quickened. "Then let's make it Monday. If it'll help you."

"That would be much better."

Earl's roommate often sat on the other side of the room in his wheelchair facing the TV, which belonged to him. He didn't seem to listen in on Jean and Earl's conversation, but now and then he broke into it. He seemed to be talking to them. "Those boys they put in the CCC camps during the Depression got thirty a month and we got fifteen. That caused a lot of resentment," said Earl's roommate. "And there was this colored girl had a baby right on the trail."

"Goodness," Jean said. She turned back to Earl.

"Those garbage-disposal units, they all have a reset on them," Earl's roommate said.

"You want your TV on?" Earl called from his bed.

"I don't care," said his roommate from his wheelchair.

Earl picked up the remote control. His roommate some-times had trouble operating the thing. Earl flicked on the TV. "He likes soap operas," Earl explained to Jean as voices full of intrigue and passion, from *Days of Our Lives*, filled the room.

The TV seemed a comforting presence at this moment. It made a barrier around Jean and Earl in their corner of the room. They talked about the trip to Florida that they had planned for March. "I was hoping we'd go, but it doesn't look like it," Earl said. "I just want to get home. The doctor gave me a week to six months."

"But you mustn't think of that as a sentence," Jean said. "That's just a guess. I wish he hadn't said anything."

"I did say, 'Now, lookit, Doctor, I'm not a kid anymore.' And he said, 'A week or six months.'" Earl looked pensive. He pursed his lips. "If I'm gonna go, I'd just as soon go fast and not suffer through another heart attack." Then he looked at Jean again, as if trying to read her face, and said, "But I want to die at home. The point is, the atmosphere here isn't helping."

"I don't think it's the atmosphere." Jean leaned close to him. She touched his leg. "It's what's happening to you. You have a nice room and services at your fingertips that you wouldn't have at home. You've got to be creative about it. You know that little poem about God give me the ability to change what I *can* change?"

"Yeah-ell," Earl said. "Remember that poem we read in Florida? 'When I'm gone . . .' "

"It's on the theme of don't spend too much time mourning me," said Jean. "That's how I'd want my children to feel."

They talked about Earl's children, and which would take his death hardest. They paused when, over on the other side of the room, a press conference about the war in Iraq interrupted the soap opera. Earl had stayed up late a few nights ago to watch TV, because there was talk that the war might begin then. "If it did, I wanted to be part of it," he'd said. What they were calling the air war began just yesterday.

"Well, I hope it doesn't go on too long," Earl said now, as the press conference on the TV went on. Then Earl asked Jean to excuse him for a moment, which was code between them for the fact that Earl needed to use the urinal bottle. Diuretics, to lessen his heart's labor and prevent congestive heart failure, had long since become a fact of his life.

Jean went out. She stood at the glassed-in, west-facing end of the corridor, looking out at the parking lot. The landscape was sunny and icy. Jean looked tired around the eyes. Her phone had rung, back at her house in Northampton, at seven o'clock this morning, an odd hour. She heard her own heart pounding as she went to pick it up. But it was just someone from the security service saying there'd been a burglary in the neighborhood last night.

For six months she'd lived with her nerves on edge, dreading every phone call when Earl was in the hospital and, when he was at home, lying awake half the night, fearing the worst. Five times Jean had driven Earl to the hospital, had left him there, and come back to her empty house, wondering whether this time she should prepare for a funeral or another less than joyous homecoming. Several times the doctors predicted that Earl wouldn't rally, and the whole family gathered. Jean couldn't remember how many nights she'd spent on couches in the hospital's waiting rooms, sometimes sneaking past the nurses into Earl's room for a late-night chat. For months she'd had her house invaded by medical strangers and medical equipment. A compulsion for privacy and order was a weakness of hers, she knew. "I'm a picture-straightener." It seemed cruel and ironic, though, that when one was weakest, one had to rely on strangers for help.

Jean wished all this news about war would cease. There was too much death around her already. She didn't know whether she had the strength to take Earl home again.

The sun was so bright on the icy grounds it made her squint. Her first husband had died in the early spring, many years ago. Memories of the aftermath were fresh again. As if standing outside herself, she had watched her hold on sanity slip away. The times when she felt lost, literally lost, in the middle of a supermarket, and her daughters, teenagers then, had to lead her down the aisles and finally out of there. Then one day a friend told her that she had to keep herself together for the sake of her children. Those simple words helped a great deal then. So she had to hold on now, for her own sake as well as Earl's.

Jean would not express regrets about either of her marriages or declare one better than the other. But she had found, for herself, advantages in a second marriage in the years after children. One came to such a marriage fully formed. Knowing herself, she felt free to be herself. Of course, Earl had a lot to do with that. He let her feel that way. Another man might have bridled at the thought of living in *her* house, and that would have been hard. She loved her large old house, on a tree-lined street in Northampton. Earl had adopted it, not possessively but comfortably, naturally, just as he had adopted her children.

He'd been a marvelous father to them in their young adult lives, she thought.

They had an almost perfect partnership. She tended to get fuddled over little things, like balancing a checkbook. A routine notice from the IRS could upset her greatly. She'd worry aloud, and Earl would say, "Don't worry. It'll be all right." And it always was all right. She tended to be shy. Earl seemed to know everyone, and everyone he knew seemed ready to do him a favor. Confronted with a problem he couldn't solve himself, Earl had only to pick up the phone to make everything all right again. He had strength and boundless energy. Those qualities, Jean thought, were attractive to a woman, to this woman especially. She felt very safe with him.

Jean's family was one of Holyoke's most prominent. She grew up on the other side, the wealthy side, of the canals of Holyoke from Earl. When she was a young woman, she enlisted in the World War II Army. Her mother was horrified. Jean enlisted partly because she wanted to fight evil in the world and partly because she wanted to test herself — she believed her life too sheltered. Jean was intellectually adventurous. But what others could do easily in the physical world required strong acts of will from her. She marveled at how comfortable Earl was in the world, a way that she could never be. She was the philosopher of their union, always trying to look beneath the surface of things. Earl was not very philosophical or introspective. But Jean never wished him otherwise. What charmed her most about him was that he remained the same — cheerful, competent, friendly, unpretentious — whether alone at home with her, or in the company of his golfing buddies, or in a park in Yugoslavia feeding pigeons.

They traveled all over the world. On one trip they conceived the wish that they'd die together, in a big bang in the sky, *coming back* from another trip somewhere. But things weren't turning out that way. Sometimes Jean wished that Earl had died from the heart attack, without foreknowledge. Philosophically, she didn't believe in keeping people alive just for the sake of doing so. But in the particular case, how did one know when to stop applying for help from medicine? Earl wanted to live. *She* wanted him to live, for his sake and her own. She hated the thought of facing life alone again, without her buddy, as she often called him in her mind.

Jean understood why Earl wanted to come home to die. But she meant more than she'd said back in the room, when she'd told him that she didn't want him dying at home. She didn't want to be complicitous in his death, and she felt all worn out with anguish and the effort, more mental than physical, of keeping him alive. She was afraid of failing him. While Earl was here at Linda Manor, others were responsible. Standing at the windows at the corridor's end, Jean rubbed her hands as if to warm them against the chill on the other side of the glass. Behind her and in front of her she saw months of wakeful nights. She couldn't bring Earl home yet.

5

The morning sun lay on Lou's neck. This winter morning's conversation began with child rearing.

"I don't think we ever hit any of our kids," Lou said. "My

wife washed Harold's mouth out with soap for calling Ruthie a bum once. We didn't have TV. We couldn't take that away from them." Lou squinted his eyes shut behind his thick glasses. "We got Ruth a player piano. Harold played the violin for a very short period and then he said, 'You should have hit me over the head before you went to the expense.'"

Not all of the reminiscing that went on in this room was Lou's. For both men, memories seemed to expand spheres of action backward, the way a wall of mirrors seems to expand a room.

"I played the violin for years and years," said Joe, reclining. "My father started me when I was five. Two or three people in Berkshire County could beat me. Them were the days when you didn't have TV or anything, so everybody . . . My sister played piano, my father played the sax."

"They used to sell song sheets at the five-and-dime," said Lou. "In Philadelphia. And they used to have a piano player and a vocalist to advertise the songs."

Joe remembered a classmate who could really play. "He got killed by a tree. He was good, but none of 'em was good enough to play, uh, Boston Symphony Orchestra."

"I wish I could remember the name of that piano player we used to hear at Fairmount Park. He ruined his life with alcohol and drugs," Lou said.

Joe hummed a snatch of a song, one he'd heard as a boy.

"Very good, Joe." Lou lifted a hand, extending the index finger. "In Fairmount Park they used to have bands come and play for the public. That's where I heard him."

Joe was still thinking about the boy who had been felled by a tree. "I think he was good enough to play in a symphony orchestra."

"The one I'm thinking of?" Lou asked.

"The Boston Symphony," Joe said. "Plays at Tanglewood. They wouldn't let me *carry* the fiddle on the Boston Symphony."

"That place on Lemon Hill in Philadelphia and the gazebo was the first time I took Jennie to a park to hear music."

"When I was a kid, every Jewish boy and Italian boy played a musical instrument, that's all."

"Each one was gonna be Jascha Heifetz, huh?"

"He went to Juilliard School of Music and played piano and cello," said Joe, speaking again of the boy he'd known, the best musician in Pittsfield in his time.

"How come I didn't play an instrument, Joe?" Lou closed his eyes, and he smiled. "I wish I could remember that piano player's name."

"I know who you mean," Joe said. "I think his first name was Oscar."

"I think you're right, Joe."

"Last name begins with an *M*?" Joe asked.

Lou would call his daughter Ruth. Maybe she'd know. But there was no answer. He sat back down by the window. "It's a shame," Lou murmured. "He ruined his life on alcohol and drugs." More loudly, he said, "Who's that other *meshuggener* who hammed it up too much?"

"Victor Borge?"

"I liked what he played. I didn't like it when he clowned." Lou again lifted a hand from the arm of his chair and turned his palm upward. "Speaking of music, in Philadelphia we had the Settlement Music School. It was a Red Feather agency. Like the United Way. It was in a big old home in South

Philadelphia. Had a stage on the first floor, for plays and dancing. They had a Russian ballet teacher."

"Mmmm." Joe's brow was knitted. "Oscar something. He had a face only a mother could love."

"Yup," said Lou. "Towards the end his face was all puffed up." Then he said, in his smoothed old voice, "The man who ran the Settlement School would go to the waterfront docks when the boats came in and find an immigrant with an instrument and invite them to stay at their boarding house."

"All right, goddamn it!" Joe said. He began getting himself upright, grunting a little. He started putting on his shoes, calling over his shoulder to Lou, "I betcha I know who'll know the name. Phil or Eleanor. Or Art."

From the hallway outside came the sound of Fleur's voice saying, "Can somebody call my mother and tell her to pick me up?"

"Oh, shut up," said Joe under his breath. He limped toward the door, heading out to find someone who might know the name of that piano player, first name Oscar, who ruined his life with alcohol and drugs.

In his chair by the window, Lou returned to the Settlement Music School in Philadelphia. Every Saturday Jennie would take Ruth down there for piano lessons. On the trolley. The number 50. And Jennie would give the neighborhood children dancing lessons at their own house on Ruscombe Street. They said it was an entirely black neighborhood now. Back then it was mixed. Jennie would tie up the chandelier and roll up the rug. She tried to teach Lou to dance, too, but he had two left feet. And there was always cookies and milk for the kids who came. It was never "Don't bring your friends." Everyone was welcome. That's how Jennie was. "She always gave of herself." Lou lifted his chin, squinting his eyes hard.

A knock at the door intervened. By the time Lou had said "Come in," an aide had already entered, pushing the blood-pressure machine. It was mounted on wheels. It looked like a tool for fixing cars. The aide was doing weekly vitals.

Lou said, "How is it?" as the aide removed the cuff from his arm.

"Excellent."

"Careful. Bob's got a patent on that word. Gonna take my temperature?"

"No. One of the other girls."

"Everyone's a specialist." Lou lifted a hand. "You know the definition of a specialist? A doctor who knows more and more about less and less until he gets to the point where he knows everything about nothing."

The aide laughed. "Ain't that the truth."

Lou settled back, wearing a rather satisfied-looking smile.

In a moment, Joe limped into the doorway. "I couldn't find Phil," he announced. "And I had to come back to go to the bathroom." He laughed. Joe Torchio not only liked bingo, he had to go to the bathroom a dozen times a day.

"Tell me," the aide said, "for my diary." She meant the BM Book. "Did you or didn't you?"

"Yes," Lou said.

"I'm about to," Joe said.

Joe went to the bathroom, the aide went off on her rounds, then Joe came out and, limping toward the door again, said, "I'm gonna go find Art or Ellen-er, Lou." Joe paused in the doorway, leaning on his cane, and called back, "And after I find

out, Lou, don't bring up any more names to me today. God-
damn it!"

Lou chuckled. He stretched his neck, resettled himself in his
chair, and went back again to Philadelphia, back to the place
where he'd left off, at the Settlement Music School. Jennie
would take the kids to the Sugar Bowl on the way back from
the music school to Lou's mother's house, where Lou would
meet them on Saturday afternoons.

Among the photographs that covered the wall to his left,
there were only several of Lou, and none bridging the gap
between Lou at seventeen in his World War I uniform and
Lou in a suit with gray hair and the mustache that he grew
when the company where he'd worked for thirty-five years
finally went bankrupt. He was back now in the time between
those two pictures. All he had to do was close his eyes and
he was again at work on Saturday mornings at the fountain
pen factory, across the Delaware in New Jersey. Them were
the days. Lou didn't have to work Saturdays, but he wouldn't
have denied himself the pleasure. He pretty much ran the
factory on weekdays. On Saturday mornings he could experi-
ment with the machinery without interference from his im-
mediate boss, Whitehouse. Mr. Whitehouse. With his Brooks
Brothers shirts and big Chrysler sedan. It had special exten-
sions on the driver's foot pedals, so that Whitehouse could
reach them. One of the men at the factory once called Whitehouse "a little sonofabitch," and Whitehouse replied, "I'm little,
but I'm not a sonofabitch." Whitehouse was nobody's fool. Lou
learned a lot from him. But truly he *was* a sonofabitch.

One time Whitehouse called Lou from one of the other
factory buildings. He and Lou argued about something. What

was it? Anyway, Whitehouse said over the phone, "You couldn't run a peanut factory." Lou told him to come on over and run this one, he was going home. But Whitehouse knew Lou wouldn't be so irresponsible as to leave a factory in full operation, and Lou knew he knew it.

They were using leftover pen materials to make lipstick cases, and Lou found a better way to get rid of the seam in the cases. Whitehouse took a look at the modification in the machine and said, "It won't work, *I* didn't think of it." But Whitehouse didn't tell Lou to stop doing it. Whitehouse didn't always get the better of him in technical matters. Already back there in his mind, Lou was about to get the better of Whitehouse when Joe's voice said from the doorway, "Art. Art thought of the name. Oscar Levant." Joe limped in and sat down on the edge of his bed.

"You're right," Lou said.

"No, Arthur was right." Joe's shoes clattered on the floor. Joe grunted, heaving himself onto his bed.

"Oscar Levant, that's the name," Lou said.

"It took Art a little while to remember it," Joe said. "Phil didn't remember it."

"I ever tell you about the time I got a hundred-dollar bonus?" said Lou.

Joe grunted, on his back now.

The big boss, Whitehouse's boss, had a lot of different factories. One of them made carbon paper, and there was a problem, and Lou was trying to solve it one Saturday morning. "This carbon paper used to be wound on a fiber tube, which was comparatively expensive, and it had to have a square hole in it." Lou's wrists had shrunk to frail thinness, but his hands, though veiny under papery skin, were still supple and robust enough to deliver firm handshakes — he hated limp handshakes, and if his right hand ever got too weak to deliver a firm one, he'd quit offering it. Lou's hands now described the tube on which the carbon paper was wound, his hands pulling apart as if pulling taffy. Then his fingers drew the square hole that had to be made in the tube. To make this tube, they'd extrude nitrocellulose, through a machine like a very large meat grinder, onto a square rod. That process worked all right, except that, as it cured, the nitrocellulose would shrink and it was hard to get the finished tube off the square rod. "I came in one Saturday to run a sample core," said Lou from his chair. He closed his eyes. He was smiling. He stood alone in the factory, over the extruding machine. Something had gone wrong. The square rod had gotten bent and was stuck at the mouth of the extruder. But the nitrocellulose tube kept coming out, perfectly formed, with a square hole in it and — this was the important thing — no rod to remove. "I thought, 'This is pretty good.' "

Joe looked thoughtful. "You know, I don't think Oscar Levant took dope."

"Yes, he did, Joe," Lou said.

Joe mouthed silently, "He didn't take dope."

"Getting back to my invention," Lou said. "The tube kept coming and it didn't collapse. I didn't know what to do. If I told Whitehouse, he'd say, 'It's no good unless I thought of it first.' So I went to a vice president of the company. He said take it to S.A. That was Mr. Niedich, the boss. So Mr. Niedich said, 'Try it a couple more times, and don't say anything to the old man.' That's what he called Whitehouse. The old man. It was successful. *They* told Whitehouse about it, and he never forgave me for that. But that year I got a hundred-dollar bonus."

Lou shifted in his chair. "You know how we tested fountain pens, don't you?"

Over on his bed, Joe turned his head and looked at Lou. Joe smiled gradually.

6

Earl sat on the edge of his bed, the blue nose catheter across his upper lip, his hair mussed up in back as always after lying down. Holding his shoulders erect, he picked up the silvery, helmet-like cover from his lunch. He stared at the plate of stir-fry. He drew air between narrowed lips and said, "I don't know what it is." He stared down at it. "That's enough to make me *not* eat." He picked up the fork and paused again. He had to eat or he'd have no chance of beating the doctor's prediction, or at least of getting well enough to go home. He scooped up a small bite and quickly slipped it into his mouth. The food had no taste to Earl, but he ate on, a thoughtful pause and a deep breath preceeding every forkful, every swallow strenuous.

The all-important diuretic was tormenting him with diarrhea. He couldn't go home this week, not in this condition. Meanwhile, his doctor thought it best that Earl not make the trip to the dining room. He would eat in his room. He didn't mind. It meant fewer trips past that lineup at the nurses' station. In the dining room, he'd shared his table with a hearty fellow who told him that he himself had trouble eating when

he first came here, and that Earl's lack of appetite would surely pass. But there was also a woman at their table who had
seemed perfectly rational until one day Earl saw that she was
trying to eat her soup with a fork. She began complaining that
her utensil didn't work. Another time she mixed her ice cream
with her mashed potatoes. Earl missed the company, but not
the dining room. He just wished that he had appetite, and that
his diarrhea would go away.

Earl got the last wish. The next morning, when the Sunrise
daytime charge nurse, Mary Ann, came in with his pills, Earl
grimaced and said to her, "Now I have the opposite problem."
Mary Ann, buxom and jolly, was Earl's favorite nurse here. She
was one of those who believed that older, simpler forms of
medicine should supersede drugs. "You've *got* to touch," she
liked to say. "I kiss the women, too, and the other day one said
to me, 'Do you know how long it's been since I've been kissed?'
It's part of the healing therapy." Now she sat down on the bed
beside Earl and put her arm around his shoulder. She sat there
for a few minutes, talking with Earl about nothing of consequence, until he seemed somewhat cheered up.

The next day, his diarrhea returned. Earl lay on his bedspread after another attack. "Sometimes I don't want to live,"
Earl said. "I *want* to live. But not in this condition. I was an
athlete. I was involved in every civic activity known to man."
He shook his head. He looked down at himself, at his now
baggy trousers. "We had the Florida trip all set up. A month.
All of March. But unless there's a big turnaround, we're not
going. I would like Jean to go with one of her children. She
probably won't want to. She'll be afraid I might die while she's
gone. Of course, I could be gone by that time."

Earl didn't want to think too much about that. He wanted to be busy. He always wanted to be with Jean. Color returned to his face in the mornings when she appeared at the foot of his bed, especially when she carried mail. "I love going through the mail."

Sorting through it, Earl found a check, a small refund on their car insurance. He wet his lips, found a pen on his bedside table, which served as his desk, endorsed the check, and told Jean not to forget to deposit it. Today.

"A banker and a Scotsman," said Jean.

"I don't like checks sitting around," Earl said. "Oh, it irks me!"

Earl had a large capacity for vicarious enjoyment, especially when it came to Jean. He liked to hear that she was going out to lunch with friends. He'd discuss the details with her, where they'd go and what she'd eat, often insisting that he pay through her. Afterward, he'd want a full account, and out of long habit, knowing this imaginative capacity of his, she would oblige, telling him every detail, down to a description of the view from the restaurant table.

It didn't take much to make Earl happy. Among some of the Sunrise staff, however, Earl had begun to acquire a reputation for being troublesome. "Demanding" was the word of choice for residents like Earl. In the staff break room or within the enclosure of the nurses' station, that word sometimes acquired a cold significance. Earl had now been here for going on three weeks, and nurses' entries full of irritation had begun appearing in his chart:

> Very demanding of staff — ordering them to do things for him that he is able to do for himself, i.e. change TV control buttons. Otherwise resident had an active day w/ visitors.

Each of the three separate nursing units had its special reputation. Meadowview was toughest emotionally, because of the many deaths that occurred there. Forest View was toughest psychologically, because of its many demented residents. And Sunrise was toughest physically, because of its many heavy, inert residents. That was the general and by now conventional assessment, but some staff, including some who worked on other units, would say that Sunrise was just plain tough in every way, the toughest of the three.

Many of Sunrise's residents presented special difficulties, especially to the nurse's aides, who in any nursing home stand near the bottom of the pay scale and do the most arduous work. The aides cleaned and dressed and often fed the residents. They lifted and transported them. Often they received harsh words or worse for their pains. Sunrise had several notable curmudgeons who growled at the staff. It had only a few residents who could do much for themselves. It had some fussy residents, including one old schoolteacher whose bedtime preparations alone could consume an hour of an aide's time. It had Winifred, very unhappy now because of the Hoyer Lift. It had the bellowing man with no legs, and a stroke victim who couldn't speak or walk but whose arms were still strong — he had injured several aides by punching them or shoving them away.

The problem wasn't that the work revolted the nurse's aides. Those who couldn't stand the smell of other people's excrement rarely made it through their probationary period. The work was simply hard, and harder now since the staff cuts. These had begun after New Year's and, to none of the aides' surprise, had fallen heaviest on them. "That's the way it always is. No one ever takes people off the top, just off the bottom," one remarked. On Sunrise the cuts meant that every aide had at least one more resident, and often two more, on her list, and the difference for them was profound. For most aides, the cuts meant they had less time to spend consoling residents and listening to their life stories. For a few, the cuts just meant more work, and more work left undone. One day around this time, the daughter of a resident of Sunrise found that her father had been lying in his own excrement for about two hours. That was not supposed to happen at Linda Manor. The administrator was furious. Nothing excused such negligence. Eventually an aide was fired. Morale had never sunk so low, especially on Sunrise. Earl had arrived at the wrong time, in the wrong part of Linda Manor.

The last thing the Sunrise staff thought they needed was another demanding resident. When a resident rang the call bell, a beeper went off at the nurses' station and a white light went on above the resident's door. To the aides on Sunrise, it seemed as if every time they looked, Earl's light was on. Sometimes it was Earl's roommate who pressed the call bell. Sometimes Earl pressed it on his roommate's behalf. But even then, it seemed, Earl had something he wanted done for himself as well. What did he think this was, some of the aides asked each other and the nurses, a hotel?

As Earl's stay had lengthened, some of the staff had decided that Earl was dominating his often inarticulate roommate, answering questions for him and assuming command of the television, even though the set belonged to his roommate. And Earl seemed upset when the staff didn't answer his bell right away. The policy was that they should answer the routine bells within fifteen minutes. That was the best they could do. Earl ought to understand that.

But to Earl, fifteen minutes could mean eternity. He kept his alarm near at hand — a small capsule with a nipple-like red button on the end, attached to a white electrical cord that snaked out from the wall. This was Earl's umbilical now, but it didn't make him feel safe, the way the same alarm device had made him feel inside the hospital. "Here, they come when they get a *chance*," Earl fretted.

Earl's Medicare coverage had run out. He paid out of his own bank account to stay here now — $130 a day, nearly $5,000 a month, counting the additional costs of oxygen and medications. Earl understood, as most other residents did not, that he was helping to subsidize the residents on Medicaid. He paid more for his care than its actual cost, to make up for the fact that the state paid less than the full costs of some others. Having his call bell answered promptly didn't seem too much to ask in return, especially when his life might depend on promptness. The other evening an aide, answering the call bell, said to Earl, "Boy, this is the busiest room."

"Not on my account," Earl said. He felt offended at the insinuation. About half the time, it seemed to him, he rang to get assistance for his roommate.

Then last night a nurse came in and took the TV's remote control away from him and placed it on his roommate's table. "You're not supposed to have this," the nurse said.

She seemed to think Earl had stolen the control, when in fact his roommate had asked Earl to keep it. True, Earl sometimes put on programs that he wanted to see, especially golf tournaments and evening mysteries, but he always asked his roommate's permission first, didn't he? He didn't want to buy his own television. He didn't plan to be here long enough for that. But Earl resolved that he would offer to pay half of his roommate's cable TV bill. He wished he'd done so sooner. Earl had not dared to protest to the nurse, though. "I'm afraid if it got around, even though I was right, some of the nurses would take it out on me." He wasn't sure to whom he might complain. He wasn't always sure which of the staff were aides, which nurses. He wished that they wore uniforms.

From the perspective of bed, every aide looked large and infinitely powerful. "You have to be careful," Earl thought. "If you get on their wrong side, they won't do *anything*." He felt safe in the daytime and completely safe during the many hours when Jean sat with him in the room. When she left late in the evening, he'd remind her to be sure to watch their favorite TV mystery, telling her that he'd be watching, too. In this way, he felt, they'd be together, sort of. The TV mattered now. It took his mind away from here, and it connected him to Jean.

He needed something to get his mind away from here. Many of his old friends from Holyoke hadn't visited yet. Maybe some of them still didn't know where he'd gone, though he'd called many of them. A few old friends had visited, and his children came whenever they could. He loved to see them all. He hadn't seen that old fellow Lou for a while. He'd enjoyed Lou's visits, but they were brief. He preferred the company of people he'd known before he came here. They made him feel he hadn't been taken permanently from the world. Indeed, their visits promised restoration to the world, because they made him feel much better, both in mind and body. He preferred Jean's visits above all.

She had come early this morning and had stayed until long after dark. He'd had a very good day, the kind of day that made him think his condition might have stabilized at last. But when Jean left, his spirits drooped. "I think about kicking the bucket. But not much. I want to get *home*," Earl said. "I could go in five minutes. I don't want to do any suffering. I want everything, I guess. I just want to get out of here. I'm not really a patient like the others. Jean thinks it'll be too much for her. It will be a chore. But she won't be without help."

These were the worst hours, after dark, when Jean had left. If he lay on his bed without his roommate's television on, he'd hear televisions in other rooms and the aides discussing their own lives away from here, the coughs and moans from nearby rooms, and that low, purring, underlying sound, like a ship's engines, like the building's sustaining force, which was the ventilation system. Five minutes could be a long time if one lay in one of these narrow beds and stared at the rectangular panels of the suspended ceiling. He kept the alarm device near at hand, clipped to an edge of his blanket. But if he had to press that little red button in an emergency, would these busy, businesslike young women — the ones on these after-hours shifts seemed the least congenial — answer it in time?

It was always this way now, before he got his sleeping pill. Thank God for his roommate's television and a sleeping pill. Without them he would lie here all night locked up with his own worst thoughts, thrown back at him, like the images of hospital beds and privacy curtains and medical furniture — metallic, functional, disposable looking — reflecting in the night-blackened window.

The last few nights a certain aide had made these hours almost unendurable. Whenever she came in, she looked cross and seemed impatient. He'd been trying to think of a way to let her know who he was. No one around here seemed to know who he was. This aide didn't seem to think he was even human. But the thought of offending her, and the possible consequences of that, chilled Earl. He'd held his tongue and suffered her coldness.

The windows across the room were black. His diarrhea had abated, but Earl wanted to wear a diaper just in case. The aide answered the call bell — that same cold, unfriendly aide. He made his request. She said, "No, you cannot have one." No explanation, just that curt answer.

Confrontation had never been Earl's style. He thought he ought to speak up, but just the thought in his mind frightened him. And yet he felt he couldn't bear this, being denied a simple disposable brief. Should he or shouldn't he? He took a quick breath and said, "You know, young lady, you don't like me very much."

The aide seemed surprised. "Why do you say that?"

Earl felt safer now. "Well, you come in here, you never wear a smile. It's almost as if you're doing me a favor."

Earl told Jean the whole story the next morning. "She took it pretty well. She said she was sorry she was acting that way. She didn't realize it. I was afraid to do it, but I figured I'd better take the bull by the horns."

"That's good," Jean said. "Because, you know, you sometimes have a grouchy expression and people don't know how sweet you are inside." She sat in the armchair beside his bed. Earl sat

149

on his bedspread, upright against the pillows, fully dressed as usual, as if he were merely resting for a moment here.

"You sing your happy song so people know how sweet you are," Jean went on. "I might be afraid of you if I didn't know you."

"Yeah, sure." Underneath the blue tube Earl's lips curled in a little smile.

Domestic routines survive even in foxholes. Jean had brought in Earl's laundry. Now she put it away for him in his photo-wood-grain-finished Linda Manor bureau, took off her coat, and, leaning down, gave him his morning kiss. She offered him her hands, to feel the coldness of the air outside, and did up a couple of the shirt buttons that Earl had missed.

"What did you have for lunch yesterday?" he asked.

"Veal, which you know I love. And we sat near a sunny window . . ."

"A long lunch," said Earl, dreamily and smiling. "But when the girls get together, it takes a long time."

These mornings on the way to the nursing home, Jean always stopped at a favorite diner for breakfast. "Tomorrow," Earl said now, "when you leave the diner, get the paper automatically." This was his way of reproving her for not having brought today's paper.

"I would have," she said, "but it was so cold. My hand would have frozen to the machine."

"We can't have that."

"Besides, you just throw it away," she said.

"I scan it," Earl said.

"Whatever you say, dear. You're the boss."

"I love that statement."

"Enjoy it while you can."

This was what a wife would say to a husband on the mend. Earl beamed. The morning sunlight shone on the floor, improving it. For now Sunrise seemed aptly named. Earl and Jean might have been just another well-matched couple, savoring the start of another day together. Musingly, Earl said he thought he'd go to hear Lou's daughter read at Literary Hour next Tuesday. Then he turned to Jean, his eyes searching her face, and said, "If I'm not home by then."

Jean looked away toward the bright window.

"Hear that, dear?" Earl said.

"Well, I don't know. I heard you." She looked at him and placed her hand on his leg. "I have to go to the dentist Tuesday. So you just have to take it easy."

"Okay," Earl said, "Wednesday."

Jean didn't answer, and soon changed the subject. Jean couldn't say yes, she'd take him home next Wednesday, because she believed in keeping promises. But she didn't believe in telling him everything that was on her mind. She often visited Earl three times a day and stayed for several hours each time. After her last visit, she'd go out to her car in the dark. She would not let herself begin to cry until she was safely inside the car, but would cry all the way home to her empty house.

7

The state bureaucracy had done a lot for residents of nursing homes. It had curbed the worst of the real estate scams through which unscrupulous proprietors used to loot the Treasury. One Linda Manor nursing supervisor remembered from the bad old days a case in which a dentist was caught extracting healthy teeth from aged, helpless residents of another nursing home, in order to increase business and get the gold embedded in those teeth. The state's nursing home bureaucracy had greatly curtailed such egregious sorts of crimes. But policing always has a price. One was lots of paperwork. It seemed that there was always more, never less. The new monthly forms, for instance, that obliged the nursing staff to describe the ways in which each resident's care had improved. Those forms took up so much time they virtually guaranteed that no improvements could take place. And the array of regulations was bewildering, even to the people who enforced them. Recently, a state inspector had ordered Linda Manor to make alterations in the dining room. The inspector cited regulations — wrongly, as it happened, but no one knew that then.

As a result, Bob's Stupidvising chairs were sacrificed. A dining table replaced them in the doorway. Bob scowled. Joe felt a little disappointed, but philosophical. "Oh, well." He assumed this was the end of Stupidvising. But he underestimated Bob.

A week went by without Stupidvising. Then on a winter morning just before lunch, Joe limped into the activity room and found five chairs arranged, once again, in the wide doorway to the dining room. Bob sat in one of the chairs. He was grinning at Joe. The chairs were all in one row now, instead of two, and they didn't face in on the dining room. They stretched perpendicularly back from the doorway. Bob had left just enough room between the table in the doorway and the new row of Stupidvising chairs for others to pass through. Bob jabbed his cane at the chair to his left for Joe, at the chair to his right for Lou, at the other two chairs for Art and Ted, and when everyone was seated, Bob said, "Excellent! Beautiful!" Stretched out in a line this way, the five men couldn't talk among themselves as easily as before or look directly into the dining room. But by bending forward and turning his head to the right, Joe could still see the dietary aides as they emerged from the kitchen.

"Lou-weese!" Joe called in his falsetto as the dietary aide by that name appeared.

Suddenly Art, in the chair to Joe's left, began to sing, with brio, in his ringing baritone. "Every little breeze seems to whisper Louise." Joe joined in, then Bob. And Lou, who never could carry a tune, chuckled, squeezing his eyes shut.

"Suuuu-zeee!" Joe called.

"If you knew Sue-zee like I know Sue-zee," Art sang.

"Excellent! Excellent!"

They used to sing only before Wednesday's lunch, when a piano player from outside would play songs on the upright. Now they began to serenade the dietary aides before almost every meal, and when the nurse's aide called out "Okay!" and the men rose and began to file in toward their table, Art would begin right on tune, "Glory, glory halle-lu-jah." Bob and Joe and sometimes Ted and sometimes even Lou would pick it up, the five men in their line, each leaning on a cane, proceeding through the dining room in slow rhythm to "The Battle Hymn of the Republic."

Joe took up the rear. As the men trooped in, single file and singing, Joe suddenly felt as if he saw his companions and himself in a mirror from above, five doddering old men on canes, earnestly and carefully limping in their line toward food. Joe stopped. He leaned on his cane, threw his head back, and started laughing.

"It's nice, you know," Joe said. "Art laughs, Bob laughs. Lou. Ted. I laugh. It's nice. Jesus Christ."

8

Lou had been the first resident to tie a yellow ribbon to his cane. Now yellow ribbons flourished everywhere — yellow ribbons tied to all the walkers, canes, and wheelchairs, yellow ribbons designed for packages fastened to all the doors inside, yellow ribbons looped around the columns of the portico. Meanwhile, at the direction of the activities department, residents were making valentines to send to the troops in the Persian Gulf.

Several Linda Manor residents claimed to have seen combat in their generation's wars, though their accounts lacked realism. Joe, by contrast, refused to say much about what he'd seen in the Pacific, besides the fact that he'd been at Leyte Gulf, the first battle of the Philippines campaign, where the first kamikazes struck. "Young people want to fight because they don't know war. Old people make up their minds, and young people fight, that's all," Joe said to Lou while watching the war in Iraq on TV.

Joe declined without comment to make valentines. But the old combination of Cupid and Mars proved very popular. Day after day dozens of residents, more even than turned out for bingo, sat at the long folding tables in the activity room and worked with paste and pens and construction paper. Even Phil joined in, parked at a table in his wheelchair, his head cocked to one side. He worked all alone, by choice it seemed, quickly turning out his messages to the troops, the same message on every construction-paper card:

Have a nice day.
Phil

"Some of the people are writing whole diaries, for cripe sake," Phil muttered, glancing at the women at the other tables.

At the end of January the activities department decorated the dining room with red streamers and rounded up a class of elementary schoolchildren. Two residents and two children sat together at each table. There at a table by the windows sat Lou and Bob and two young boys. Bob fidgeted and chewed at his mustache. The boys were asking questions. "I can't talk," Bob told them. Lou was smiling beneficently. "I can talk but I can't see," he was saying. In a moment Lou was cane-walking rather quickly from the room. A couple of the teachers who accompanied the children had approached Lou and said that they were friends of Ruth's. Lou was hurrying back to his room in order to phone Ruth before he forgot the teachers' names.

At a table near the center of the room sat Winifred — in her wheelchair, in one of her gowns and lots of costume jewelry, a boy on one side of her and a little girl on the other, all of them busily cutting big hearts out of paper plates, Winifred chatting away as she worked her scissors. "I've got my tongue hanging out," she declared, "so I'm happy."

Eleanor, well rouged and neatly coiffed as always, sat over near the coffee machine, her chair half turned to face a handsome little boy. Eleanor looked radiant. She wasn't making valentines, she was recruiting talent. The little boy was telling her that he'd played Cobweb in a production of *A Midsummer Night's Dream*. He came right out and said that he was a great actor. "I *like* him," Eleanor said later. "He's very conceited and he loves to act. I'm going to try and put him in my next play. I'd love to get back into children's theater."

Rosa was at a table over by the dining room's mirrored wall. She had two schoolgirls to herself, pink-cheeked sixth graders with silky hair and dainty wrists. Rosa had dressed up. She wore a string of pearls and a pink sweatshirt with the legend "Spoiled Brat" on the front. Rosa leaned toward the girls with her elbows on the table — she was so short that this put her elbows almost at shoulder height. Rosa, the poet of Forest View, the maker of salty limericks, had her hands clasped before her on the table. She looked as if she meant to be on her best behavior. One of the staff stopped at Rosa's side. She wasn't helping the children write any poems, was she? "Nah," said Rosa. She smiled from the side of her mouth.

From the Stupidvising doorway, the activities director called, "Thanks again for all your help in this wonderful project for helping our troops." She asked that all those with relatives "over there" raise their hands.

At Rosa's table, meanwhile, one of the girls asked Rosa, "Do you want to write something here?" The child had a card prepared and was offering it to Rosa.

"Nah," Rosa said. "I don't write very good." Then a sneaky little smile came over her face. "Roses are red, violets are blue,

I'm in love but not with you," Rosa said. She grinned, looking at the girls.

The schoolgirls looked back at Rosa with widened eyes. One of them said, "Want to put, 'Roses are red, violets are blue, sugar is sweet and so are you'?"

"Yeah," Rosa said.

The girls got busy concocting a card on pink construction paper, pasting paper hearts all around the poem. Rosa cocked her head, leaned over, and watched.

"There. How's that?" said one of the girls.

"Ohhh," Rosa said. "Good. That's nice writing there."

"Thank you," said the girl, dropping her eyes modestly.

"What do you want to put on the front?" the other girl asked Rosa.

" 'I'll see ya when you come back,' huh?" Rosa said. She frowned. "Well, we don't know when they're comin' back, do we?"

Outside the activity room the corridors were all but empty. Faint sounds of merriment reached no farther than the Sunrise nurses' station. Down at the end of the west corridor, Earl's door was open. He lay on the covers of his bed in street clothes, fast asleep.

By the time Earl awoke that afternoon, the party was over. He regretted missing it. He wanted to do his part.

❖   ❖   ❖

Valentine making in the activity room continued daily. Several days later, Earl and Jean sat together at one end of a table, Earl in his wheelchair, and worked on valentines. Winifred and several other female residents sat at the next table.

Jean, recalling her own Army days, told Earl, "No one ever sent me a valentine when I was in the service."

"No," Earl said. He looked at Jean and winked. "But they have ever since." Earl came of age between the wars and never served in the military. He leaned over to see what Jean had written on her card. "Don't write a book on it."

"Why not?"

"Okay." He smiled.

Earl fingered the cup of paste before him. "This looks like milk of magnesia," he muttered to himself. He got to work designing his own card. He looked like an executive at his desk now, in spite of his thinness, his wheelchair, his oxygen tube.

"You're going too fast," said Jean, leaning over to look at Earl's work. "Why don't you make a little cherub or something?"

"Me? Oh, come on."

"Think of a few messages, dear."

"Oh, come on."

"If you were a soldier out in the desert, what would you want to hear?" she asked.

Earl looked at his card and said — there was great conviction in his voice — "I'd just want to hear from someone." Perhaps he was thinking of the many friends who hadn't yet visited him here.

Jean went back to work, and Earl started to do likewise. He meant to pick up his pen, but he took the paste brush instead and made as if to write with it. It was only a moment before he realized the mistake. He put the paste brush back. His hands were suddenly fumbling.

Winifred now raised her voice, addressing the whole room.

"I put on all of mine, 'Our minds are on you, our hearts are with you, our love is for you.' And then I said, 'Thank you and God bless.'"

Jean turned around in her chair. "That's very nice," she said to Winifred.

Winifred looked, in her wheelchair, like a person immobilized in traction, sprawled out, feet up, and yet she was managing to turn out valentines at a staggering rate.

"On some of them I said, 'God loves you and so do I,'" Winifred went on.

"That's nice," Jean said more softly.

"And on some of them I wrote, 'We support you and will work to bring you home safely and soon.'"

Earl didn't seem to hear any of this. He had dropped his pen. He was staring at nothing, wearing the sort of look a night watchman might wear who has heard a suspicious noise behind him.

Jean turned back to Earl. "I didn't know you got involved in this sort of thing."

Earl was breathing more rapidly now. "I get involved whenever I can help," he said, staring at the table.

Winifred was telling the room, "I've got a friend with two daughters, and . . ."

Earl stared fixedly in the general direction of his card. The color in his face had all drained away. "I'm going to have to go," he said to Jean. "Can you finish this?"

"You're getting tired?"

"Yes."

9

Slow, tenacious traffic moved up and down the first floor's central corridor. A resident out for exercise bent unsteadily over her walker. A white-coated physical therapist followed close behind, towing an empty wheelchair with which to catch her if she should lose her contest with gravity today. A few aged figures limped by on canes and caterpillar-walked in wheelchairs, pushing with their hands and padding with their feet, their eyes fixed on distant goals — the beauty shop, the dining room, the library, the elevators halfway down Sunrise's northern corridor.

Lou and Joe joined the northbound traffic. Lou got a little ways ahead. He probably didn't realize it. He was concentrating on the perils in his way.

It had surprised Joe when he'd found out that Lou could walk faster than he. It had surprised him more when Lou had told him that he had almost all his teeth. Ninety-one years old and Lou still had his teeth. Good God. Dragging his right leg along down the corridor, Joe grinned. He called out loudly toward Lou's back, "He didn't drink. He didn't smoke. He didn't chase women. He's dead, for Christ's sake!"

A woman in a wheelchair heading the other way smiled up at Joe. He smiled back.

Lou turned in at the door to the left, labeled "Physical Therapy." Joe paused at the door. Across the hall, in the activity room, Bible Study was in progress. The minister was talking about the immortal soul. "Oh, Jesus Christ. Goddamn fool," Joe muttered.

Anyway, this was M&M's time, the body's hour. Joe looked forward to it. M&M's was better than bingo. More constructive.

Joe limped into the M&M's room. Daylight from the small adjoining greenhouse and overhead fluorescent lights gleamed brightly on the floor. The clean, bitter smell of geraniums filled the room. Lou was already seated in a straight-backed armchair, his eyes squinted shut against the brightness. A couple of the other M&Ms regulars were already there, too: Carol, the instructor, seated beside a small tape recorder, and Lou and Joe's next-door neighbor Mary, in her wheelchair. Mary was only in her sixties, but a brain tumor had twisted her face out of symmetry. The left side drooped; it looked the way one's face feels when numbed on one side with Novocain. Mary spoke out of the right side of her mouth, rolling her head to that side. Her speech sounded garbled but she spoke slowly and distinctly enough. "Go' morning, Joe."

Good-mornings were passed all around. Joe sat down beside Lou. "Mary, I'm going to take off my shoes."

"All right, Joe. I know you just took a shower."

From the hallway a rhythmic sound of creaking metal approached. "Here she comes," Mary said. "Miss 'merica."

Dora came in on her walker. Joe watched her enter, and a little smile blossomed on his face.

Though he liked Dora, Lou was weary of her predictable discourse. Back up in the room, he had said to Joe, "Don't get Dora started." But the sight of Dora put Joe in a sportive mood. Knowing her answers as well as he did, Joe could not resist. "How *are* ya, Dora?" Joe asked.

Dora stopped halfway into the room, standing behind her

walker, gripping its front rung as if at a balcony railing, and she declared, "I was never better. I was never better than I am this minute."

Dora's *t*'s were very crisp, like several other female residents'. Did schoolteachers early in the century insist on the emphatic *t*, along with good penmanship and right-handedness? And was it the girls, back then as now, who paid attention?

Dora continued: "I went to bed at a quarter past eight and I never got up until quarter past seven. That's what I call a good night's sleep. Can anyone beat that?"

Joe leaned forward, bowing his head, so that his face was hidden from Dora. He laughed silently.

"I slept eight hours without interruptions," Dora went on. "My next-door neighbor's snoring didn't bother me a *bit*."

Joe, his grin under wraps, looked up at Dora. "You told me how old you are."

"Nine-tee-four," Dora said. "I'm going to be nine-tee-five next month. I'm in no pains. I eat everything put in front of me. I'm in good health. My doctor says, 'Dora, I've got some good news for you. As of today, you're one hundred percent well.' I told him the other doctors say, 'Get out of here, Dora, you're gonna live to a hundred.' "

"You dream when you sleep?" asked Joe.

"Yes, I dream every night," said Dora, who still hadn't moved to a seat. "I have *good* dreams. I dream that my folks are still alive. But they've all passed away. They're all in the Colrain cemetery."

"You're an inspiration, Dora," said Carol.

Joe's face turned serious. He looked Dora in the eyes. "Yes, you are," he said. Then, smiling again, Joe asked, "Do you feel like you're twenty?"

"Just her mind," Mary said in her garbly voice.

"You think like a twenty-year-old," Joe said.

"Yes, I do," Dora said. She recited exactly what she'd had for breakfast.

"I feel like a seventy-two-year-old man, that's all," Joe said.

"You're not. Are you?" Mary said to Joe. "You don't look like a seventy-two-year-old."

Suddenly Joe was frowning. "Bullshit I don't."

Carol began to say, "It's all in your —"

"No," Joe said, and, evidently hearing the warning in his voice, Carol abandoned the sentence. The scowl left Joe's face as suddenly as it had appeared.

Lou, in the meantime, was starting to look restive. "Dora, you better sit down before someone steals your chair," he said.

"All right," said Carol. "Everybody ready? Deep breath. In. And. Out." And to the strains of Mitch Miller and his band singing "I'll Have You to Remember" on the tape recorder, Music and Motion began.

They exercised sitting down for about half an hour. The routine, which Carol had invented and kept tailoring to fit her ever-changing clientele, demanded gentle exercise of all movable parts from head to feet. Joe sang along to the taped music now and then, in a tenor much more fluid and mellifluous than his speaking voice — to old favorites, Lawrence Welk taking up when Mitch Miller finished, slow music for the slow stretching. Joe grunted sometimes, especially when he had to lift both arms over his head. He grasped the right one and pulled it up with his left, and the right arm shook. Carol called out instructions. "Now chin up and head back. Nice and slow. Now gently to the side."

"Your neck creak, Lou?" Joe asked over the music.

"Yeah. I should keep a little can of oil."

"Now reach to the side. Very carefully. Pick up those hundred-dollar bills off the floor."

"Recession," Joe said. "Ten-dollar bills."

"Are we still picking them up?" Carol asked.

"Just on the right side," Lou said. "I can't reach all the way with the left. Somebody's gotta bring in a tape measure, see if my right arm's longer than the left."

"Maybe your hips aren't straight," Carol said.

"Well," said Lou, stretching left. "Years ago I used to carry a toolbox on my right shoulder."

"Verrrrry good, everybody," Carol said. "Everybody still breathing?"

"Oh, for Christ's sakes!" Joe said.

"I just say that so you'll have something to say."

"Oxygen in, whatever coming out," Lou said.

"If we didn't breathe we'd turn purple!" Joe said.

"But some people hold their breath," Carol said.

"Yes, I agree with you," Joe said.

When they started to work on their feet and legs, Carol switched to a Scott Joplin piano rags tape, and they went walking in place, did a piece of the Charleston with their feet, made cancan kicks if they could, all without ever leaving their seats. In a while Lou took a break. Soon Joe did, too.

"Anybody worn out?" Carol asked.

"We're *all* worn out," Lou said.

"Or we wouldn't be here," Joe said.

They concluded with more slow, gentle stretching, and everyone thanked Carol, who said, with evident feeling, "It's a privilege for me. How's that? I'll see you all on Monday, God willing."

At the doorway Lou and Joe split up. Lou would go back to their room. Ruth would be here any minute for her daily visit. Joe said he was going to ride the exercise bike. Lou said, "Don't push it, Joe. Don't try and go all the way to Chicago. Maybe just Cleveland."

Joe limped down the central corridor toward the occupational therapy room. "I *glide* across the floor," Joe said as he hobbled along. "God almighty." He looked forward to the bike. Riding felt like progress, carrying him back.

The OT room was small and sunny, full of exercise equipment, the most hopeful-looking room at Linda Manor, promising rejuvenation. Carol arrived to supervise. "Don't get too fancy," she said. Joe grunted as he began pumping the pedals.

After he got up some momentum, he'd talk. He spoke of his wife. "She wore herself out. Soaking my foot twice a day, helping me in the shower. Good God."

"Basically, you do what you can," Carol said.

"That's right." Joe's voice sounded testy for a moment. "Adjust. Adjust," he said, as if quoting from a despised text.

"How's your knee?"

"It's, uh, fine."

"You lie," Carol said.

Joe said, "Uh, Lou. He asks you how far? Don't tell him."

"Keep it fuzzy when he asks?"

"Yeah."

"Yes, because he does worry," Carol said.

Joe pedaled on. He said he wanted her to increase the resistance in the machine. Since the blister, Carol had kept it at the lowest level. She said, "No, no."

"I know," Joe said, "but Jesus Christ."

"Because all tension does, Joe, is build up the muscle."

"I don't want that."

"No, you want endurance."

"No," he said. "All I'm doing it for is get my belly flat."

Joe pumped and pumped. The muscles in his jaw flexed, he breathed heavily, sweat beaded on his forehead.

"Going back to Pittsfield," Carol sang.

10

Earl came out into the hall for his morning walk. He pushed his wheelchair down the corridor toward the nurses' station, a portable oxygen canister hanging from the handlebars, the blue tube still looped around his head. Every time he'd felt that he was making progress with his physical therapy, he'd had another setback and been obliged to stay in bed. Earl wasn't feeling very well today, just better than he had. His doctor had visited again, and had told Earl that he wasn't ready to go home. He needed to get some exercise, the doctor said. Earl understood this to mean that exercise might get him out of here. So Earl resolved to take these walks, two walks per day, no matter how he felt.

Earl walked out of Sunrise, passing the lineup with averted eyes. Walking slowly down the central corridor, he glanced in the tall narrow windows of the physical therapy room. M&M's

was over. The room was empty now. He planned to go to M&M's himself soon. Earl walked down to the administrative corridor, turned around, and walked back to his room. Then he lay down to rest, awaiting lunch.

Everything he ate here had a funny taste to it now, except for the cans of liquid dietary supplement, a product called Ensure. Earl sat on the edge of his bed, his tray on the table before him. He smacked his lips over the Ensure. He picked at the solid food on his plate. He got a little down. Then he rested again, and at around one o'clock he saddled up for his second walk.

Earl hitched up his trousers to a spot not far below the sternum. His belt wasn't tight enough anymore to hold up his trousers securely, even though he had it cinched to its last hole. Earl attached his nose catheter to his portable oxygen canister, fumbling a little, breathing rapidly and noisily. He set the oxygen on 2, and he was ready. He'd go a little farther than this morning. He'd walk behind the wheelchair all the way out to the lobby, around the piano, and back.

A friend of Earl's had called the other night and offered to talk to Jean about taking Earl home. Earl had demurred. He'd work it out with her himself. "It'll be a chore for Jean," he said, walking on. "But I won't go upstairs to bed. I'll get a bed downstairs, and a toilet. But Jean's afraid I'll fall sometime and she won't be able to pick me up. I know it's going to be a chore for Jean, because even though we can afford help, she likes to be independent, and I will be a chore at certain times. Jean's trying to be nice to me. At the same time, she's a little afraid of having strangers in the house." He made it to the piano, which he circled. On the way back, Earl began running short of breath. By the time he turned down the Sunrise hallway, he looked as though he'd run five miles. He climbed right back on his bed and lay there, concentrating on his breathing, wearing the night watchman's look. He had asked one of the maintenance men to poke a new hole in his belt so he could cinch it tight, but the man hadn't come to do it yet. A simple thing like that. A lot of things around here took longer than they should.

II

Outside Linda Manor's windows, some snow appeared. It soon melted. For many days there were views of flapping flags and cold gray skies, and then bright sunshine lit the grass. The days warmed up a little. The temperature inside didn't vary much. It was always warm. Many residents wore sweaters and shivered at the slightest drafts. From outside, in the afternoons, bedroom windows stood out dark against the sunlight. Now and then a resident's face swam into view behind the glass and lingered, looking out. Weather was observed but not experienced. Art sat in his favorite armchair in the lobby, beyond the full reach of the jets of fresh air that visitors brought in.

"It's a beautiful day," said a visitor, stopping in front of Art's chair and unbuttoning her coat.

"Yes," Art said. "That's what the people tell us."

The visitor passed inward, and Art went back to his own thoughts, gazing at the windows.

Joe stood at the window in the room upstairs for a moment.

"It's a nice day, Lou." Then Joe lay down. Today being a shower day, Lou lay on his bed, too. Showers wore him out. He wished he knew exactly why. In the room the lights were off. The view of woods and brown meadow out their window was brightly lit. It was as if their room were a dark museum and their window a backlit diorama in which a bear or a red fox might appear. Joe began watching a movie. His son still brought him videotapes regularly, and Lou still shook his head and said, "I don't understand why Joe wants to listen to some of those tapes." Joe's movies remained Lou's trusty soporific, though. Lou was dozing now. When he awakened he'd say to Joe, "I slept two hours between car smashups."

Soon Joe, too, dozed off. The TV played on unwatched, the afternoon light slowly fading in their window, the sound of gunfire emanating faintly through their door into the corridors of Forest View. Throughout Linda Manor, from closed and half-opened doors, came voices broadcasting news of the bombings in Kuwait and Iraq, mingled with the sounds of soap operas and game shows. Now and then the elevator bells rang — *Boing, boing,* as in a department store. A monotony of sound is a kind of silence. The lengthening afternoons were full of silences.

Jean peeked in the door to Earl's room. He was napping. She withdrew to the corridor and looked out the windows at the sunny, spring-portending February afternoon. "He's a good scout," she thought. "He's puzzled by these things that are happening to him." She thought Earl had finally resigned himself to staying on at Linda Manor. At least yesterday he said that he realized what a trial it would have been for both of them if he'd lived at home these past few weeks. But he kept saying to her, "This isn't me." He was still having a very hard time believing that he wouldn't get over this sickness one day. Optimism, Jean thought, had tenacious roots in Earl. He believed in the lessons of the Frank Merriwell books that he read in his youth: work hard and think good thoughts and help other people. But he found it difficult to say what his motto should be now. And Jean was having some of the same difficulty. Now and then she had thoughts like this: "At least when Adam and Eve left the Garden, they went out together."

Where did people get joy and energy? From their families, and especially their children, she thought. But where could she get those things, returning every night to an empty house? What would it be like to work here? She hoped the people who worked here had home lives that restored them. Maybe the fact that they were helping other people was enough. Everything seemed to revolve around that, she thought. To have a vital connection. She felt disconnected. Her own health wasn't sound enough for her to work at a real job. She still had some responsibilities away from here, but she wasn't having much fun at anything, because she was doing almost everything alone.

Jean wished that she could garden, but gardening was still two months away. Driving over this afternoon, she found herself thinking about the difference between looking and seeing. At a museum, she thought, most people just glance and move on. But every so often a person stops and really *sees* a painting. That was the way she wanted to live, she thought driving over. "I want to experience things," she thought. "I don't like just to pass by them. That's the part I miss. I like to live connected."

Linda Manor was a good place, Jean believed. But there was

too much sadness here. The other day she sat out in the lobby with Earl and the one friend of Earl's from Holyoke who regularly visited, and a woman in a wheelchair across the lobby began weeping, waving at her departing husband's car. Jean wanted to do something, but could think of nothing to do. She wished she saw more residents like that fellow who sat like a guard at the front door. She liked his songs of hello, which she overheard in the hallways. This place needed more of that, a little energy. She smiled, thinking of Bob. He reminded her of Art Carney in *The Honeymooners.*

Jean hadn't taken off her coat yet. "We say, 'March forward. Don't look back.' But most of the stuff is back!" she exclaimed toward the windows. Then she turned away and tiptoed into Earl's room. She sat in a chair beside his bed until he woke up from his nap.

❖   ❖   ❖

Earl had constipation problems once again. They lingered for a few days. Finally, after several younger nurses tried without success, one of the veterans managed to give him a full-fledged enema. "I finally had an enema today," he crowed. "I yelled and screamed, but I feel much better." Earl lay on his bed. There was some color in his face. His thoughts were rambling, though, this morning while he waited for Jean to arrive. He spoke even more rapidly than usual.

"I still want to go home. But I couldn't go with all the stuff that's going on. I could, but Jean doesn't want to go through that. She's such a fastidious woman. Everything has to be spick-and-span. I'm careful, too. I don't smoke. But I notice she's always cleaning up things that don't need cleaning up. I know she'd love to have me home. But — this is a terrible thing to say — she doesn't want me to disrupt her household."

Earl wet his lips and readjusted his nose catheter. He thought of the many hours Jean had spent in here at his bedside, never missing a day, often bringing in picnic lunches and dinners in the hope of arousing some appetite in him. Her own health was far from perfect, too. "She's been very faithful," Earl said. He wouldn't talk to her again about going home. It would upset her. But when he felt as well as this, he couldn't help but think of going home. And if he kept on feeling this way, he wouldn't be a chore.

❖   ❖   ❖

Earl took his two walks Saturday. On Sunday morning his two young grandsons visited and played Monopoly with him. Earl intended to lose, but he'd forgotten the game and old banking instincts asserted themselves. He managed to lose the rematch.

"When I get company it helps me immensely," he said afterward, when everyone was gone. "Even if I just *know* someone's coming." Now he faced another week in here.

Earl still took the sleeping pill Halcion every night. He'd felt afraid to try to sleep without it ever since his doctor told him he probably had a week to six months left. About a month had passed since then. Some days lately Earl believed he might have more than five months left. But last night, just when his bowel problems had cleared up, a tooth fell out, a front tooth.

He'd awakened mourning it. "Everything's happening," he said. "Now I look worse than ever, dammit."

The gap did add a few years overnight to Earl's visual age. He had to get his mind off it. Today he'd shaved and dressed without assistance, which was good for him, he felt, though he figured help should have been offered. By ten o'clock he'd made four phone calls, to various friends. Then he made some more notes on his family's history. "You know, keeping your mind active is so important."

On his bedside table lay a calculator, a spiral notebook with his notes on family history, and a fat neat bundle of checkbooks and bills, bound together with a rubber band. Jean's bookkeeping skills were another project. She had some distance yet to go, Earl felt, but then again Earl had exacting standards. It wasn't just a question of *paying* the monthly bills, he liked to say, but also of knowing *when* to pay them. Pay a few days late and you risked a penalty; pay a few days early and you lost interest on your money. Anyway, he had to get Jean self-sufficient on the bills, in case the doctor's prediction was correct.

Jean arrived smiling, carrying the morning paper. She always wore a cheerful look when she arrived, even if she had to compose it at the door. Earl was very businesslike today. "Here's that check for St. John's," he said, undoing his financial bundle and handing that item to her.

She tucked it in her pocketbook. "What are you trying to do, look like one of those rockers?" she said, leaning over and buttoning up his shirt, which had been partway open on his thin chest. She moved some mail to one side of his bedside table, his desk. Earl moved it back, saying, "Be careful now."

She smoothed out his half-elevated collar and sat down.

In his notes, Earl had gotten to the story of a brother's untimely death, in the railroad yards of Holyoke. He retold it now. "John was hopping onto railroad cars. He had to go through the railroad yard to deliver lunch to our father. He was hopping onto the ladder of a moving train and he slipped and was mangled. He was only six years old."

"Probably someone dared him," Jean said softly.

"Two or three years ago I went to the Holyoke Public Library and found the story of his accident," Earl said. "I was only a couple of months old when it happened. At the cemetery there's a tiny headstone. Forestdale Cemetery. I was president for fourteen years."

"Three or four lots belong to our different families. And you and I don't know where *we're* going," Jean said. She had a soothing way of confronting sorrow. Sometimes consciously, and sometimes without forethought, she was trying to help Earl find a way of confronting death. He wasn't built in such a way as to make that easy. He was the doer in their family. Jean said to him now, "We were brought up, we were taught that taking care of gravesites was one of your familial duties. Almost like the Japanese. My grandmother took me there as a little girl, and I was afraid of dying a lot when I was six years old. She made a lovely outing of it. She cut down some lilacs. 'Where are we going?' I asked. 'To take some nice flowers to all our lovely relatives in the cemetery,' she said. 'Isn't this a pretty day? We'll put some flowers here, these here.' We came back and sat on the porch and drank lemonade. I wasn't quite as anxious about it after that."

Earl sat upright against his pillows. "Probably helped you a lot."

"I think what happened was my grandfather had died," Jean said. "And I'd prayed every day and I was resentful about that. What's the good of prayers if this is what happens? I thought I had a direct line to God."

"What a jolt in life you have," Earl said.

"Well, you know," Jean said, "you don't see the big picture when you're young. I wasn't as secure about heaven as I was about earth."

Earl did not comment. Jean was going out to lunch soon. He turned to business. She was to pay for lunch. First, she should go to the nurses' station and get his portable oxygen bottle refilled.

"And try to get a little exercise," said Jean, rising. She nodded toward Earl's midsection. "But be sure to zip up. Don't let the horse out of the barn."

Earl had missed another item when dressing himself this morning. He looked down, then zipped up his fly, murmuring, with a little smile on his face, "Horse out of the barn, I love that."

As Jean went off for the oxygen, Earl picked up his phone and dialed. "Can I talk to someone in the kitchen? This is Mr. Duncan in one thirty-one. Oh, Dave. Fine. How are you? What's the alternate on today's meal? Pot roast with gravy. What else have you got in lieu of that? Baked chicken. Let me have that. Everything's working out fine on breakfast now. Two eggs. Now supper. What else besides macaroni and cheese?"

Earl seemed more like his old self than ever before in here, in spite of the lost tooth. He hung up the phone and said, "I'm getting to know the people here." He had plenty to keep him busy today. He'd get his favorite aide to help him with the tape recorder, so he could begin dictating the family history. Technology makes it easy for younger generations to earn the admiration of their elders. Earl couldn't seem to get the recorder to work right, but that aide could. "She's a world beater."

12

"Dad? How's Earl Duncan doing?" Ruth asked Lou upstairs in the room.

"Well, I went down to see him the other day, and he was doing fine. Then I went down yesterday and the nurse said he wasn't feeling well, so I didn't go in."

"Oh," said Ruth.

Joe changed the subject. The subject was the weight that Joe couldn't lose, in spite of diet Jell-O and long rides on the bike.

Lou, from his seat by the window, said, "The best exercise, Joe, is —"

Joe sat up and said, "Pushing yourself away from the table. Jesus Christ, my grandfather said that."

Lou made a pantomime of shrinking back in his chair and swallowing his last words. Then he smiled and said, "I'm quoting your grandfather."

"And his grandfather told *him!*"

Lou's thoughts were already elsewhere. He had heard that three oranges cost a dollar.

"Jesus Christ! Three oranges for a dollar?" said Joe.

"I can't believe what Dave was telling me about coffee," said Lou. "Three dollars a pound." He shook his head.

"Well," said Joe, "we don't know what real life is. We're in a nursing home."

The price of things was one of Lou and Joe's continuing subjects. They agreed — vehemently sometimes, as if they were arguing — that the price of things nowadays proved they were superannuated. In the real world a pound of coffee cost almost as much as Lou had once earned in a week. There was no point in trying to keep track of such a crazy world. In agreement with Joe on that point, Lou got his cane and headed downstairs for Current Events. "See ya late-ah, Joe."

In the activity room every Friday, for about half an hour, the activities aide Rita read aloud articles from the regional newspapers. The turnout was usually thin. It would have been thinner if the Forest View staff hadn't routinely rounded up four or five demented residents and sent them down to hear the news. This was a way for the staff to get some respite, and was perhaps a silent protest against the general lack of activities designed for Linda Manor's demented. Zita, the gray-haired woman who paced the halls and tried to pluck flowers from the carpet, had already fallen asleep in her chair. The former inner-city schoolteacher was trying to read a newspaper upside down. The tiny Fleur, the woman who was always wanting to call her mother on the phone, asked the room in general, "We havin' a party or somethin'?" A couple of able-minded women were there. They were regulars. Lou and Joe's neighbor Hazel asked the aide to read *all* of the local obituaries. "The Irish comics," Hazel called them. Being Irish herself, she was entitled. She smiled sadly, hearing a couple of familiar names. To outlive one's contemporaries is, after all, a species of accomplishment. Lou was the only man there, as usual, and once the obituaries were read and the demented residents had fallen into attentive but puzzled-looking silences, he and the aide carried on, the aide reading the news and Lou offering commentary. "Here's an article about another beaching of whales on the Cape," said the aide, Rita.

"I think it's pollution that's causing it," Lou said.

"Bringing them in," Rita agreed.

Lou said, in a slightly higher voice, "What I don't understand — they claim the whales have to stay wet — why the fire department doesn't hook up its pumps."

"I like to read a few *good* things," Elgie put in.

"That's why I say we should write our own newspaper," said Rita.

But Lou was not afraid of bad news.

"They're expecting a big fight in Moscow today," said Rita.

"Maybe they'll bring the czar back," said Lou.

"Ooooh," said Rita. "Richmond, California. It says there's a rash of —"

Lou interrupted. He'd already heard this news. "Legionnaires'. It's in an area where they failed to clean their air-conditioning filters. That's what happened when they discovered so-called Legionnaires' disease at the Bellevue-Stratford in Philadelphia. They didn't clean the filters as often as they should."

"Isn't that something," said Rita.

"The problem is," said Lou severely, "they don't do the maintenance."

"Oh, here's something! A bicycle for eight."

"*That's* what this country needs," said Lou.

"Here's a bit of slightly good news. 'The Persian Gulf War should not cost the United States any money.' "

"So far the other countries haven't come across with their share," said Lou, wearing a dark look.

"I think they will," said Rita.

"I don't know," said Lou. "I think they're gonna hem and haw on it, that's for sure."

Rita read some figures. One country was going to give $12 million, another $11.5 *billion*.

"Promises, promises," intoned Lou.

Joe liked these hours and half hours when Lou went to activities. Over this last year he had discovered — it seemed like for the first time in his life — a capacity for calmness. Lou might have been astonished to hear that, but Lou hadn't known him before. The other night, for instance, Joe had called his wife and gotten no answer. At such times he used to fill up with worry. He would call his son to ask where the hell his mother was. But the other night he waited and called his wife back later, and sure enough, everything was all right. She'd just been out to dinner at the neighbors'. In his newfound calmness, Joe could see himself more clearly. He remembered how as a young man he'd imagined himself like the movie actor Leslie Howard, suave, urbane, insouciant. Joe guffawed at that old fantasy, remembering himself back then, jealous, combative, always anxious. He was different now, both inside and outside. Somewhat more on the outside, he thought. "I still have things inside me."

Lou would return soon. Today being Friday, there'd be scrod

for lunch, and before lunch Lou would probably tell his scrod joke, one of Lou's two or three off-color jokes. Lou would probably say again, "You know the story about the proper Bostonian lady. She said, 'I'm going to Boston to get scrod.'"

Joe wouldn't mind hearing the joke again. "He's seventy, eighty, ninety, ninety-one, for Chrissake. He can *tell* his joke. Good God."

But when Lou came back to the room, he had something else on his mind, obviously. He gave Joe his usual summary of Current Events, and then, shifting in his chair, lifting a hand, index finger extended, Lou said, "Changing the subject a little. Talking about tools . . ."

Joe grinned. He sat up in his bed and, still grinning, said toward Lou, "I wasn't aware we were talking about tools."

"I was up last night trying to figure this out," Lou went on. "Millers Falls. They made tools somewhere around here. Are they still in business?" Lou didn't wait for an answer. He lifted an index finger again. "The first tool I ever bought myself was a hand drill. I was working in a shop that made electrical fixtures. I had to drill small holes. And I paid three dollars and fifty cents for that drill, and three dollars and fifty cents was my wages for the week, and that tool is still in good working order. I gave it to my grandson. It has the Millers Falls label on the handle."

Still grinning, Joe sat up again and said toward Lou, "Changing the subject a little."

"A hundred and ninety degrees." Lou smiled. "Go ahead, Joe."

"I don't have anything to say." Joe lay back and let his laughter out. Then, the trace of a smile on his face, Joe lay listening to Lou reminisce.

Lou said he knew where all of his old tools had gone, and it was true. Joe had overheard Lou on the phone on Saturday mornings asking his grandson about the well-being of that old hand drill. Afterward, Lou had told Joe that the drill was still "in perfect working order." Over on the table beside him was Lou's album of photos of knickknacks and furniture he had made. Lou had shown the pictures to Joe, and often Joe had lain here watching and listening while Lou, who could no longer see those photos himself, showed them to various visitors and staff. Joe had listened many times this past year as memory summoned Lou back to his workshops. Knowing where his old tools were and having pictures of things he'd made with them kept that part of his life real. Sitting there by the window, Lou would reconstruct the furniture, telling how he'd used this and that tool, now in his son's workshop, to make that grandfather clock, now in the album and in a grand-daughter's living room. And lying on his bed, Joe listened.

That first tool, the seventy-eight-year-old Millers Falls hand drill, was like the fertilized egg of Lou's memory. It seemed to carry all the information Lou needed to reconstitute his long life. The drill took him back: Lou finishing up eighth grade on a Thursday in 1914 and skipping the graduation ceremony in order to start his first full-time job. Turning over his $3.50 paycheck to his mother, who somehow managed always to put food on the table for a large family. His father's delivery service that ended in failure, like all his other ventures, in this case when his horse went lame. The restaurant and boarding house in South Philadelphia, Lou's father's voice calling to his mother in the kitchen, speaking about a man who had ordered beef stew, which cost a nickel, "Take the beef out, the bum's only got three cents." Shutting his eyes tight, Lou described Philadelphia, in whole and in parts, and repopulated it, with that Irish cop with a voice like Joe's and that hawker down in the Tenderloin.

That old hand drill took Lou forward from boyhood, through his long succession of jobs, helping to wire up factories and shipyards. With that drill and a can of shoe polish, for covering up scratches in baseboards, Lou once again brought the first electricity to a number of houses in Philadelphia.

Joe could imagine the hollow feeling of unemployment that lay upon Lou these days. It lay upon Joe, too, sometimes. Probably it was that feeling that took Lou back once again to the time, in his late fifties, when after thirty-five years of running the pen factory in Burlington, the company went bankrupt and Lou was left with neither pension nor job, and at every interview he could see that his gray hair was being studied, and he waited to hear the interviewer say, "We'll get back to you." But that was all right, Lou would say. He and Jennie always lived frugally, and Jennie never complained. "She was never demanding." Lou got a job finally, working with industrial machinery again. "I invented a few things for them, too." Then he was sixty, moving to California, where their son Harold, who was an engineer, found Lou a job in the model shop at Lockheed. There Lou, who'd started out in the early days of electricity, made pieces of models of rockets and space stations. Then Lou was being forced to retire at the age of sixty-eight, and was enlisting as the maintenance man for the apartment complex where he and his wife lived, fixing locks and windows and appliances until he was seventy-five. Then he was in his workshop, building furniture.

Joe listened to Lou inventing things as a boy, working on

designs for a perpetual motion machine, for a bobbinless sewing machine. When remembering the hand drill led to remembering the job for which he had bought it and that job led to his next jobs, which he sometimes skipped over, and he came finally to the fountain pen factory, then Lou was rising again at 4:30 in the morning, reriding the trolley through the quiet streets down to the ferry terminal, to cross the Delaware. He crossed it every day except Sundays for thirty-five years, wondering, when there was ice in the river, about the strength of the ferryboat's hull. He boarded the train on the other side. He remembered all the stops. Joe could hear the conductor calling them out. Lou also remembered the names of the factories that lined the tracks of his daily commute through that part of New Jersey. Once in a while he'd pick up some information from other commuters bound for other factories. He made it a point to visit the factories of his factory's suppliers. Lou was amazing, Joe thought. He still knew everything there was to know about how fountain pens were made, about the invention of ballpoints, about the fabrication of carbon paper. He had watched tinkers make their little dams of clay to catch excess solder, and then throw out the ruined clay, which was why, of course, tinkers' dams had become synonyms for worthlessness.

The first times he heard Lou repeating himself, nearly a year ago now, Joe had decided to say nothing about it because Lou seemed like a nice guy, and he was old, really old. Joe felt differently now. He liked to hear Lou repeat his stories. He actually liked to hear them again.

There was something beautiful about Lou in the act of storytelling, opening up his storehouse of memories and bringing them back to life. He summoned up his memories with what seemed like the force of necessity. Telling his stories, he sat quite still in his chair but his hands became animated, and if he was interrupted midcourse, by a visit from an aide or a nurse, he would stop. He might even chat with the intruder, but his fingers would stroke the arms of his chair or drum lightly upon them, and when the intruder departed, he would pick up his story just where he'd left off.

Joe recalled the old story about two prisoners locked up together so long that they no longer tell each other their jokes. One simply says, "Thirty-six," and the other at once begins laughing hysterically. Maybe he and Lou resembled those prisoners, two old pensioners who had run out of new things to say to each other. It was true that local news was scant. Around here, what qualified as a new story usually had to do with someone's new ailment. Lou's stories were more entertaining than most contemporary local ones. Heard only twice, Lou's memories could seem monotonous. Heard many times, they were like old friends. They were comforting. They lent stability to Joe's life in this room, and there was little enough of that around here, in many rooms in this building. Lou's memories seemed like an immortal part of him. They existed right now forever. Lou's memories contained such a density of life that in their presence death seemed impossible.

Here in the room, he was often at the business of keeping his wife alive. The fact that some of his memories about her were painful was part of the point. Joe understood this. His voice turning high and reedy, Lou would say, "I have a mental picture of my wife on the day she had her first stroke, which I can't eradicate from my mind. And which I don't *want* to eradicate from my mind!" As he said those last words, Lou's gentle countenance would turn stony, as if he meant to warn Joe against telling him to put such thoughts away. In a softer voice, Lou would describe that mental picture again. Though he couldn't smell anything in the present, in his mind he smelled the meal Jennie had been cooking — Canadian smelts. "Ahhh, beauty-ful." He heard the thud from the kitchen again, and he saw Jennie lying on the floor by the stove, and also, lying on the floor beside her — this detail had weight and was never omitted from Lou's telling — her wire-rim eyeglasses with the temple pieces bent.

Jennie didn't seem to be breathing. Lou had never been trained in artificial respiration, but he had read about it. He knelt down and breathed into Jennie's mouth, and she revived. Lou didn't always tell that part of the story, and when he did, he seemed to think it incidental. Joe did not agree. "How old were you?"

"It was a couple years ago," Lou answered.

He'd have been in his eighties when he did that. Good God.

Lou also worked on his memory now, Joe realized. That is, Lou maintained and improved his bank of memories. One of the nurses had brought in a collection of clocks. Nearly every time he and Joe passed them in the display case in the central corridor downstairs, Lou would stop and peer in and wonder aloud what had happened to that clock of his mother's that used to rest on the mantels of their many homes. "I've got to remember to ask my sister next time she calls." Next Saturday on the phone, Joe would overhear Lou asking his sister. Lou's mother used to tell him that when he was a baby, before the family moved to Philadelphia, Lou witnessed the return of Admiral Dewey's fleet from the Philippines. His mother said she carried him down to the New York City waterfront and stood among the crowd, holding him in her arms. Lou had carted this memory of a memory around for the better part of a century, but it was only recently, here at Linda Manor, that he had set out to verify the story. He asked his son-in-law to look up the date. Lou was born on May 2, 1899, and Admiral Dewey returned from Manila on October 3 of that year. These facts had become a necessary addendum to Lou's telling of the story. "The dates checked out," Joe would hear Lou say.

Lying on his back, listening to Lou today, Joe had watched himself scissor the fingers of his good hand, and had kept silent. Now Lou had left off. He'd left off too soon to suit Joe. Watching himself scissor his fingers, Joe said, "Hey, Lou, who was the relative you were visiting in New York and you got the cot and she was still talking?"

Lou smiled. "Oh, that was my sister-in-law, who called up a friend to borrow a cot."

Joe laughed.

"What are you laughing about? I haven't told the story yet," said Lou.

Joe backed off at once. "I just think it's funny, that's all."

Lou went on: "Harry and I walked a few blocks to the friend's house, said hello, got the cot, brought it back, and she was still on the phone talking to the person we borrowed the cot from."

"*That's* funny," said Joe.

"The story I like," said Lou, "my sister-in-law's sister was being courted, and her father came down in his robe and said to the young man, 'You expect to see my daughter again?' 'Yes.'

'Well, how you gonna see her again if you don't go home first?' "

Lou was on a roll now, once again. "In Philadelphia, shortly after I was married, my brother had a Ford. There was no regular shift in those days."

"Well, they hadda crank it up first," Joe said.

"That's not the main part of the story."

Joe, looking at the ceiling, made an exaggerated closure of his lips.

Lou went on: "And they didn't have signals at the crossings. The cops stood in intersections with signs. Philadelphia from Broad and Fairmount, going west on Fairmount was a real wide street." Lou drew a map with his hands. "And at Twenty-second and Fairmount there was a big prison. Eastern Penitentiary. Just before you come to Twenty-second there's a big steel gate." Lou shifted in his chair. "Anyhow, this Sunday morning my brother called me up. He said, 'There isn't much traffic, I'll take you out and teach you how to drive.' Out on Broad and Fairmount, he puts me in the driver's side. I couldn't see any traffic. I was tense as hell. We were riding along pretty good."

Joe chuckled at what was coming.

"Anyhow," Lou said, "we got out to Twenty-second. I don't know what happened. I drive up on the pavement, and where do we do that but right beside that prison gate. Fortunately we didn't hit it, and my brother says, 'Let's get the hell out of here before someone sees us.' And that's how I didn't learn to drive. That's my one and only time behind the wheel of a car."

"Wait a minute," Joe said. "You had another thing happen to you once. You drove a thing through a plate glass window."

"Out in California," Lou said. "A big department store. They had small hand trucks and . . ."

Lou went on for a while. Then he returned to the present. "Hey, Joe, incidentally, what's the definition of 'hospice'?"

Joe shook his head. Lou was amazing. Sometimes Lou would get to thinking about his wife and say, "I think I've seen about everything God meant me to see." And then, often moments later, he'd raise his index finger and say, "Incidentally, Joe . . ." He'd want to know if Joe knew what this term they kept using on the radio, "Dolby sound," meant. If humanity continued to extract such vast amounts of minerals, oil, and water from the earth, would the globe collapse? Did chickens raised in incubators lose their nesting instinct? Could hail be used as ice cubes if it was tainted with acid rain? Could you eat salmon after they'd spawned? If vultures ate tainted meat, why didn't they get sick? "Sitting here, I think of some of the damnedest things," Lou said once. He didn't have to tell Joe that. Lou would sit in his chair, his brow knitted, his lips pursed, like a student at an arithmetic problem, and Joe would know that pretty soon a question would be asked. What was chicory? Someone had said a wild duck had been seen on the grounds outside. What did a wild duck look like? What was the origin of the expression "freeze the balls off a brass monkey"? Did anyone ever try filling a football with helium? If someone down on the first floor and someone up on Forest View each simultaneously pushed the button to summon the same elevator, what would happen? Where did the expression "sow your wild oats" come from? What kind of wood were George Washington's teeth made from? They'd been discussing that one for three months.

When Joe didn't know the answer, which was often, Lou

would hold the question until Ruth came in. The other day Lou asked Ruth, "I wonder what lesbians actually do?" Then, with sudden force, Lou said to his sixty-five-year-old daughter, "But don't *you* tell me."

Ruth told Joe that it had gotten to the point where her friend the reference librarian wouldn't even say hello to her. The librarian would see Ruth coming and say, "All right, what does your father want to know now?" The man was almost ninety-two years old and he asked more questions than any child Joe had known. Joe used to think seventy-two was old. Well, it still was, as far as Joe was concerned. Life was mysterious. Maybe ninety-one was, in its way, younger.

What was the definition of "hospice"? Lou had asked a moment ago.

Joe looked thoughtful. "I don't know," he said finally.

Then, suddenly, Joe sat up. "Here. I'll go get the, uh, medical thing. They got a, a . . . Oh, what the hell."

Joe's steel brace clattered on the floor. He was putting on his orthopedic shoes.

"Where ya goin'?" Lou asked.

"Well, I'm gonna find out what 'hospice' means. They got a, uh, medical dictionary."

Lou rolled his shoulders and settled back in his chair, his eyes shut, like an old cat in the sun.

Joe headed out toward the nurses' station. He limped along on his cane down the carpeted hallway, then stopped for a moment to rest and catch his breath. "Lou's always thinking of these things. It's good. It keeps him active."

Joe started on again, limping toward the nurses' station and the medical dictionary. "Keeps *me* active."

13

Earl was growing a mustache. "I wanted to for a long time, but I was too chicken," he said. "If I'd known I'd be tied up this long, I'd have started it sooner." He had taken off his oxygen catheter. "All in all I'm a lot better. I shave myself. I dress myself. I'm walking a little better."

He'd gotten part of his family history onto the tape recorder, with some help from that aide who was so adept with the device. Sitting on the edge of his bed, in street clothes and slippers, he'd turned the table into his desk again and done some work on his income tax. From the other side of the room came sounds of explosions and goofy voices. His roommate was watching cartoons. Earl was making a list for Jean of the bills she'd have to pay in the months to come, in case he wasn't around. His lawyer had visited him the other day, and he'd asked the lawyer to go see Jean. Earl wasn't going to leave her untutored in these matters, as her first husband had — though through no fault of his own, poor fellow. "There are a couple of things she can't find," Earl said of Jean. He chuckled. "I kidded her last night. I said, 'Look in *all* your pocketbooks, dear.' Because if I give her something, she folds it up and puts it in her pocketbook." He'd also written himself a couple of memos about matters to discuss with a fellow Red Cross volunteer, his most faithful friend from Holyoke, who was coming to visit. And Earl still had some mail from various companies to review. "These are things Jean doesn't know about that you've got to *study*. AT&T's coming up with a new plan, and I've got to study it."

Earl glanced at his roommate, who sat in a wheelchair in

front of the TV, his stroke-disabled arm in a sling. A lot of the time Earl still changed the channels for him. "You want that on?" Earl asked him. "Or do you want channel forty?"

"Is forty," his roommate murmured without looking away from his TV.

Earl had too many of the wrong thoughts hovering at the doorway to his mind. If he didn't keep busy, they'd enter in a crowd. He was still thinking about getting out. Sometimes it seemed like the most important goal of all. Sometimes he wondered if he wasn't a great deal less afraid of dying than of dying here. "If I don't make myself do things, I'll go bananas. I'm always worried about not having visitors. But I think it's awful to be here and not have anyone to talk to. My goal — I don't know if Jean'll go along with it — my goal is to get out of here next Monday. I don't think I can do any more here. The food here is like all institutions'. I look at it and that does it for me. I'm not perfect, but last night when the nurse was here, she walked out and the bed wasn't made at all. This morning the nurse said, 'You don't need a brief anymore,' which was nice to hear. But this atmosphere here is *very* depressing." He wet his lips, drawing quick breaths. "Very depressing. I think getting home, even though it would be hard for Jean, would improve my morale and I'd eat better. She may fall over. I got here January eighth and Medicare paid till the twenty-fifth, and I've had to pay from then on in. It costs a pile of money. I really think I could go home. I'm not perfect. I'd get better food, and we could have a VNA girl come in and test me."

A few mornings later, Earl awoke and found his oxygen catheter lying beside him. It must have fallen off in the night, and yet he had slept soundly. There was excitement in his voice when Jean arrived and he told her, "Last night my oxygen thing fell off and it didn't bother me at *all*. I woke up and felt like a million dollars." He added, "I'm always going to be short of breath."

"I think that's true," Jean said.

He walked with her behind his wheelchair to the lobby, to meet his friend from the Red Cross. He got a little winded, but he recovered. Back in his room, they settled down to talk awhile.

"You're very flexible," Jean told him. "I'm pretty flexible."

"You're coming," Earl said.

"You've been good for me, pal." She patted his knee.

"So have you."

Earl gave no hint of the subject uppermost in his mind, but as they talked he must have been waiting for an opening, which did not materialize. Finally, just before she left for lunch — as he often urged her to do — Earl said to her, "I'll talk to you later."

"About what?" Jean asked, standing by his bed, buttoning her coat.

Earl looked up at her. "I want to go home."

Jean walked out through the lobby. The sun had some real springtime warmth in it. The only snow lay in small piles, more sand than snow, at the corners of the visitors' parking lot. Her mind was full and troubled. She'd thought he had resigned himself to staying on. Now he was getting restless once again. He wanted out of here. She didn't blame him. She wouldn't mind having him come home for a few days. But not for the duration. The other evening Earl called her up from his room, and in the midst of the conversation he abruptly said he couldn't talk anymore because he was out of breath. She felt that sudden fright, and the wave of weakness that follows, of a driver who has nearly had an accident. She was all worn out with worry. More than ever she needed those times when she could feel that others did the worrying, so that she could prepare herself for being on her own in the world again.

Jean always looked composed. The illusion came from her neatly done hair, her tweed skirt, her tasteful silver earrings. But now, as she stood at her car door, there was strain in her face and in her voice as, looking back at the façade of Linda Manor, she said aloud, "I don't want you to die." She didn't want to watch him gasping for breath. She didn't want to lose her strength with him at home, and aid in his demise. The white balconies and balustrades and windows glistened in the sunlight. Earl lay back inside. Knowing that he couldn't hear, she spoke aloud to him the words that filled her mind, as if they might cross the morning air, turn the corner, and enter softened through his window. "I have to fight back sometimes. I understand what you're saying, but I also have to think of myself."

Jean didn't come in that afternoon. She called him instead. She said over the phone that she couldn't take him home for good. "There's nobody here to take care of you," she said.

Earl called her back right away. He promised he wouldn't discuss going home again. And the quarrel was patched up. But a door had been closed as well. He could no longer dream of going home.

His roommate had left for supper now. The window across

the room was darkening. "I'm thinking too much. I just made out a check for forty-five hundred dollars to this place. The services get less and less. Last night my bed wasn't made. And, of course, the food is . . . unbelievable. Push a bell and no one gets here for twenty minutes. You go down to the front there and you see people it's awful to look at. I thought I was only going to be here nine days, and now it's been a year and a half. A month and a half. I've got to get this depression out of my mind. But I don't know."

He glanced at the snapshot of himself on the bulletin board. "I've got a lot to be thankful for. Our children and grandchildren are all healthy. I've got Jean. I was such an active guy. I wish I'd had a *little* heart attack. But anyway, I'm here. I've gotta live with it, I guess."

Earl stared at his plate of shepherd's pie. "I've lost my appetite. Just looking at it. Jean loves the same TV programs. That's one thing. So we're watching the same programs. If I wasn't such an active guy, I could maybe take this better. I'd just as soon kick the bucket. It's my future. At the moment I can't see what's in store. I have to stop and think about things to be thankful for."

Earl went on staring at his plate.

"I just feel caged in here." He looked again at the photo of himself on the bulletin board. "That's how I looked till last July. Robust and everything. Most of my friends are so far away, they don't often come here. People don't like to come to a place like this. There's a friend I played golf with all the time, and he's *never* been here. Of course, this is depressing right here, this news about the war. Well, I guess I better get going while it's still warm."

He took a little bite.

"That's about as tasteless as can be. Boy. No taste. Not to me, anyway. I thought Jean would be here by now. I think she's afraid of coming, except I told her I wouldn't discuss it. Thank God there are TV programs like *Matlock* and *Murder, She Wrote.* That gives me a lift. Simple a thing as that."

The next morning Earl got out of bed and didn't return to it. He sat down in an armchair and worked on the family history. "I'm feeling great." He lifted his thin right hand and crossed two fingers.

He had called up Jean right after shaving. "I told her I was sorry about the way I talked yesterday. I upset her terribly. So I made up my mind I'm going to try to keep my morale up. I asked her to bring up a folder I kept on Florida. The way I feel now I could *almost* make it. I want to go in March. But it's a tough time to get in." He had canceled their reservations. He'd call today and ask to be put on a waiting list.

"I didn't use oxygen at *all* last night, and I slept like a, oh, beautiful. Of course, I had a pill. I can walk a little bit now. I'll pay another bill for this place today. I hope it's deductible. My former wife was told she had six months. She lived *seven years.* She had a lot of guts."

Jean felt somewhat restored. They'd had their argument, out in the open at last. She told Earl to go ahead and try to make reservations for Florida. Why not? she thought. She recalled that conversation back before Earl's heart attack when they agreed they'd like to die together, on the way back from a splendid trip. So why not try to go to Florida? What if Earl died on the way? He could live to be a hundred and have nothing but bad days, she thought. Would that be preferable?

Earl awoke and looked at his roommate's clock on the wall above his TV. It read 8:30. Earl could not remember the last time he slept so soundly and so long. "I slept till eight-thirty! *Without* oxygen!" he told the nurse. He'd see if he could go without oxygen for the entire day.

He made it until afternoon, but then, while merely lying on his bed, he started panting. His fingers fumbled with the oxygen catheter as he looped it around his neck. He set his jaw. "I want to get the doctor over. So I can find out something about myself. I'd like to go to Florida. I'd need a wheelchair to the plane. I might have to bring a urinal along. That's embarrassing. Something could happen. But I'll take that chance. I don't want to get depressed."

14

Behind Winifred, in her window, out by the drive, stood an old dead maple tree. Crows often gathered in it. Winifred liked to study them, especially on Sundays when she would watch *The Chalice of Salvation* on television and the crows — it seemed to her — would hold their own church service in the tree. The maple's limbs were empty now. The crows must have taken shelter from the latest cold snap.

The Hoyer Lift had come and gone and left Winifred in her recliner. She'd had her cry. Now, her native sanguinity restored, she was making use of time. She sat surrounded by her cordless phone and many wicker baskets and plastic bags stuffed full of correspondence, magazines, and projects. Winifred paged through back issues of *Ideals* magazine for an inspirational poem to read at next month's Resident Council meeting. She wrote a little poetry of her own. She spent some time separating raffle tickets. Then with scissors and paste she resumed the endless task of turning old greeting cards into new cards and also into bookmarks. She had prepared an advertisement for her bookmarks, which read:

> A bookmark is a simple thing
> But oh what helpful joy it brings.

In her earlier life, Winifred kept a house and raised a child. For many years, she worked as a governess at other people's homes. Retired and widowed, the elderly but mobile Winifred, out in the wider world, cut a notable figure on the streets of Amherst. Bound for committee meetings, get-togethers, and banquets, she limped along behind her wheelchair, which was her mobile office, the seat stacked high with papers and refreshments for her various affairs. She helped to organize the local chapter of the Gray Panthers. She also served in eight other organizations. She said she was president of seven, including the tenants' association in the subsidized apartment building where she last lived, mainly among other elderly, widowed women.

"And I used to be the Band-Aid for everybody, and the mouthpiece, and their hearing aid. And, oh, how they miss me. Because I love people and my old cliché is, Life is people helping people." So saying, Winifred was apt to break into poetry. "Life itself won't give you joy unless you really will it. What life *does* give is time and space. It's up to you to fill it." She carried on for twelve years in that life, right up until the stroke that landed her in here, at the age of eighty-four.

She was born for raising funds, she often said. Confinement in a nursing home had not stopped her. Last summer she raised $200 to send her favorite aide's son to camp. But she was only warming up with that. Her plan to buy a chairlift van for the nursing home's own use was what raised her spirits these days. She contemplated with relish the freedom of a wheelchair van at her disposal — and at the disposal of other residents, of course. She figured she'd have to find at least $15,000 to buy a good used van and at least $35,000 to buy a new one, and never mind the costs of a driver and insurance. She had organized and named the Linda Manor Chairlift Van Fundraising Committee. She had taken the position of co-chairperson. Dan from Forest View had agreed to serve as her co-chair. So far he and Winifred were the committee's only members. That did not faze Winifred, however.

She had a lot of plans. Some of what she was doing now was merely waiting — to see if she would win the $10 million Publishers Clearing House Sweepstakes. A while back she received an entry blank and filled it out. Right on the front of the envelope it said that she might already be the winner. "If I should become a multimillionaire, I'll buy the damn van myself."

Winifred paused in her morning chores to contemplate her chances. She had received many follow-up letters from the Sweepstakes people, all of them encouraging. "I have been working on it and answering every letter for months. My daughter keeps telling me, 'Read the fine print.' I keep saying, 'No! I am reading every word that comes and there's nothing that sounds negative.' So I say to my daughter, 'Okay, you skeptic, if you don't go along with me and wish me the best, I'm not going to give you one red cent.' "

Winifred knew this was a long shot, but as she thought about it, she felt pretty sure that she'd improved her odds. "The one thing that they accentuate in their correspondence is timeliness. And every time a letter comes, I fill out the questionnaire and put those silly stamps on. You're not supposed to have to buy any magazines from them, but I believe it helps. And they praise me for my choices. I just buy one each time I get a letter, and usually as a gift for someone else." The winner would be announced soon, on late-night TV, and she would be watching.

❖ ❖ ❖

Ideas of progress, like old habits, die hard. Earl still believed that this was no kind of place for a person who loved life. But he'd always felt at home in groups of people, and he was going to try to get involved in things a little more. Jean had urged him to do so. He loaded up his portable oxygen canister and walked behind his wheelchair to Ruth's Literary Hour, out in the activity room.

Earl didn't say much before Ruth began to read, and he simply sat and listened to the conversation after she had finished. He was a newcomer here. Besides, Winifred was there and very voluble today. As Literary Hour began to disband, Winifred asked her fellow residents to wait for just a moment.

But they were already leaving their places. Winifred said she had something to sell today. She was managing a mail-order contest, all proceeds for the Chairlift Van Campaign. The prize would be a stuffed Easter bunny. Ruth, smiling politely over her shoulder at Winifred, pushed one resident to the door. Lou was following. "You press the button and it plays 'Easter Parade' and 'Here Comes Peter Cottontail,'" Winifred said.

The procession of wheelchairs was moving out the door. Joe limped along behind them. Winifred, meanwhile, rummaged through a sheaf of papers on her lap, the papers for the contest. "Ah, here it is. Now on the back are all these names," she said, but everyone had left, everyone except for Earl. Never mind. She still had an audience.

Earl sat across the table from her, staring at her, nodding now and then.

"And there are thirty-six chances," Winifred said. "And I have to fill them all in before I can scratch them off and see who is the winner." She shoved the contest card across the table toward Earl.

He glanced toward the door. He looked back at Winifred. "I'll take one."

Earl rubbed off one spot on the card, as directed. Winifred took the card back and accused him of rubbing off two spots. Earl denied it calmly.

"Well, just let me see." Winifred studied the card through her magnifying glass. "Well, you're all right. You just owe me whenever. Just don't rub off another, because that belongs to somebody else. And when we get this all rubbed off, we can see who the winner is."

"Yup. All right." Earl stood up slowly, carefully, and made

his way back to his room. He was still feeling better generally, but he couldn't eat much. His hands, strong and supple on a golf club a mere six months ago, were skeletal. The other day his wedding band had fallen off his finger. Jean had put it on her own for safekeeping.

Earl had not forgotten how, almost two months ago, he'd felt desperate for a telephone and Winifred had offered him the use of hers. He was less than interested in stuffed, musical Easter bunnies.

Earl lay down on his back, thinking of Winifred. She certainly did have a knack for clearing out a room, he allowed. "But she's *alive*, I'll tell ya."

15

Joe's movies were one thing. There was no accounting for taste. As for Joe's eating and dieting and exercising habits, it was obvious, as Lou often said, that Joe was his own worst enemy. But Lou could understand all that. Joe savored his luncheon outings, and he liked riding the bike. However, Joe's inability to say the three simple words "I love you" — that was simply unfathomable.

The other day a family friend who'd been visiting and was getting ready to leave asked Joe if he had any messages he wanted carried back to his wife. Joe said, "Tell her I love her."

Lou recalled again his father-in-law's precept: No one knows what goes on between the sheets. But this was too much. "Why don't you tell her yourself on the phone!" Lou cried out.

"I do sometimes."

Lou couldn't help himself. "I'll get out of the room, if you're bashful."

"Wait a minute," Joe said. "I've only been married forty-seven years."

He was trying to wriggle out of this. "That has nothing to do with it, Joe."

"I know it. But, see, compared to you —"

"I never went to bed without telling Jennie I loved her."

Then Joe said, "Open the window or not?" It was the last week of February. Word was, the air had some spring in it again.

Lou let the subject be changed. He'd had his say. "We'll give it a try." He got up and groped his way to the sliding window to the right of the picture window. "Quite a breeze blowing in," Lou said doubtfully.

"It hasn't reached me yet," said Joe from over on his bed.

So Lou left the window partway open and went back to his chair. They talked about the trouble Art was having with his legs, about Bob's vigilant ways, about George Washington's false teeth. Joe wondered if they'd been made of mahogany. Lou pointed out that the Father of Our Country wouldn't have wanted *red* teeth. Lou thought they were probably made of white oak. He would remember to ask Ruth tomorrow to ask her dentist. Supper interrupted their conversation. Later, Joe called his wife.

Lou sat across the room listening. His face looked stern. He felt stern again. It sounded as if Joe was arguing with his wife. Soon Joe hung up, simply saying, "All right, we'll see ya."

Lou didn't comment. He'd said what he had to say earlier. It was none of his business. Joe just had a different way. Lou wasn't going to say anything about what he'd overheard. They'd talk about other things.

But then Joe said, "Ahhh, dear." He said that he wished he hadn't argued with his wife. Joe sounded sad and remorseful.

Lou thought of Joe's lying over there feeling miserable. And for what? The solution was so simple. Lou was old enough to be Joe's father. Well, he'd play the part again.

"Joe. Next time before you hang up, why don't you tell her you love her?"

From the direction of Joe's bed, through the gauze of his cataract, Lou saw the outline of Joe shift jerkily. He heard a brief series of sobs.

"I'm sorry, Joe," Lou said. He was truly sorry. He shouldn't have said that. He should mind his own business.

But Joe had recovered his voice. "No. No. I agree with you."

16

Sometimes Earl's roommate got confused, and the man was prey to those abrupt fits of weeping that strokes often induce. Once, over a month ago, he had been parked out by the nurses' station and had started weeping, saying that he couldn't watch what he wanted on TV. But that had all been straightened out, Earl thought. It was long past dark. Earl had asked his roommate, "Mind if I watch this show?" His roommate had said he didn't mind. Now Earl was watching a mystery. As always, he had reminded Jean to be sure and watch this show at home tonight. He lay propped up on his pillows. Now and then he'd remind himself that Jean was watching too, at home. Suddenly, two young women entered. One of them picked up the remote control from Earl's bedside table. She put it down on his roommate's table and said, "Mr. Duncan, you can't have this."

But Earl's roommate himself had given Earl the control to handle. Earl tried to explain.

"*Mis*ter Duncan," said the other young woman, "you *cannot* have that."

Earl was not a wrathful man. But this was the second time this had happened. When the social worker visited him the next morning, he simply asked her how many days' notice one had to give before leaving Linda Manor. She sat down and asked him for the story. Earl told her that he felt as though he'd been treated like a five-year-old. She questioned Earl's roommate, who said there was no problem, that he got to watch what he wanted, and that Earl helped him find the channels. The social worker went back to her office and wrote a long note addressed to all of the Sunrise staff, a politic version of her thoughts, which were: "This really pisses me off. Earl shouldn't be sitting in his room worrying about what two twenty-five-year-olds said to him last night. That's the last thing he needs."

Earl worked hard on his family's history off and on the rest of the day. He made his call about reinstating the reservations in Florida. The resort was booked. Earl had them put his name on the waiting list.

Within a few days, by Thursday, the last day of February, Earl had shed the humiliation of his scolding. Earl's sense of who he was could withstand much stronger blows. But everyone who has been mistaken for someone he is not feels lonely. Earl couldn't shake the loneliness he felt in here when he was without Jean or other people from his former life beside him.

If he lay in bed somewhere down in Holyoke, he'd have a steady stream of visitors, he thought. "See, they don't know me here." That was the problem. There were no biographies hanging on residents' doors. It was all too apparent that this was a place where biographies ended. He had more visitors than many people who languished here — Jean and his children and a few old friends from Holyoke. But the majority of his old pals still hadn't come. Earl could imagine why. Linda Manor was a twenty-minute drive each way for them, and most people didn't need stronger excuses not to visit nursing homes. Earl didn't feel angry at his absent friends, only disappointed. He'd just like to see them.

His family doctor, the same who had given him the bad news about two months ago, was due in this morning. Earl had asked for the visit. The prospect worried him, but he had to know if anything had changed to improve his prognosis. He'd like to hear his doctor say that Florida was possible. Just now he missed Jean. She came in early this morning and stayed briefly. She promised to return this evening for a lengthy visit. She said she had a busy day ahead of her. Earl didn't begrudge her that, a day of her own. Far from it. He looked forward to hearing all about it, every detail she could think of — for Earl, the next-best thing to being there.

Right now his friends would be sitting in the booths at Friendly's on Northampton Street in Holyoke. If only he could join them. He'd love to go down there some morning with his health restored. He'd just show up at the door. He'd gladly put up with a few bad jokes about where he had been the last eight months. Maybe he could go there some morning even as he was. His friends would know that he was still himself in every way that counted. He needed something like that to look forward to. He had held his tongue with Jean this morning. But most of last night, lying awake in spite of his sleeping pill, he thought of pleading with her, *pleading*, to take him home. All he said to her this morning, though, was that he'd like to visit home and go through his desk. Right now he'd settle for that, a trip back to their house in Northampton. He really would like to see his desk and go through its drawers. But he wasn't sure if he could travel even that far right away. This morning, in the bathroom, he'd dropped a towel and, bending down for it, he'd fallen to his knees. To his astonishment, he couldn't get up. He had to pull the emergency cord to summon help.

Now he lay on his bed with the catheter at his nostrils, breathing carefully. The canned oxygen left a funny taste in his mouth. His roommate lay in bed beside him, but the privacy curtain was partway drawn. His roommate was probably asleep. A soap opera played on the TV screen, and nobody was watching it. It had snowed again yesterday, just a couple of inches. The snow would be gone by lunchtime. It looked like a pretty day, what Earl could see of it, around the privacy curtain, through the picture window on the other side of the room. A rose in a vase and a vase full of jonquils stood on the sill.

Earl's doctor didn't keep him waiting long.

He was a stocky figure in the doorway, dressed in a dark, slightly rumpled suit, with a stethoscope around his neck. He sat down on the edge of the chair beside Earl's bed. Leaning forward, his hands clasped, he asked Earl how he felt. Earl said he felt depressed, frankly.

"That's the tragedy," the doctor said. "Your mind is perfect, and your body can't keep up." He had a quiet voice and a laconic manner. He seemed the sort of man who preferred listening to talking.

Earl spoke in a hasty-sounding way, taking quick shallow breaths — it is hard to speak normally while breathing through a catheter. "I've gotta get out of here," Earl said. "I told Jean I wanted to go home and just go through my desk."

"That's a good idea," the doctor said. "Do it in small steps. Take some short trips. It'll be easier on Jean."

The doctor sat down on the bed behind Earl, to examine him. Earl sat bolt upright, his mouth open, as the doctor applied the stethoscope. Earl looked distressed, perhaps from trying to oblige and take deep breaths, and his eyes were wide. Then the doctor took off the scope and went back to the chair beside the bed. Earl lay back against his pillows.

"You're not better. You're not any worse." The doctor said there was some fluid in Earl's lungs; he'd increase the Lasix.

Earl looked at the doctor's face. "About two months ago you told me I had between a week and six months."

The doctor nodded. "It's probably. That's all I can say. It's because your heart is functioning so marginally. Because of that, I didn't think you'd be here in six months."

Earl raised his head from the pillows, an eagerness, a near smile, on his face. "Oh, you meant I wouldn't be in *here?*"

The doctor looked squarely at him. His voice was very soft, almost a whisper. "No. Among the . . . living."

"Oh."

Earl told the doctor he hoped to go to Florida next week, but that it looked as though there wasn't space for him and Jean. "It's March, you know."

The doctor nodded. He said, again in a very soft voice, "You're not going to Florida."

Earl said, "I'd like to go in my sleep."

"You probably will."

Suddenly Earl's voice had an edge to it. "I could just walk out that door and do myself in."

"Probably not," said the doctor, his own voice resigned. "You're not strong enough. They'd probably catch you."

For a long moment the two men didn't speak. Earl stared at the wall across from him. To his left, a commercial flickered across the TV screen, the images mostly washed out in the sunlight. Then the doctor said, "We have to make the best of where we are."

"I know it," Earl said. "I'd like to make some short trips. Not for long, because I get tired."

"Just an hour or two. You don't have much reserves," the doctor said. He added quietly, "You don't have any."

Mary Ann, on her morning med pass, came in as usual, carrying a cup of pills and another of water. She hadn't seen Earl's doctor, let alone talked to him, but it wasn't hard to tell that something was wrong. Earl was breathing rapidly. He struggled to sit up. Finally, he swung his legs over the edge of the bed.

"Trouble getting up today," said Mary Ann, sitting down beside him. He took the pills and water. "A Duncan donut," she said. "I made a funny." She hugged him.

It was an odd tableau, the very thin, pale Earl hanging limp in big Mary Ann's embrace. "That's what we need, a sense of humor," Earl said. His voice sounded rueful, but he was smiling a little.

"We only do this when your wife's not around. You were single, I could kiss you."

"You can kiss me anytime."

"She's a good nurse," Earl said when Mary Ann had left. "But the others, they aren't nurses. They have no personality, some of them. So I guess my gripe this morning is . . . Not a gripe. At least I know where I stand, maybe. But to get away from the business world and the social world . . ."

From behind the privacy curtain came Earl's roommate's voice. "I spent thirty-four years and nine months workin' at the VA." A raucous game show was playing on the TV now. His roommate, it seemed, was talking to himself.

Earl went on: "I guess my Florida trip is definitely out. I could've maybe died on the way down . . . That'd be fun if I could go down to Friendly's on Northampton Street. Not all the gang'll be there. A few are in Florida. If I'm gonna die, I'd like to see some friends . . . When I think of all the things I was involved in, and all the civic things I tried to do . . ."

The phone rang. It was his daughter. "Well, pretty good," he said into the phone. "I'm having a hard time breathing. The doctor was in this morning. I said, 'Would you repeat to me what you said about two months ago, about a week to six months?' He said, 'That's right.' I'd like to just go in my sleep. I was going to tell Jean I wanted to go home, but I guess I can't. I fell in the bathroom this morning, and I couldn't get up. Yeah, if you could come Sunday, I'd appreciate it. By the way, did you ever buy anything for your birthday? Whatever you did buy, I'm going to give you a check Sunday for fifty dollars."

In a moment the phone rang again. "Hi, Joe." It was his fellow Red Cross volunteer, his most faithful Holyoke friend. "My doctor was in this morning. He doesn't come in very often. He gave me the same news he did two months ago. I said, 'Well, I hope I go in my sleep or something.' "

When he got off the phone, Earl wet his lips. He readjusted his nose catheter on his cheeks with both hands, pulling up-ward on it. "Well, I don't know which way to think. I'd like to tell it to Jean. I think she'll be coming in after lunch."

It was evening at the window of Earl's room. He lay under the covers. Jean sat beside him, stroking his leg through the sheet. He was exhausted, clearly, after his day of bitter news and too little air. Now and then his eyes closed, then opened quickly. He said he'd like to go and see the gang at Friendly's tomorrow. Jean laughed. "Hold your horses. You've to get your strength. We'll go next week." Earl smiled up at her.

After the incident with the TV, the social worker had invited Earl to come and talk to her about his fears. He'd told her, "I'm almost afraid of using the word 'death.' " He said he was afraid the word would upset Jean. Earlier this afternoon, when Jean had arrived, Earl came right out with it and told her he was worried about dying. He said "dying," not "kicking the bucket." "As long as you're here, I'm okay," he added.

Jean had felt sure over these last six months that Earl was struggling only partly for his own survival. She'd sensed that he also wanted to leave her and his family with an inspiring last view of him. Now it suddenly occurred to Jean that Earl was more worried for her than for himself — whether she could withstand the blow of losing another husband — and that Earl was asking her if it was all right now if he let go. Sitting beside him, Jean said, "When the moment comes, it's not as bad as you think. You've already been through so much. It'll just come quickly and whatever adventures lie ahead you'll just enter them." In her mind, Jean thought, "I don't know if I'm lying through my teeth or not." But this was a moment to speak of these things with certainty, and this was certainly what she hoped for, for him. She leaned over Earl and said that his father and mother and brother Bill, and his brother John, who'd died in the railroad yard, would all be there. Earl reached out his arms and hugged her.

Now Earl was nodding off, his eyelids flickering open and shut as Jean stroked his leg through the covers. He asked her to stay with him a while longer. He seemed to doze. Then he opened his eyes. He smiled at her and said, "You can go home now." He'd never said that before, in all the many long days he'd spent at Linda Manor. He had always asked her to stay longer.

17

Earl died in his room the following morning. Across from the Sunrise nurses' station sat the usual lineup of residents in wheelchairs — the woman in the turban talking to the caged parakeet, the man who sat there playing the organ in church and competing in a turkey shoot, the several others who sat silently and seemed to gaze at nothing, and a very old woman who sometimes declaimed prayers aloud. She was chanting loudly, eerily, "The Lord Jesus Christ. We may die according to the flesh and live . . ." No one had told her that someone had died, but she clearly sensed something amiss. Her voice trailed off into incoherent mutterings, and rose again as she cried to her God, "Help! Me! Help! Me!" Earl's roommate sat across the way, in his wheelchair in front of the nurses' station counter. He was weeping. Several aides and nurses hovered around him. "At least he didn't suffer," said Earl's roommate through his sobs. Behind the counter a nurse stood holding the telephone, saying to someone in the kitchen, "I want to let you know that Earl Duncan has died. Just so you won't send us a tray for him." It was the sort of scene Earl would have hated, the sort that had intensified his hopes of escape.

Alone in her house last night, Jean awakened nearly every hour, carrying up with her into consciousness, like a vivid dream, the thought that Earl was in trouble. When she got the call this morning, Jean felt stunned, but not surprised.

Earl's doctor later said he didn't think that people get to choose their time of death. They merely receive signals from their bodies, alerting their minds to the imminence of death. But Jean believed that all of Earl, his body and his mind, had decided last night. She was glad that he had chosen his time to die and that, in the end, he had been granted a quick death. Driving out Route 9 toward Linda Manor, Jean wondered if she could have done something to prevent his dying. She wondered why, after knowing for so long that this was bound to happen soon, she still could not believe that it had.

A veteran nurse-administrator whom Jean scarcely knew

hugged her, then led her to the room. Jean sat in the armchair beside Earl's bed. He looked like himself, but waxen. Jean sat and stroked his arm. Now and then she patted the sheet that covered his leg. "I never take steps now without a lot of emotion, which is hard for an old Wasp," she said. She cried without sound, just a steady mist of tears. "He's the most social animal I have ever known. I got jealous of his time sometimes, because I wanted more of him. He's a dear man, a very spiritual man, but not holier than thou. He loved going to church and he worked for the church. I don't know what he thinks of the life to come, but he lived this life wonderfully, every minute. He was totally comfortable in the world. Feeding the pigeons in Yugoslavia, wherever. Just himself, totally himself. Everybody was delighted to see him after they knew him for about five minutes. It's so wonderful when a person has a simple heart and has a lot of honors poured on him and remains just himself, the same with everyone."

Jean stood up, leaned over, and kissed his cheek. She picked up her pocketbook and left. She got all the way to her car, and then decided to return. "I just like to be with him," she explained to the social worker, who stopped by for a while.

Sitting there in the small and barren room, stroking Earl's arm, Jean suddenly thought she felt him move. She shook herself. "I just can't believe he isn't going to wake up."

Where was he now? "Certainly every good person has enriched the world," Jean said aloud beside the corpse. "Anybody who had a family such as he has, has an immortality through them. The mysteries, the paradoxes, we have to let go of knowing the whole design. Somebody said the tapestry weaver works from the other side, not seeing the beautiful design till later.

Maybe there's more and more. Another chapter." She lifted her chin and said in a much louder, urgent voice, "But everything he *loves* is here!"

Jean sat with the body until the undertakers came. Then she went home and began to make her calls.

18

Deaths were first announced on the erasable bulletin board inside the kitchen, out of the view of residents. The name would be printed with felt marker, followed by "Deceased." The "In Loving Memory" form would be posted within a day or two on the obituary board in the main corridor. Sue, the activities director, or her aide usually wrote the brief encomiums. These included a standard line or two — "A loving woman," "Will be missed by family, friends, and staff." Sue and her assistant strove to convey something of the person's individuality, but there wasn't always much to say — "A lover of plants," "An avid bingo player," "Enjoyed children." Not in all, but in many cases, the deceased had been essentially anonymous in here. Earl's memorial was of a piece: "A kind and gracious gentleman, who loved his family, friends and the sport of golfing."

The residents who came to the monthly memorial services, held before bingo in the activity room, sometimes knew much more. Winifred, who always attended, would have a lot to say about many of the people who died that month. But even she would come up short on one or two. "I don't recall ever seeing him," she'd said of one of the dead who had been honored at last month's service. "But I miss knowing that he's not with us anymore."

The morning of Earl's death, several female residents sat in the activity room, sipping coffee and munching donuts, a downstairs late-morning coffee klatch. "Too bad," said one. "But it's a good thing. He had cancer."

Earl had been proved right. No one here had really known him.

Lou had never gotten to know Earl well. Joe wasn't sure he'd ever spoken to him. Joe read the notice on the bulletin board and said to Lou, "He was seventy-one, -two, -three, seventy-nine. If I had a heart attack at seventy-nine, I'd say all right. I feel bad about him, but Jesus Christ, his age and all."

"Let's get our mind off that," said Lou.

Evenings had lengthened. Twilight was still lingering at the windows when Lou came out to the nurses' station to turn on the night lights. Fleur and her roommate had gotten their false teeth mixed up and had been bickering all day. Fleur stood at the nurses' station counter. Phil sat nearby in his wheelchair. Tonight Fleur thought Phil was a policeman. She was ordering him to arrest her roommate. From the east corridor came the cries of another demented resident: "I want my washing! Now!" A special restlessness came over the demented in the hours just before and after nightfall, or so the evening staff believed. "Sundowner's syndrome" was the name for this phenomenon. But didn't it apply to other worlds outside, to everyone who hoists a cocktail during so-called happy hour? The windows blackened. Art and Ted didn't have a lot to say to each other lately. Inside their room on the west corridor, each man sat in his electric recliner, each watching the TV on his bureau, each TV tuned to the same show. Zita paced the halls. She paced by a white-haired woman who sat beside the water fountain, holding a damp washcloth to her forehead. She was trying to ease the vertigo she'd suffered ever since a car accident many years ago. This woman's roommate was stone deaf. She got lonely in her room. She'd sit out here by the water fountain until she thought that she could sleep.

In Lou and Joe's room, the curtains were drawn across the picture window, and the light brown shroud of the privacy curtain now fully separated the two men's beds. The night light, situated low down on a wall, cast a thin, yellowish glow across the floor. Joe lay on his back, illuminated by his TV. The nurse brought Joe his last pills of the day, then fetched Lou's and carried them around the privacy curtain. Lou lay on his back with his bed covers drawn up to his chin. They were drawn so tightly over Lou that they held the outline of his body, like the cover of a sarcophagus. There was something exotic about Lou's face. Perhaps it was his very full lower lip. In the eerie light, with his glasses off, his chin lifted, his face composed for receiving eyedrops, Lou might have been a pharaoh laid out in state.

The night shift took over. They turned out the lights, and the corridors lay in that dim, cherry-colored glow of the exit signs, the corners in shadow. Around midnight, an aide thought she heard a noise from the northern hallway. She thought that one of the demented residents, Norman, must have slipped out again somehow, past the barricade of laundry hampers that they'd placed in front of his door. Thinking it was only Norman, the aide went off to investigate. Finding no one there in that darkened corner, she hurried back to the well-lighted nurses' station and laughed about her little fright.

Forest View slept fitfully. Around 2 A.M., the woman with the washcloth and Eleanor appeared from different doorways, dressed in bathrobes. They sat down side by side at the water fountain, and the night nurse, as was her custom, fixed them snacks of milk and toast. Then they went back to bed. Every two hours the sweet-tempered night aide, a hefty woman, went down the halls from room to room and crept to each bedside, listening for breathing. She was older than the other aides, and, for all her bulk, as stealthy as a cat burglar. She did not awaken Lou or Joe. The aide's wide shadow, cast by the night light, lengthened as it crossed their floor, then shrank and disappeared.

Lou awoke all on his own. He awoke three times a night. He could set a clock by these middle-of-the-night awakenings, he often said. The TV, his sleeping pill, was silent. Some nights Lou dreamed that he was back at work, sometimes that he could see clearly again. In the dim light he could almost make out the numerals on the clock on his bedside dresser. Lou ran his hand along his headboard for the plastic urinal bottle that he'd left hanging there before turning in. Lou didn't grope his way into the bathroom at this hour anymore. He didn't want to wake up Joe. Joe needed his rest. Afterward, Lou drifted easily back to sleep.

Joe had a recurring dream. Several times in the past year he awakened in the dark and said to himself, "No, I passed the bar exam." Once he dreamed that he was in a factory and couldn't find his way out. He awakened with relief that time, and, on another night, with relief that he didn't have to worry about not being able to remember where he'd parked his car. Sometimes in the small, dark hours before dawn, Joe woke up to re-encounter worries, remembering that his beloved granddaughter had a cold. "Oh, dear God, the baby's sick." Or he awoke remembering with a jolt that his daughter was planning to drive *all by herself* to New York City, or that in a day or two he had to go to the VA hospital for a routine check of his cholesterol. Joe hated to go back to that hospital.

When Joe awoke, the room was quiet except for the windy sound of the ventilator outside the door. Joe lay still and listened. He couldn't hear a thing. This silence contained Joe's greatest fear, the one that seemed most pressing at this hour of the night. Joe pulled back his covers and swung his legs over the side of his bed. He pulled back the privacy curtain and leaned toward Lou, cocking an ear. Joe listened. Lou was still breathing after all. Joe lay back in bed. Usually now he'd sleep straight through to seven.

Bob, on his way to prepare the dining room for breakfast, would wake Joe up. There'd be a rapping at the door, and then Lou, already awake, and Joe, still half asleep, would hear Bob's abrupt, loud voice calling in to them, "All right?"

Spring

❧

I N THE ATTEMPT to understand and control the biology of aging, medical science has long drawn a distinction between the "pathological" and the "normal." The term "normal aging" still survives in the medical literature, in spite of many ambiguities, in spite of the fact that an old age free of pathology isn't really normal, but ideal.

The term "normal aging" arose in the nineteenth century, along with a morality that celebrated individual success and individual control of health. According to a cultural historian named Thomas R. Cole, this new morality stripped away the spiritual solace that former conceptions of aging had offered every elderly person, and replaced it with a dual view, glorifying the healthy old age and denigrating the unhealthy. Cole writes: "Middle-class American culture since the 1830s has responded to the anxieties of growing old with a psychologically primitive strategy of splitting images of a 'good' old age of health, virtue, self-reliance, and salvation from a 'bad' old age of sickness, sin, dependency, premature death, and damnation." Over the last century and a half, American culture has swung between those two poles, emphasizing the positive in some eras, the negative in others. This tendency, Cole argues, even infected the recent, well-publicized campaign against "ageism." "The fashionable positive stereotype of old age showed no more tolerance or respect for the intractable vicissitudes of aging than the old negative stereotypes."

By insisting on the difference between the normal and the pathological, modern medicine has tried to avoid old erroneous notions that would stifle research and encourage wrong diagnoses — about dementia, for example. A lot of symptoms that used to make doctors throw up their hands and declare, "It's a case of senile dementia," turn out not to be signs of true dementing illnesses but of reversible, treatable afflictions. And the notion that a person can carry good physical health late into life, through the cultivation of good habits, undoubtedly promises benefits for the general public health and Treasury. But there's a problem. Ideal aging — these days also known as "successful aging," often depicted in photographs of old folks wearing tennis clothes — leaves out a lot of people. It is estimated that nearly half of all the Americans who make it past sixty-five will spend some time in a nursing home. More than a million live in nursing homes now. The celebration of successful aging leaves out all of them. Ultimately, of course, it leaves out everyone.

❖   ❖   ❖

Spring weather first comes to Linda Manor in Dora's diary. On March 22, as hailstones clatter against the windowpane beside her, Dora sits in her rocking chair and writes, "Beautiful morning here."

Dora says she met her husband on the telephone — she was an operator in the early days of telephones. "He put a diamond on my finger in September 1916. And he had to go to the First World War, and he went to sunny France and he was there three years in France, and he came back without a scratch." Her husband died young, over forty years ago. "He passed away on the twenty-fourth of February, 1951, and I've been a merry widow ever since," says Dora. "He died with a smile on his face."

She says, "I never had an unhappy day. I had a wonderful mother. She brought us up in a very rigid way. We had to be good girls. We had to clean our plate every meal. I didn't cut up any capers. I was just a good girl." Dora admits that she feels sad sometimes, here at Linda Manor. But when sadness comes, she keeps it to herself. "Because I don't think anybody else is interested," she explains. Dora adds — and it is easy to imagine her mother's voice echoing down across the century — "Why should anybody else have to worry about Dora?"

On April 22, a day reminiscent of November, when all the world outside is gray and visitors cross the parking lot huddled in raincoats and the still-leafless maples by the drive stand dark and dripping, Dora wets a thumb, turns to today's page in her diary, and writes, "Beautiful morning here."

This is a prophecy. The next day the sun comes out, and for weeks blue skies prevail. The limbs of the hardwoods in the groves around the building give off the reddish glow of incipient growth. Spring has not exactly entered Linda Manor, except in rooms like Lou and Joe's, where the windows are cracked open. But Dora's interior weather and the objective weather have begun to coincide, and pictures of a bountiful spring have arrived at every window.

The Judge, a courtroom drama, has unfolded toward a climax, and Bob is thrilled. He sits in his room upstairs, on the edge of a chair, poking a finger at the screen. "Oh, boy. I'm tellin' ya."

Up on the witness stand, an elderly man says, "Of course the way *I* took care of my parents . . ."

"*Bull* shit," says Bob.

"Now *he* wants to throw away five generations of craftsmanship and lock us up in a retirement home," continues the old man. He is speaking of his son.

Bob looks thoughtful, as if considering changing sides in the dispute. He runs a finger back and forth across the cleft between his lower lip and chin. He leans forward toward the screen.

Suddenly, the old man clutches his chest and topples forward onto the courtroom floor. He must be having a heart attack. And who should rush to the old man's side but the son's despised fiancée.

Bob is chortling.

The old man lies on the courtroom floor, twitching all over.

"Told ya! Damn it all!" cries Bob.

The courtroom fades into another commercial. "Come on, for Christ's sake," says Bob. "Yak, yak, yak. It's ree-diculous!"

When the courtroom fades back in, the stricken father has vanished from the floor. The judge tells the son that he is free to sell the family business and marry his fiancée.

"Hoo-ray!" says Bob.

The judge says to the courtroom, "A family relationship should be built on love."

"*Bull*shit!" says Bob.

The son's fiancée starts to speak about filial piety. Bob stands up, says "Goddamn fool," and snaps off the TV. "All right, let's go."

Bob hurries, limping on his cane, through the halls of Linda Manor like a fire truck in traffic. The lobby is his destination. His doorkeeping chair awaits him. It appears to be exactly where he left it, but must be a few inches out of place. Bob makes the corrections, sits down, scratches his nose with his good hand — "Goddamn nose. Itch, itch, itch" — and then extracts a roll of wintergreen candies from his shirt pocket. He works a candy off the roll with his lips, slides it into his mouth, crumples up the excess wrapper into a little ball, leans over, and deposits it in the pot of the plant beside his chair.

Bob keeps watch as the afternoons lengthen. Warm weather lures a few of the more mobile and determined residents outdoors. They wheel themselves past Bob and sit outside in front of the portico. Every so often, a resident gets positioned so as to block Bob's view of the drive and parking lot. "Goddamn-itall!" says Bob, shaking a fist at the figures out there in the window. Rising, Bob hurls the front doors open, stumps out, and shakes his cane at the obstructionists. Usually, they move.

The soil in the potted plant is disappearing gradually beneath Bob's little foil balls of candy wrapper. On the lawn outside, maintenance erects a yellow tent, under which on Father's Day — mothers are also invited — a noisy crowd of residents and relatives and staff gather for a picnic lunch. The white-haired combo, the same that played here New Year's Eve, sets up their music stands just outside the greenhouse. Between them and the tent Winifred is parked, her legs sticking out on her wheelchair's extenders, dressed in one of her best silky gowns, about to give a speech.

Yesterday and the day before, Winifred sat out here happily for hours, behind a table laden with a hundred different things assembled from the corners of her room — gifts she'd gotten and hadn't used, or had used only a little, and things she'd purchased through the mail, and things she had recycled, such as her bookmarks and pictures of cute puppies torn from old calendars, and things that she had made, such as her collection of embroidered handkerchiefs, attached to a large piece of cardboard, which bore this beguiling hand-lettered advertisement:

Assorted Handkerchiefs
Some hand Tatted edge
Some crocheted
Some for Doilies
Some for Framing
Some for Blowing or Weeping

She assembled all her hoarded treasures and offered them for sale, all proceeds to the Chairlift Van Campaign. At the center of her table she propped up a sign that read:

Raffle
Tickets $1.00
5 Fine Prizes
$1000 Goal
We Need Your Help

Today there is no selling, but Winifred has seen an opportunity. She has conferred with the leader of the combo, and he has obliged her by ordering a dramatic roll on the snare drum. A hush falls over the crowd at the sound, and Winifred leaps into it, calling toward the tent, "Can I have your attention briefly, please. I am speaking as chairperson of the commi-tee for the Linda Manor chairlift van. Isn't that a mouthful?" Winifred laughs resoundingly. Her *t*'s, like Dora's, are very crisp. "On Friday of the two-day Craft Fair, I sold for-tee-seven raffle tickets. I have sold a total of seven-tee-two! Leaving a total of twen-tee-eight of my allotment unsold." Beneath the tent the picknickers turn back to their food and conversation. The staff now move to and fro around the tent again, carrying trays of food. "From the sale of miscellaneous merchandise, I realized a total of eigh-tee-two dollars and thir-tee-two cents!" cries Winifred. "The total for Saturday, a lesser day but appreciated, was for-tee-two dollars and eigh-tee cents. Bringing us to a grand total of one hundred and twen-tee-seven dollars and eigh-tee cents! We are pleased and grateful and thanks goes to . . ."

Behind her, the white-haired combo stand with their instruments poised. Winifred looks small, all alone out there in her wheelchair. Her voice, loud and cheery, rises into the warm June air, sweetened with the smell of new-mown grass, but her voice meets a barrier of babbling voices from the tent. Perhaps she doesn't notice. "I don't come from the George H. Beane Yankee auction family for naught! Today's object is to realize an additional fund of *one hundred dollars!* I urge you to consider the urgent necessity of owning our own van, even without state assistance. It's a scary and an ambitious undertaking! But with belief in our cause, we shall prevail!"

The members of the combo shift from their left feet to their right and back again. "Thanks for listening," cries Winifred toward the noisy tent. "But listening isn't enough. We appreciate nickels and quarters, but we really appreciate green!"

Winifred has absorbed her earlier defeat. How many bedridden people lay awake with her that night back in the winter, figuring they had a chance to win the Sweepstakes because of all the magazines they'd bought? Winifred, however, went right back to hatching schemes for chairlift van fundraising, plans for raffles and teacup auctions, plans to put the squeeze on a dozen local restaurants, then sell the donated food to residents and staff at a "social box lunch," plans for getting residents to remember the van in their wills.

But the intervening times of enforced idleness torment Winifred. On many mornings, from her room on Sunrise, though her open door, comes the sound of weeping, mingled with TV. Winifred still sobs about the Hoyer Lift. "I still have that strength of will. Oh, I cannot, I will not, let anyone destroy it. I believe miracles will happen, but sometimes you have to give them a shove. And if I can't touch my feet to the floor, how can I walk again? It just breaks my heart to think that I can't use my own will, my own strength, to put my own feet on the floor. When they use the Hoyer, it just denies you the chance to see what you can do. I really, really feel deprived. You have no idea how I long to slip out of bed, and sometimes I feel that I could do it. I could hold on to something."

She sobs at this image of herself trying to stand beside her bed. And yet a little company and a chance to say all that almost always cheers her up.

The staff has not yet wheeled the Hoyer in. Winifred lies on her side in bed, looking out her window. Spring has passed too quickly for her. "Before you feel that you're gathering years, you have the misconception that as you get older time is going to lag. But even bad days — it doesn't matter — they are just fleeting. I look at the calendar and I think, 'Where did the months go?' I get almost in a panic and I think, 'I must harness myself, hold myself back and not let it race so. I accomplish a lot, but I want to do more before this day goes.' On wings. Time goes *on wings.* I wish I could reach out and put a leash on it."

There's clover in the grass outside. From Meadowview windows the surrounding bits of field are likely-looking pasture for a horse. Perhaps it is the grass that stirs Cliff's memory and brings him out of his room down on Meadowview. Cliff is lean and gnarled. He wears a baseball cap with a legend above its brim that reads, "We Are All In This Alone." He wears a cardigan sweater and has draped a down vest over the front rung of his walker. Cliff is ninety-three, partially deaf, and very unsteady on his feet, and he usually keeps to his room. The two nurses on duty and Meadowview's lone male aide look up, surprised, as Cliff comes slowly down the hall and stops near the nurses' station. They ask him where he's going. Cliff says that he is looking for his horses.

The male aide stands beside Cliff and shouts his questions while the two nurses bustle here and there, listening in.

"Cliff," shouts the male aide, "you used to deliver the mail up in the hill towns, didn't ya?"

"Yup," says Cliff.

"How'd you do it? With horses?"

"The first four years," Cliff says. "Then they started clearin' the roads, and I could go by car. I had a Reo Speedwagon."

Cliff leans on his walker and peers down the long corridor as he talks. He says that in the wintertime he used to take the front wheels off his Reo and replace them with skis. "I made some money the first few years I had the Reo, but I spent it. And, shit, I haven't made any since."

"What'd you spend it on, Cliff?" shouts the aide.

"Liquor," Cliff says. "There were thirteen places between Pittsfield and Adams where you could get something to drink."

"You didn't drink on the job, did ya?"

"Sure!" exclaims Cliff, still peering down the corridor.

One of the nurses, passing by, lets out a hoot.

"Cliff," shouts the male aide, "were there any women on your route?"

"Oh, sure. A lot of 'em," Cliff says. "All accommodatin', too. Up through there."

The two nurses, heading in different directions, both hear this. Both make simultaneous, mock cries of distress — "Oh!" — and move on, laughing.

"How old are you, Cliff?" asks the aide.

"Ninety-three, I guess. I was born in '98."

"Where were you born? Plainfield?"

"No, Plainfield," Cliff says. "Well . . ."

"Well, what do you say we head back to your room," says the aide.

"You think I better head back?"

But only minutes later Cliff reappears, with his down vest still draped over his walker. "Hi," says a nurse. "Where you goin'?"

"I don't know," Cliff says. "Goin' down there where I live."

"Got a hot date?" asks the nurse.

Cliff, halted on his walker, once again peers down the long

corridor toward Sunrise. People all the way down there look small, like figures seen through the wrong end of a telescope. Cliff is breathing heavily from his walk of thirty feet. "No," he replies. "I got some hosses down there. That's one thing that irritates me. Been there about two days."

Cliff moves on, grunting, and stops after a few steps. A female aide comes up to him and asks, "Where you goin', Cliff?"

"I got some hosses way down at the other end," he says. "Ain't seen 'em for three days, want to see how they are." Poking his chin forward, he peers hard down the long corridor. "Well, Jesus Christ, I'm on the right way to go down to the other place, ain't I?"

"You live down there," says the aide, pointing in the other direction.

"I just came from down there," says Cliff. "Christ, I came down through there. My room ain't down that way."

"Yes, it is."

"How the hell *can* it be?"

The aide hurries on. To himself Cliff mutters, "My God, I don't know if they're right. Prob'ly are." He looks around him. "Oh, I see where the hell I come out."

A nurse emerging from another resident's room stops beside Cliff. She tells him he looks tired. Doesn't he think he should go back to his room? Cliff guesses that he should. The horses will have to take care of themselves for another day. They'll be all right, he figures.

"How old are you?" the consulting psychiatrist asks the woman, who lies propped against her pillows in her bed on Meadowview. The curtains are drawn. It might be any time of year.

"Eighty-two," the woman says.

"What year were you born?"

"You're trying to check up on me," she says. She smiles, not warmly but brightly.

The psychiatrist laughs in a friendly way.

"I was born in 1907," she says.

"I hate to tell you. You're eighty-three."

"Well," she retorts without so much as a pause, "I give myself the benefit of the extra year."

Do her breathing problems frighten her?

"I don't think I'd go so far as to say *fear*, young man."

He asks her the date. She offers one. He tells her, gently, that she is a month off. She says, "Don't fool me. Don't ask me what year it is or I'll throw you out."

"I was just about to ask you that," the psychiatrist says, smiling.

But before he can, she asks him, "And where are *you* from, sir?" She traps him in a long digression.

Finally, the psychiatrist finds a way back. "I've always been very interested in someone who's had an intellectual life, and what happens as we get older. Do you think your memory's —"

"I don't think my memory's as sharp," she snaps. "I think I started losing some of that back when I was sixteen. The things I've forgotten are things I don't mind forgetting."

He'd like to give her a simple memory test. Would she be willing to take it?

She looks thoughtful. "I'm being an awfully good sport to say yes, I will."

He gives her three words — feather, car, bell. He asks her to repeat them. She does so. He says he'll ask her for those three words again in about a minute. She says she'd prefer to repeat them now.

"I want to distract you first."

"I know. But I don't want to be distracted."

"But it's part of the test." Quickly, he asks her to do some subtraction in her head — 7 from 100, then 7 from the remainder, and so on. She falters after 86, and in a moment the psychiatrist asks, "Now do you remember those three things?"

"No," she says.

"A feather," he says.

"Oh, the *things*," she says. She falls silent for a moment, and when she speaks again, her voice sounds small and plaintive. "A feather and a broom?"

He names the three items.

She looks pensive, then suddenly declares, "I wouldn't have remembered those in a hundred years. I think a smart person such as I am would forget them right away, because you said you were not going to ask me to repeat them." She looks quite regal, her head framed against white pillows, a lofty-looking smile on her face.

"Well, I thought I said I would," says the psychiatrist.

"I think you tricked me," she says.

"I don't like to trick people," he answers. He might be her pupil, in spite of his gray hair. He looks down at his feet. "I apologize."

"I accept your apology."

The warm weather, the long green afternoons, beckon Martha out more often now. She walks steadily along, a determined look on her face, her pocketbook dangling from her arm, through the lobby, out the front doors, and down the drive toward Route 9. A nurse runs after her.

Martha imagines that she is walking home to get supper for her husband. Martha was a nurse, a big nurse in charge of surgery and pediatrics in a hospital. From time to time, she issues orders to the Meadowview nursing staff, sweetly but firmly, often cogently. She'll come upon a fellow resident in need of "toileting," as it is called, and she'll tell the charge nurse to get on that job immediately. Once, a resident's grandson skinned his knee while visiting, and Martha bandaged it herself. She told a fellow resident's granddaughter that she would give her some doll clothes, and, a full week later, Martha, who could not have named the date or this place, made good on her promise to the child. Once every week or so, when one of the staff has coaxed her back from the brink of the highway, she will surface completely in this world of impoverished present time. Eyes wide, her voice choked with sobs, she'll say to one of the staff, speaking of her husband, "He's dead, isn't he." She'll weep over her husband for an hour or two. By dinner she will return to a time when her husband is alive. Whenever she remembers her husband's death, it is as if for the first time. Alzheimer's — that's what the doctors think she has — has fastened Martha to a wheel. About once a week it brings her back to mourning. She has intermittent but never-ending grief.

Martha is escorted inward, and Ted, the fifth Nudnik, sits alone in the lobby, his cane between his legs, looking through bay windows at the afternoon, like so many afternoons that he recalls and yet so strangely empty. "Just waiting for some company that isn't gonna come," says Ted. "She's comin' down. I can't remember when. I can't remember anything anymore."

Ted's wife died here last summer. During parties and events like bingo Ted often stands outside the activity room, looking as if he'd like to enter, but he doesn't. "That's the way I like it," he has said. "I just want to sit by myself and think about my wife. I do like pushing somebody down to a meal in a wheelchair. Physically I feel fine. Well, I thank God for that. But there's nothing else I can do."

In old age, memory often fades in the absence of apparent disease, through a process for which science has no real explanation but does have a name: benign senescent forgetfulness. A basic principle of neurology, promulgated in the nineteenth century, holds that failures in memory tend to proceed inversely with time. As memory fades, the past comes nearer. No doubt there's a biological cause, but the psychological result has a logic of its own. In old age, many people seem to remember best what has mattered most to them, and often it is work. Ted sits alone here in the lobby recalling his days on the railroad. He was a telegrapher, manning the key in switching towers in the remotest sections of the Berkshires, all alone in his high perch except for the occasional hobos who would come by and ask for a place to sleep. Ted would accommodate the hobos. They were, after all, just workingmen down on their luck. Ted can still see those towers in his mind, and though he often can't remember if any of his family has promised to visit on a given day, he can name all of the stations he worked at. "I can tell you every station, from the East Deerfield station to the Rotterdam station. Thank God I've got a good memory," he says. "I can still remember every letter of the Morse code today." Now and then, while sitting here in the lobby, or upstairs in his electric recliner, Ted drops his right hand to his thigh and taps out his thoughts in Morse code on his trousers.

A new summer decorates the windows, and the rooms are full of yearning. One woman has imagined she is having an affair with a demented fellow resident. She doesn't care who knows. "He makes my ovaries ache," she says to a nurse. The nurse returns to the privacy of the medication room to laugh. "That's a new one on me," the nurse says. "I must be missing something."

Through the squawk boxes in the ceilings — the in-house paging system is used only occasionally — a supervisor's voice calls out, "Attention staff. Attention staff. Norman has found his room." Norman is presumed to have Alzheimer's. The drugs he is given are supposed to curb his restlessness. They don't always. The evening charge nurse tells this story: On an evening last summer she took him out for a walk, and suddenly he asked her if she owned a car. Then he said to her, "Let's get out of here." The nurse told him her car keys were upstairs. In his low whisper, but quite distinctly, Norman said, "I can hot-wire it." The nurse coaxed him back to Forest View, and by the time they got there, he'd forgotten that plan of escape. Norman still walks the halls of Forest View, pausing at doorways, rubbing his forehead worriedly, looking for his wife as well as for an exit, which he still finds sometimes.

Upstairs in the Forest View living room, the staff clears away the remnants of breakfast, the breakfast of those residents too demented for the dining room. It isn't summer in this room. It is, as always, a season of memories all mixed together, and there is no season here. Norman, in his porkpie hat, his escape aborted, now dozes in a chair in a corner. Phil, who has not set foot outside for over a year, has come up from the dining room and sits in his wheelchair in front of the TV, watching *The Regis Philbin Show*. Today Regis and his sidekick Kathie Lee preside over a men's underwear fashion show. A succession of mostly potbellied men model jockey shorts, and the studio audience howls at the spectacle while Phil, his head cocked to one side, smiles as if mesmerized at the screen. In the room, there is the usual hustle and bustle of aides and nurses, taking away breakfast trays, readying medications. In the hall just outside, Fleur says in a chirpy voice to a nurse, "I don't know where I am."

"You're in Linda Manor and your apartment is right down there."

"Oh, I still don't know where I am!"

"You look lovely in white," the nurse says.

Fleur looks down at her white cardigan sweater. "I wish it was mine."

Behind Phil, at one of the church-social-type tables, Zita sits facing two white-haired women. They do not seem to notice the hubbub around them. They seem to be having a post-breakfast chat. "He wouldn't be, wouldn't be. Nine billion!" says one of the women seated across from Zita.

Zita looks at her but says nothing. Zita's eyes look sleepy.

"I told you once, I don't want you back here," says one of Zita's tablemates.

"That's all right," the other says. "The one little thing. That's what you've got to have." The woman looks across the table at Zita and adds, "You've got a dead stump and it isn't worth anything. That's what you've got and you haven't got any."

The studio audience is howling on the other side of the living room.

Zita nods. She speaks very softly. "If she wants."

"Throw it in," says one of the women across from her.

"Just let 'em sit," the other says.

"He is the *best* I've known," says the first.

"Cage to them," Zita murmurs.

One of the other women coughs. "Goodness crispies," Zita says. She smiles. "Now I know he's a snot."

Gradually, those voices cease. Soon, for no apparent reason, but as if sleepwalking, Zita rises and exits the living room.

Just a few years ago, when she was in her mid-sixties, Zita was holding down a job as a machine operator. Then people from the factory began calling her daughters to say, "Something's wrong with your mother. She's getting lost on the way in from the parking lot."

Zita's parents came from Poland. She was born and raised on a farm in the Connecticut River Valley. Zita worked all her life, in fields and her own household and factories. She was a gentle and undemonstrative mother. If two of her children fought, she'd make them sit on the sofa and hold hands. She was fond of practical jokes: once she dressed herself up as a boy at Halloween and went trick-or-treating at a daughter's house. Zita's descent took a path often described in the burgeoning annals of Alzheimer's disease. Her children and husband first assuring one another that everyone forgets things. Then the slow realization of a general decline in Zita's abilities, especially her once impeccable housekeeping — and her daughter's discovering in Zita's refrigerator a jar of cold cream with a light bulb stuck in it. And finally the first of many grim family scenes. Zita didn't recognize her own house. She said of her husband, "A strange man is following me." She sat on her daughter's couch and wept while her husband paced the floor in great, understandable fury.

Her children had never before seen her weep. That was the worst stage, for her family and Zita, when her mind still clearly grasped its own trouble and she would say, "Something's wrong with my brain."

A year's worth of tests confirmed the worst. Zita almost certainly has Alzheimer's. But at least she no longer seems to realize it. There is no telling where she lives now in what remains of her mind. Today, an average day for her, she will walk about two and a half miles indoors, up and down the corridors of Forest View, only stopping now and then to pluck at flowers in the carpet.

In the afternoon, at Eleanor's request, one of the staff places a wicker armchair at the west end of Forest View's longer corridor. Eleanor calls this spot "my little pretend porch." She would like to sit outside in the new summer air, but the door to the real porch behind her is locked, because it has no screening. Seated here, Eleanor tries to read a little, but puts down her book to watch Zita pace up and down the hall in front of her.

A while back Eleanor thought that she might write a play about the denizens of Linda Manor. *All Set? All Set!* was to be the ironic title — "All set?" being what every nurse and aide and doctor asks a resident, and "All set!" the response that they expect. For a time, from her lookout posts in the corridors, Eleanor kept a keen eye on all of her potential characters, especially her demented fellow residents. But Eleanor's interest in writing the play has flagged. And none of the demented amuse or interest her anymore. Except for Zita. To Eleanor, she appears to be the quietest and most inoffensive of all of Forest View's demented, more attractive to her indeed than most of Forest View's nondemented residents. Eleanor wonders if at bottom she and Zita aren't a little bit alike, both as restless in their own ways.

Though always an actress, Eleanor also worked as an English teacher and speech therapist. She has the teacher's knack for reaching the hard to reach. Some months ago Eleanor set out to make contact with Zita. Whenever she paced by, Eleanor would speak to her. "Hi, Zita. What you up to?" Small questions like that. For the longest time, Zita didn't answer. But Eleanor felt encouraged, because sometimes when she spoke to her, Zita would stop nearby and speak herself, in disconnected phrases, saying incoherent things usually, and sometimes uttering amazing phrases that made Eleanor wonder if she had heard her right: "Way, way, and you could hear the wind blowing. The way of the god was a white crow. It'd wake me up."

Eleanor would reply as if Zita had been speaking to her. Eleanor would try to imitate the inflections of Zita's voice. Then, a month or two ago, when Eleanor was sitting in her wicker armchair on her pretend porch, Zita stopped in front of her and said, "I came over to your house and you weren't there, and I missed you."

Maybe she mistakes Eleanor for someone in the past. It is

clear in any case that Eleanor has now become a distinct personage to Zita. Sometimes she stops and takes Eleanor's hand, rocking back and forth and speaking incomprehensibly. Once, Eleanor had her feet on a stool, and Zita walked up and said in a sympathetic-sounding voice, "Didn't you sleep well last night?" Just the other day, Zita bent down and planted a kiss on Eleanor's cheek. Eleanor was delighted. "When you've been treated like someone out of *One Flew Over the Cuckoo's Nest*... Well, I think Zita's much better since I've been talking to her."

Better perhaps, but not miraculously restored. As Zita approaches, Eleanor waylays her, saying, "Hi, Zeet. What you up to?"

Zita stops in front of Eleanor, looking over her head toward the windows.

Seated in her wicker chair, Eleanor studies Zita's face. "My, it's nice outside," says Eleanor.

"It's about time," says Zita.

Eleanor beams, but then a mask seems to descend over Zita's face, and she turns and walks away. It is as if one's car radio had caught with perfect clarity a station a thousand miles away, only to lose it in static moments later. Eleanor expects this, but it's a daily disappointment that mirrors larger ones — to succeed at making contact and then to have it break.

Eleanor has changed rooms and roommates. She finally had it out with Elgie. Elgie is ninety-four, but Eleanor could not abide the way that woman seemed to like to lie in bed — "I hate bed," Eleanor says. She had several noisy rows with Elgie. Eleanor made all of the noise. Now she lives in a room on the eastern half of Forest View's longer corridor. She has reasons to regret the change. She doesn't see Art as often now that she lives half a hallway farther from his room. He is still a *bon vivant* as far as she's concerned. But it seems as if it's always she who must search out Art, never the other way around. And the morning coffee klatch has all but died. Eleanor used to be awakened by the sound of Bob's shoes squeaking as he passed by her room at around 5:30 every morning. She stays in bed later now. But even when she does get up in time for the klatch, it just isn't the same. She can't say why. She's sick of Bob and Phil anyway, she tells herself, and yet, she must admit, she misses those morning get-togethers.

For company, Eleanor still has her confidantes on the staff. But they are all too busy to talk long, and they are limited in other ways. Striking up a chat with one of the passing aides, Eleanor mentions Maria Ouspenskaya.

"Who?"

"The Russian actress."

"I don't know her," says the aide.

"You're too young," Eleanor says. "I get so *sick* of you young people."

The cabaret is long since over, so are the invigorating little dramas of her cataract operation and her fight with Elgie, her new play is merely in rehearsal, she can't seem to get interested in reading anymore, the coffee klatch is moribund, she doesn't see Art much. Eleanor feels bored, estranged from the younger generation by their ignorance and from her own by geography, illness, and eternity — bored with all the routines, sick of almost everyone around here, and lonely. Her new roommate is no help. Eleanor has one of the presumed victims of Alzheimer's for a roommate now, and Eleanor can't even complain about it, because she was the one who chose her. She thought the woman would resemble Zita, but Eleanor has found her quite annoying.

It is evening, a green and golden evening, outside the window of Eleanor's new room. Eleanor sits by the window and stares at her roommate. The woman is short and stout with gray hair cut very short. She sits in a chair chewing gum — the same piece of gum she stuck in her mouth this morning — and knitting. She has been sitting there knitting for hours, her television alight in front of her. "She says her prayers right through the mud wrestling," says Eleanor. The woman never watches her television, and she almost never says anything to Eleanor, unless Eleanor tries to turn it off. Then the woman says, "Oh, please, please, I want to watch this." Eleanor now has a method. She makes several trips to the bathroom, and each time she passes the television, she turns the volume down a little. The volume is all the way down now. The TV is on but soundless, and her roommate doesn't seem to notice.

Looking toward her roommate, Eleanor sees Zita go pacing past the open doorway. "I wonder if Zita dreams," Eleanor says. "I wonder why she paces like that. I think she's trying to get away from something. There's a lot of loneliness here. I wonder if loneliness has something to do with Alzheimer's. Loneliness in disguise." Or maybe, Eleanor thinks, it isn't a matter of disguise but of depiction, Zita depicting the loneliness that hangs in every corner of this place.

That is the most discouraging fact of this life to Eleanor — not all the illnesses in the building or that she has to live in a little corner of a little room, but the separateness of all these lives around her. This community hardly deserves the name. It takes too great an effort of will and too much energy for most people here to say, "All right, this is part of my life, too. I have to live in these moments." Too many people have too many overwhelming problems of their own and can't or won't get out of them. The physical distances inside are vast, given the difficulty many have in crossing them, just to visit someone in another room. Too many people around Eleanor seem to be giving up. Eleanor has tried. God knows, she's tried. She thinks again about her cabaret. How she got a little adrenaline flowing in some of her fellow residents. But it didn't last. She'll put on another play in a month or so, but she knows that she'll spend most of summer sitting on her pretend porch, watching the world pass by out there on Route 9.

Eleanor sits beside her bed in her fine old Windsor chair and gazes out her window. "It isn't fun. Nothing *I* do is fun. I don't suppose you're supposed to have fun, but we don't laugh the way we used to. To get out of this whole environment. I wish I could." In the dusk, Eleanor's window has begun to catch the reflection of her roommate's silenced TV and her roommate's stocky figure. Eleanor looks out through the watery image of her roommate — knitting and chewing behind her, knitting and chewing. Through her window Eleanor can see the windows of the north wing, rectangles of glass within brick walls. She looks at Lou and Joe's window across the way. She imagines they are having a wonderful conversation. She remembers other rooms, the salons of Amherst. She can almost hear the witty talk in them. "I may leave," she says. She can see the back of Lou's head behind the glass, his white hair glowing in the dusk.

Lou and Joe

❧

JOE HAD MADE himself quite fit, fitter perhaps than ever before in all the years since his stroke. He rode the exercise bike five and a half miles, then six miles, then seven. After riding the seven, Joe declared, "I could have ridden ten." He mounted the scale and found he'd lost two pounds. "I think I'll have ice cream tonight."

But then arthritis flared up in his bad arm, and it no sooner left there than it turned up in his good knee. "Where does it hurt, Joe?" asked Lou, lifting his cane as if to smack Joe's knee, and Joe laughed. But walking toward the bathroom, Joe winced, and he muttered, "Oh, Jesus Christ." For a while, he couldn't even manage M&M's, let alone the bike. Coming downstairs to dinner, he saw on the activities bulletin board a notice for Catholic services at which the Sacrament of the Sick would be administered. "Christ, I should go in there." Then Lou caught a cold and had just recovered from it when Joe, often in bed now with his aching leg, began suffering deep, long coughing fits, which Lou, on the sly, reported to the staff. A chest x-ray was ordered. "I got walking pneumonia?" Joe said that evening. "That's what the girl told me. Cripes sake, I haven't got walking pneumonia. Because I have a good appetite."

The x-ray confirmed the fact, however. Joe's doctor prescribed antibiotics and oxygen.

Joe's face flushed, he thundered curses, and his blood pressure, measured afterward, had shot up when one of the nurses first tried to loop the thin blue catheter over Joe's ears and across his upper lip. Joe lay on his bed with the outlet of the tube stuck in his nostrils, the tube snaking across his cheeks and pillow to the oxygen concentrator that stood beside his bed. It looked as though he was attached to an industrial vacuum cleaner. He looked trussed up and, at times, small and forlorn, but then again, nothing dwarfs a person like medical machinery.

Joe's daughter had recently brought him a photograph of his ganddaughter, and Joe had given it central billing, on the wall directly above his TV — the image of a mischievously smiling three-year-old with very curly blond hair hanging beside the photo of Joe with very curly black hair, mischievously smiling on his wedding day. "God, she's beautiful," Joe said, staring at the photo. "God, I love her."

To know that new generations of one's family will follow may be the greatest comfort that old age retains in modern times. It had been Joe's fate to learn the perils of succession, too. He went to war, survived himself, and then he lost his first son. In this room, Joe uttered the names of the Christian deity as often as a monk in prayer. He was, it seemed, still arguing with the God he no longer believed in.

Joe was mightily, superstitiously solicitous of his grand-daughter's health. If someone should happen to praise her beauty or intelligence, Joe would invoke the belief of his fore-bears that to praise a child was to tempt the evil eye of fate. "*Malocchio!* Don't give her the *malocchio!*" he'd say. His tone was joking. But news that his granddaughter had a cold or an earache would send him into real paroxysms of imagined grief. "Oh, dear God, the baby's sick. Sonofabitch. God almighty. Jesus Christ. Jesus Christ!" In the habit of imagining the worst, as if by imagining it he could prevent it — as if it wouldn't have to happen because it already had in his mind — Joe would depict her dead from the sniffles. "Joe, don't talk that way!" Lou would say. "Joe, if you're gonna talk that way, I'm gonna leave the room." He could not understand why Joe tormented him-self. But Lou had never lost a child.

A friend of Joe's named Neal was in the room on a visit. He said something in praise of Joe's granddaughter, and Joe sud-denly sobbed. "I'm starting to cry," Joe said.

"We couldn't tell," Neal said.

Joe laughed. Then his face darkened. "Lou leaves the room if I say it. But if something happens to her . . ." Joe, catheter-ized, threw his good arm out sideways as if cutting the air with a sword.

Lou accepted this as bluster. "Calm down, Joe. Or your blood pressure will be way up, way it was the other day."

Neal smiled. He had always conducted his friendship with Joe via insults, which was one reason Joe liked him. Neal tried out an insult now. "Joe has *creeping* pneumonia. It can't be *walking* pneumonia."

But Joe wasn't in the mood for insults. "Ha, ha," he said.

"I'm surprised," said Neal, seriously then. "You never get sick."

"I *know*," Joe said.

Then the evening nurse came in with her stethoscope and applied it to Joe's chest. "But it's all right," Joe said to her when she unplugged the stethoscope. "Because I'm coughing up clear, you know."

"It just sounds wheezy," said the nurse, offhandedly, reassuringly.

For parts of every day and evening Joe lay breathing the canned oxygen. "Run oxygen this morning, run it this afternoon. Now I'm sick of it," he said.

"You've got pneumonia, I got a sore tushie," Lou said.

Joe laughed, then said seriously, "But it's a mild, mild case."

Daily, Joe sucked on a tube attached to a little machine called a bronchodilator. He'd hold the tube with his pinkie extended, as if sipping a cocktail. He'd start laughing, the laugh would turn into a cough, and he'd go back to sucking the tube.

Joe's trips downstairs to meals and bingo left him gasping. But after those first days with the illness, Joe became quite calm. It was as if, lying on his back, he observed from a distance the skirmish going on down in his chest. Up in the room after dinner, he and Lou replayed Art and Ted's spat during Stupidvising. "Ted came down, and he's an old man," said Joe. "*I* am an old man. And Ted said, 'Nobody calls me a liar.'"

"And Art sat at the other end and said something about how he wouldn't sit next to Ted," Lou said.

"Two old men," said Joe. "What's the sense of fighting? They could be dead tomorrow, for God's sake."

Joe puffed on the bronchodilator. Lou sat in his chair, in an engineering frame of mind. "I said, 'Why don't you give him some moisturizer with that.' Because they gave it to my wife before she passed away. They said the doctor didn't order it, but the next day they gave it to him, and I think it helps." Lou added, "When my doctor first saw me, he said, 'You're too scientific.' I don't just take things for granted."

Joe seemed to be improving. That's what Lou heard the staff say. Lou considered this a likely moment for advice, and said from across the room, "Joe, you're gonna get mad at me, but I told you you shouldn't just lie in bed. You should at least raise the head of your bed up high."

Joe sat up, the blue tube trailing, and glared across the room at Lou. "Do you see my bed? It's raised up, all right?"

"All right, all right," Lou said. "I can't see it. I didn't say anything."

"All right!" said Joe, lying back down.

That sounded like the old Joe. Lou thought he must indeed be getting better.

From the intercom just outside their door came the voice of Sue, the activities director, saying, "Good morning. Today is . . ." Sue's cheery voice named the day and date and intoned the menus and scheduled activities, also the birthdays. As always, Sue closed by saying, "Have a *good* day, everyone."

"Jesus Christ," Joe said to the ceiling. "Have a good day. Wheee! The people here, uh, Parkinson's, All-timer's, cancer, bad heart, can't walk. Jesus Christ, huh?"

Joe liked Sue. What he objected to was the nearly universal voice of the helping professions in gerontology, indeed of society in general, saying "Cheer up, cheer up" to people who were struggling with the infirmities of age, to him and the other people here.

Joe waylaid Sue in the lobby later. He went there to escape

his sickbed for a while. "Why don't you say, 'Have a good day, if you can'?"

Sue thanked him for the suggestion, but said she couldn't do that. The words would sound too negative.

Joe shrugged. "Well, that's a good answer."

Lou made sure that the staff monitored Joe's oxygen machine. He'd go out and remind them if they didn't check it. From time to time, Lou focused his eye on the gray image of the machine and said, "I'd like to know how that thing works."

It was lovely weather outside and pneumonia in the room, another season of its own, an eerie contrast to the other, flowers blooming in the garden below their window, while Joe lay on his back breathing manufactured oxygen. Pneumonia's time passed slowly. The nurses monitored its progress through their stethoscopes. And then one day a nurse came in and wheeled the oxygen machine away.

Lou, returning from M&M's, brought Joe some news. The class had a new member, a ninety-five-year-old woman, and very vigorous. "She was kickin' her legs up," Lou said. "She eats garlic every day, so when the Angel of Death comes to her, she'll say, 'Whoooo are you?' Friend of mine used to tell me that story about a hundred-and-ten-year-old man."

When one has had pneumonia in a nursing home, being in a nursing home without pneumonia looks like a pretty good deal. Joe was eager to get back to Linda Manor time. "I'll go to M&M's Friday," he said.

"Make sure you got your wind before you go," said Lou. "If you do go and get winded, *stop!*"

"That's right," Joe said.

"Don't be a hero," Lou said.

"Damn right," Joe said.

"That's what my doctor said to me. If you have chest pains, take a pill. Don't be a hero."

Lou thought that Joe was clearly better. Joe seemed to manage M&M's without much difficulty. But Lou knew he wasn't altogether well. When Joe went to the bathroom, Lou confided to one of the staff in a low voice, "He's still short of breath, and he gets himself excited once in a while." And Joe had an intermittent cough. It would grip him for minutes at a time. The sound of it across the room made Lou grasp the arms of his chair. It sounded, sometimes, as if Joe was suffocating.

A chest x-ray, taken about a month ago, had shown improvement. Now that he was off the oxygen, Joe got x-rayed again, just to make sure the pneumonia had really passed. A few days later, while waiting at the nurses' station counter for his morning pills, Lou overheard a couple of the staff talking to each other about the latest x-ray. From what Lou overheard, he gathered that it showed something wrong. Lou kept the information to himself.

Joe had already heard the news, but he kept his own silence in front of Lou, for now at least. Joe didn't think he could be very sick. His appetite was all too good, as always. This occasional cough and shortness of breath would pass, he figured. He felt like telling everyone to leave him alone. He was sick of being an invalid. He was sick of the attention. It also worried him. He didn't know exactly what he had to fear from the nurses and the x-rays and his Linda Manor doctor until events unfolded, and then he felt as if he'd known all along. The doctor came in, examined him, and discussed that last x-ray. It showed a lingering irregularity in a corner of Joe's right lung which should have passed by now. The doctor couldn't say just what this signified. Joe would have to see another doctor, a specialist. Since the ultimate responsibility for Joe's health lay with the VA, Joe would have to see a specialist there.

It was the worst news Joe had heard in a long time — not the news about his lung, but that he must go back to the VA. He still went there periodically, but he never had to stay more than an hour or so. This problem with his lung could get the VA doctors going, Joe imagined. "When they get you there, they like to keep you." He couldn't bear the thought of spending another night in that place. Never again, he told himself. No one had said he'd have to stay. But there was always that chance. A worrier like Joe automatically converts the possible into the probable and, given a little time, the probable into a certainty.

Soon Joe was notified that he had an appointment at the VA. It was for a few weeks from now. He would keep the appointment. He didn't see how he could refuse.

2

Eleanor had decided to leave. The arrangements themselves hadn't been easy, and they'd been complicated when, a couple of weeks ago, she'd taken a fall in the elevator and suffered a hairline fracture in her pelvis. But she had persisted in her plan.

She had consulted with her family in Wisconsin. They had found her a place in a nursing home there. And she was going, no matter what.

In the visitors' parking lot, Eleanor's son and an old family friend paused beside their cars. They had just come from Forest View. The old family friend now shook his head and, smiling, said to Eleanor's son, "She's well organized. When she really wants to leave a place, she doesn't waste any time." The man paused. Then he said, "I just hope that in six months . . ." He left the sentence hanging.

"Well," said Eleanor's son, "she's not getting any younger . . ." But he, too, let his voice trail off. The eighty-one-year-old woman they'd just left upstairs, sitting regally in her wheelchair with her cheeks rouged, talking about how exhausting this process was and wondering where she'd find the strength to direct her new play, *The Silver Whistle*, before she left — and surrounded by several packed suitcases, even though her departure date was still a couple of weeks away — certainly looked as if she had gotten younger.

Eleanor smiled out her window up on Forest View. Hasn't everyone, traveling away from the routines of life at home in summertime, seen through the windows of a car or train other people staying behind, stuck at their daily stations, and felt enviable?

Eleanor had heard that the place where she was going had both a stage and decent food, but she'd never seen the place. It was, after all, another nursing home and therefore bound to be, to some extent, a house of grief and pain. But moving there would put her nearer to more of her family, including a granddaughter who had a child on the way. These past few months

Eleanor had discovered a great desire to be surrounded by family. Or so she'd said to everyone at Linda Manor. But she was still her nomadic father's daughter, and she knew that the main reason she was going was to go. She knew this in feelings that were hard to put in words and that none of her young confidantes would really understand. She felt like a child again, watching as her father, the receipts from his latest minstrel show extravaganza in his pocket, packed up his big black trunks. The show was over. She and her father had pulled another sleepy town out of its dull routines. They'd left the people laughing and given them something to talk about. Soon they would board the night train and leave that little burg behind. Eleanor might be eighty-one, with diabetes and a slightly damaged pelvis, but she had pulled off another escape. Where she was going didn't matter. She was getting out of here. In the meantime, there were preparations to be made. She had to make a proper exit.

Everywhere Eleanor looked, from her easy chair in her room, from her post across from the nurses' station, from her pretend porch, she saw new reasons to leave. The other night at 2 A.M. she awakened to find Norman standing at the foot of her bed. She rang her call bell, but no one came, so she led him to the door, and he urinated there on the floor. When she complained, the aide said to her, "How'd you like to run one floor all alone?" The staff had been cut again. The food, Eleanor insisted, was getting worse. There was a water stain on her ceiling. The place was going downhill fast, she thought, and she might be, too, if she were staying.

All the few remaining ties that she had to this place were breaking. The Forest View staff had imposed a new rule: residents should no longer sit across from the nursing station. Too much confidential information about residents was being passed in rumors, the staff decided. The other night, several hours after supper, Art was eating his pre-bedtime popcorn in a chair across from the nurses' station, and a nurse told him he shouldn't sit there, he must move into the living room. Art was irritated but didn't argue. Most residents never argued about policy. The next morning, though, Art came back from breakfast and found Eleanor sitting in a wheelchair in the very spot where he'd been sitting last night. Art called to the nurse behind the counter. Did the rule about not sitting there apply only to him?

"Oh, stop making trouble," snapped Eleanor.

"I'm not making any trouble!" Art yelled at Eleanor. "I want to be where I'm supposed to be." Art shuffled off in a high temper.

Eleanor tried to patch up the quarrel, but Art told her he didn't care to talk to her, since she'd called him a troublemaker.

"I didn't say that," Eleanor protested.

"Then what was I hollering for?" Art said. "You've had your ear up near the nurses' station, and you've been peddling all that stuff you hear. Who's sick, who's this, who's that. *You're* the troublemaker." She was the reason they'd made the rule in the first place, Art said.

Eleanor hadn't spoken to Art since. "You know Art," she said, "he considers himself now sort of a *bon vivant*. He's a flirt. He really is. I watch him give the nurses the eye at night, making little jokes and stuff. Anyway, I don't see that much of him now, not since I moved to the other end of the hall." All was perhaps for the best, she told herself. "I have nothing to hold me here at all." Only the sight of gray-haired Zita pacing past her, up and down the corridors, gave Eleanor pause. "She's the only one of them I'll miss."

Anyway, Eleanor didn't have much time for melancholy thoughts. She had all but recovered from her fall in the elevator. She could walk again, but still used a wheelchair, to save her strength. She had to put her affairs in order. She had to dispose of some furniture and probably some clothes. "I've got five years of stuff to sort out. But, you know, going to these various nursing places, you have to dress like they do." She had to alter her wardrobe when she moved to her previous stopping place, the retirement community of faded elegance. "There it was gloves and dresses. It was a very Victorian place. Heaven only knows what they'll wear in Wisconsin. Probably aprons and milking stools." Meanwhile, she was trying to whip the cast for *The Silver Whistle* into shape. "They want me to put it on before I leave. How can I? I'll probably leave on a stretcher," she said. Eleanor laughed gaily.

❖   ❖   ❖

"Ladies and gentlemen, I'm happy to welcome you to the Linda Manor Players' production of *The Silver Whistle*," said Eleanor from her chair at stage left — the left side of the wider dining room doorway. "This is just a reading rehearsal. We had planned to do it later, but a few things came up."

One was asked to imagine a small unkempt garden outside an underfunded, church-sponsored home for the aged. Two elderly women, played by two elderly Linda Manor residents in their wheelchairs, and an old man, played by a middle-aged male aide, sat in the fictional garden discussing their ailments as the play began. "We're all sitting here waiting to die," said one of the actresses.

Out in the audience, a male resident of Sunrise who was slightly deaf said to another resident, "I can't hear them. Why don't they have a microphone, for heaven's sake." From the kitchen of the real nursing home came the clatter and clang of dishwashing.

Joe and Lou had taken end-row seats, so they could get out quickly just in case the play flopped. But soon Lou's face composed itself in a smile, behind closed eyes, and Joe was laughing. The audience was mostly residents, with a smattering of relatives and staff mixed in. They laughed when the actors blew their lines and Eleanor snappishly corrected them, and when Dave missed a cue, because he had gone into the kitchen to mix the punch for the post-play refreshments. Dora, playing a coquettish septuagenarian, insisted that she had only just turned seventy. The waspish old-age-home resident, played by Lou and Joe's neighbor Hazel, retorted, "You're seventy-eight and you look every damn day of it." That got a big laugh, as did such lines as, "He died right here in this chair" and "He gave her an enema" and "They don't last long once they're here."

Eleanor had done a fine job of casting. There was, for instance, the resident of Sunrise who maintained that the men and women of Forest View all fornicated with each other and who had spread false rumors that Art didn't really go out on Tuesdays in order to play bingo but in order to get drunk. This woman played a puritanical old scold who, in the play, made her entry on a walker, declaring, "Sin! Sin! The whole world's gone crazy with sin!" Winifred played a drunken old woman. Never a drinker in real life, she *possessed* her part. It was said by the staff that only Eleanor could handle Winifred, Eleanor who had brooked no interruptions or speeches during rehearsals. Winifred nearly stole the show again, as she had months ago at Eleanor's cabaret. At one point the audience interrupted a scene to applaud Winifred's boozy rendition of "I want a beer just like the beer that pickled dear old Dad."

The Silver Whistle first appeared on Broadway in 1948. It was a hit, and soon forgotten. A tramp searching for some free room and board comes to the rest home posing as an indigent seventy-seven-year-old, though he is only middle-aged. He ascribes his youthfulness to a potion, a harmless concoction that in due course he administers to the residents. Naturally, once they've sipped, they rediscover the boldness and romance that have lain dormant within them.

The play ends with the tramp's departure. "God bless you," he said to the residents of the old age home. "God bless you, too," replied one of the resident actors.

The audience applauded loudly, and then Sue, becoming once again the activities director of *this* nursing home, said goodbye to Eleanor. Sue deposited a huge bouquet in Eleanor's arms. "We will miss her dearly," Sue said to the audience.

Eleanor remained seated. She received the audience's applause with a sedate smile, her chin lifted, and when the applause, her applause, died down, she said simply, in her strong, always slightly hoarse voice, "Well, I thank you all very much."

The audience was shuffling and chattering. Several of the able-bodied had stood when from the stage, the pretend stage, a high voice called, "I have a message here from our drama group. Can I keep you here for a moment to read this message?" It was Winifred. Lapsing for a moment into her bibulous stage character, she said, "And then I'll give you all a drink."

Winifred, in her wheelchair in the activity room doorway, peered through her magnifying glass and declaimed the message she had inscribed on one of her recycled cards. It went on for a few minutes and concluded with Winifred reading loudly, "It was riotous fun, even though we were all convinced of our doom, to live out our days here at the home till our demise in death and rotting. Let us here apply the stage rule: the show must go on, but not on and on and on. Let us finally say a hearty, sincere, and loving *thank you*, Eleanor. From *the* Linda Manor troupers. P.S. May we all apply these words of wisdom. It's better to wear out than to *rust* out."

❖   ❖   ❖

When she'd moved into Linda Manor, Eleanor had thought she was making the last move of her lifetime. On a summer morning, four days after the play, Eleanor made her last move again. At the Forest View nurses' station the pre-breakfast procession to the elevators, what Art called the cattle drive, had begun. But this morning Eleanor did not join the throng. She sat near the nurses' station in her wheelchair, dressed in a short-sleeved sweater, purple slacks, and white sneakers. She wore a gold necklace and two wristwatches. An aide stopped to say goodbye. Eleanor looked up and smiled. "I hate goodbyes. I said so many yesterday."

Eleanor's late-night companion came by on her walker, the

woman with whom she had shared many 2 A.M. snacks. "Bye again, honey. And good luck."

Eleanor smiled and waved, then said, "I've gotta say goodbye to Phil."

"He's already gone down," said one of the staff.

"Oh, well."

Art had already gone downstairs, too, without saying goodbye, but Eleanor didn't mention Art.

Eleanor struck up a conversation with the nurse, who was still dispensing pills. "I'm going to work with the speech pathologist on stroke cases," Eleanor was telling her, when Joe's loud voice interrupted.

"I gotta say goodbye to Ellen-er."

Lou and Joe came toward her, side by side on their canes. Joe offered his left hand, which Eleanor took with her left. "Goodbye and good luck," Joe said.

"Where's the traveler?" Joe stepped back and Lou bent down and kissed Eleanor on the forehead. "Bless you," Lou said.

Lou and Joe trooped slowly away toward the elevators. Watching them go, Eleanor said, "I've gotta get out of here quick. I hate these goodbyes." But she made no move to retreat.

There were still some stragglers, residents who chose not to go down early to breakfast. Clara, the pleasantly confused woman who used to tie Bob's shoes in the morning, came up from behind, lugging her huge pocketbook as always, and gave Eleanor a kiss. "You just remember to change your clothes," Eleanor told Clara. "And clean out your pocketbook."

"We'll miss you terrible," said Clara.

"I should get back to my room," Eleanor said. "I'm tired of

saying goodbye." But she only wheeled herself to the water fountain, from where she had a view that commanded all of Forest View's corridors. She said goodbye to yet another resident who was passing in a wheelchair, then turned her head toward the sound of a high, cheery voice. Elgie was approaching. Eleanor glanced at her, then turned her eyes away, lifting her chin. Elgie passed by. Elgie's new roommate, deeply demented and very timid, was following Elgie at a little distance, walking on tiptoes. Eleanor said goodbye to her. "Say hello to Ken for me."

"Who?" asked Elgie's roommate.

"Your son," Eleanor said.

"Oh."

"Oh, I'll be glad when all of this is over." Eleanor sighed. "But, I was happy with the play."

An aide gave Eleanor a hug. "Don't tell the pilot how to fly."

A nursing supervisor came by. "Well, may God go with you. It's nice that you've been able to be part of our lives." From the living room came the cry of the demented woman whom Eleanor had nicknamed the Banshee. And then at last Eleanor's family emerged from the elevator, her son and a grandson who lived nearby and her granddaughter from Wisconsin, big with child, who collected a large plastic bag full of Eleanor's pills and also the sheaf of paperwork. An aide passing by patted Eleanor's head.

Eleanor reached up and touched her hairdo lightly with both hands. "If you muss this . . ."

Eleanor's granddaughter laughed and said to the aide, "She's hoping to marry a rich man so she can stay in a private room."

The charge nurse gave Eleanor a hug. "You send us a post-card."

"Thank you for everything."

Most of the residents were gone to breakfast now, either downstairs or into the living room. Rosa was kicking up a fuss near the nurses' station. "I have to get my medication or something and she hasn't done it. Doggone it!" Rosa waddled off, muttering angrily. Eleanor didn't call goodbye to her. She liked to describe Rosa as "a perfect Shakespearean clown," but hadn't managed to find a part for her in a play. It was too late for that now.

Eleanor looked around. Zita was pacing west, down the longer corridor. "Hey, Zeet. Come here." It seemed for a moment that Zita would simply pass by. But Eleanor reached out and caught her hand, pulling her closer. Then, clearly, Zita saw her. She bent over Eleanor. Eleanor kissed Zita's cheek. "Goodbye," she said. "I'll see you."

"When's that?" Zita said.

At this moment, as she looked down at Eleanor, Zita's senses seemed restored. Her eyes glistened. A tear rolled out of one. Abruptly, she turned, bent down, and plucked at a flower in the weave of the carpet.

"You can pick me a flower," said Eleanor, watching from her wheelchair.

Then, suddenly, the mask descended. Zita stood upright and paced off. She headed down the corridor toward the west windows. An aide intercepted her and led her into the living room for breakfast.

Eleanor watched. "I hope someone will keep me informed about Zita," Eleanor called to the aide. "She's the only one I will miss."

Then Eleanor turned to her retinue, the three family members who stood in a circle around her, and Eleanor said, "All right. Who's pushing?"

Eleanor passed, as if in state, through the downstairs corridors, extending her hand to a couple of front office people, and then out the lobby into the hot morning air. At the car door, she rose from the wheelchair and climbed, slowly and carefully and yet rather nimbly, inside.

3

Lou remembered a fellow resident who always wore a hat indoors and liked to travel backwards in his wheelchair. (Lou once told him, "You'd make a good quarterback.") About a year ago the man slipped into a coma and was sent to the hospital. There, Lou heard, he was kept alive with a respirator. "It didn't make any sense. He was going anyway," Lou said to Joe.

Lou said he wouldn't want his family to see him dying that way, turned into a living-machine. Both Lou and Joe had DNRs, "Do Not Resuscitate" orders, on file. Like many other residents, each had a little red dot affixed to his name tag outside their door. The dot warned the staff against performing on them not only CPR but also the procedures known as intubation, ventilation, and defibrillation. Some months ago, Lou and Joe had heard about a new Health Proxy law, which allowed a person to name a "health agent" who would make medical decisions for the person if the person couldn't make them for himself. Sitting by the window, Lou told Joe that his granddaughter, herself a nursing home administrator, had the forms. "I'm gonna ask for a copy."

"Ask her to bring two," Joe said.

"We could ask downstairs in the office."

"Okay, I'll ask in the office."

"I think I'm gonna go out there right now," Lou said.

Lou ordered the forms from the front office and headed back upstairs. "Well," he said, "that takes care of one thing."

The room became again a corner of Fenway Park. Joe watched. Lou listened. Ever since his retirement Joe had looked forward to the eternal return of the grand old game. Back home in his den, Joe had discovered that the Red Sox won more often than not if he wore his Red Sox cap. In the room at Linda Manor, Joe's Red Sox pennant hung from the mirror on the wall behind his TV set. Joe put on his Red Sox T-shirt and cap for Opening Day. The Sox won, and he put his magic cap away for Opening Day next year, or, if this should be the year of the miracle at last, for rooting them to victory in this coming fall's World Series. The Sox last won the Series the year Joe was born. Perhaps, he said, they'd win the year he died. If so, he figured, he'd have to live to a ripe old age indeed.

But he was just being cautious. He had high hopes again this year, but didn't want to dash them by uttering them aloud and giving the Sox the evil eye. The team had played unevenly so far, slumping early, then reviving. Now they were playing mostly night games, and once again on many nights Lou went to sleep not to the sounds of action-adventure movies but to the drone of the Sox announcers' voices and the thumps from the bed beside him. Joe drew the curtain between their beds for night games as he did for movies, so as not to disturb Lou. With the curtain drawn, the room became two rooms in cross section, like two rooms in a dollhouse. On one side of the curtain lay Joe, his face deeply flushed, his lips fastened tightly to stifle shouts, but pounding the mattress, sometimes in glee, more often in fury. Lou lay on the other side with his covers pulled up to his chin, shaking with silent laughter.

Mornings after games, stronger oaths than usual often rattled around their room. One morning Lou told Joe again that he really ought to break the swearing habit. If he didn't, Lou said once again, Joe might start cussing during one of his granddaughter's visits. Joe said all right, Lou should correct him every time he swore. Sometimes Joe would catch himself. "Jesus Currr —" he'd say, and he'd bite off the curse. But then the Red Sox hit another losing streak. On a morning after another loss, Joe lay on his bed and said toward the ceiling, "I don't care to hear about it. I don't care to hear about it. I don't care to hear about it." Then he muttered, "Jesus Christ!"

"Joe," said Lou, "you promised me you wouldn't say that."

"No," said Joe. "I'm praying."

Lou had turned ninety-two in May. He received at least a dozen cards, including one from Winifred, an old condolence card on which she'd written birthday greetings. Joe and Bob chipped in and bought Lou a new bottle of cheap brandy, the only kind he liked. Ruth catered a special birthday lunch complete with chickpea salad, one of Lou's favorites, the Nudniks all seated at a table of their own in the activity room, Lou in a cap that read "#1 Grandpa" and Joe in his Red Sox cap. The place set for Art was empty. Art had to go to the hospital that day for a bone scan. "You stay around here long enough, and boom, boom, boom," said Joe, looking at Art's empty place.

In late June, the state surveyors arrived to give Linda Manor its yearly inspection. The surveyors held a confidential meeting with residents, in order to root out complaints. Winifred raised several, but other residents contradicted her. Joe limped into the meeting. It was the first Linda Manor meeting he'd ever attended. He got up and told the inspectors, "Nurses, aides, and kitchen workers are wonderful. And I'm not going to speak about the cooking."

Then he limped out, and Lou raised his hand. "What I have to say may hurt you," Lou said to the surveyors. "But if the state and federal governments gave less paperwork and a lot more money for nursing homes, everyone here would be happier."

The crowd of residents clapped with unusual vigor. The memory of that applause lingered for Lou. Coming from people whose faces he couldn't see, it warmed him.

The surveyors held what the manuals call an exit meeting, in the activity room. The surveyors had asked the administrator to invite all of her managers and also some residents. She invited Lou and several others.

They sat in a wide circle, as if in a session of group therapy, the chief surveyor presiding, the various Linda Manor managers and several nurses sitting solemnly and quietly. The chief surveyor was smiling. She said she'd learned a lot. She mentioned the deficiencies found in the kitchen — just a few picayune items.

"I regrettably wouldn't know about that," Lou piped up. He was the first member of the audience, including staff, bold enough to speak.

"No," said the surveyor. "And that's one of the reasons we need people to come in and look at that." She went on, "Based upon an acceptable solution to that, recertification is recommended."

There could not have been much question, but several of the managers let out long breaths and smiled at one another.

"We've discussed everything. Probably more than you wanted," said the chief surveyor. She laughed. The managers laughed, too. Lou pursed his lips.

The surveyor didn't ask any of the residents if they had something to say, not at this meeting. Maybe residents were invited merely to fulfill a paper requirement. But Lou clearly took this meeting seriously. He looked stern and attentive, his face turned toward the surveyor's voice. She went on, listing a couple of small items for correction: the ID and summary sheets weren't up to the standard of federal regulation F. 514; the receiver of the pay phone in the central corridor should be amplified; Forest View should have its own pay phone. Lou sat almost motionless, his striped cane between his legs. But Lou's fingers tapped impatiently on the handle.

Finally, the surveyor recommended that the color-coded dots outside residents' doors be removed. She'd noticed those dots right away, and she thought it an invasion of residents' privacy to have dots outside their doors announcing that the inhabitants were prone to falling and wandering, or, most important, had Do Not Resuscitate orders on file. That was deeply private information, the surveyor said.

"It's been a pleasure being here," she said after explaining her objection to the dots — she'd left no doubt that she expected those dots to be removed. "I've enjoyed it. Any questions?"

No one spoke, neither residents nor staff, until Lou raised a finger off his cane. "I question this thing about the color code. We don't always have the same nurses on the floor, and if something happens, they need to know what to do."

"I agree," said the surveyor, leaning toward Lou.

"Well," Lou said, "what's the answer to that?"

"In-service. So per diem staff are aware of residents' needs. People shouldn't be relegated to colors on doors."

"I have no objection myself," Lou said.

"There's a difference between having no objection and something you want. If you want dots outside your door, you can have them," the surveyor replied.

Sue spoke up, supporting Lou. She said she'd brought up the issue of the dots at Resident Council and no one had said they minded them. In fact, most residents hadn't known what the dots signified.

Another staff member suggested a meeting of residents to vote on the issue.

"To me, it seems incongruous," said the surveyor. She sat with her skirt smoothed over her crossed legs. "In a facility that doesn't use a paging system and goes out of its way to respect residents' rights, to have everyone know that someone doesn't want to be resuscitated."

The surveyor looked around the circle and said, "It's important to get resident input, but I don't think everything should be put up for a democratic vote. There shouldn't be a power struggle. Residents shouldn't be in the middle, where they feel they have to support the facility. It shouldn't be an adversary relationship."

"Mr. Freed," said one of the nursing supervisors, turning to Lou, "that information is readily available to the nurses."

"I have no objection either way," said Lou, both hands on the handle of his cane. He turned his head toward the surveyor again. His voice was steady and clear. "But coming back to what you just said. You have a per diem nurse come in and she doesn't know your needs. I filled out one of those forms, and I don't care who knows that I don't want to be resuscitated."

It seemed that most of the staff would just as soon yield on this point and get the meeting over with. Only Lou now stood in the way. "Mr. Freed," said one of the Linda Manor nurses, "there's a list of DNRs at every nurses' station."

Lou pursed his lips. The surveyor said again that the problem of per diem staff was separate. They should be trained in the procedures — "in-serviced." The issue of not resuscitating certain residents should be discussed with the per diem staff.

"It should be discussed with a resident's family," said Lou.

He'd gotten a little confused, obviously. He must have thought they'd turned to the subject of how Do Not Resuscitate orders get made, not the dots on the doors. The surveyor looked across the circle at Lou. She paused. Was she considering helping him get back on track? If so, she thought better of it. Yes, she said, a DNR was something that should be discussed among families.

The whole argument had been pointless anyway. She won it before it began. She was going to protect residents from the indignity of those dots whether the residents liked it or not.

"It's been a learning experience," the administrator said to the surveyor.

The surveyor smiled. "Yes, it has."

As the meeting disbanded, Lou moved to the chief surveyor's side. He said, "This is where the Nudniks sit." He gestured at Bob's row of five chairs, neatly arranged near the dining room door.

The surveyor was a little taller than Lou. She smiled down at him. "What's a nudnik?"

"A pest," Lou said. He smiled toward her voice and hazy shape. "*You're* a nudnik."

❖   ❖   ❖

It is often said that the old resemble little children. This is true in only one sense: they are often treated similarly. Many people would no more take advice from a ninety-two-year-old than a six-year-old. But many of the staff of Linda Manor had one by one found their way into Lou and Joe's room for just that purpose. Not all the advice that Joe gave was solicited or followed, vasectomy being his main solution to many family problems. But Joe had several regular clients now, invited in for consultations about alimony. Many came to see both men, to talk about their troubles and to receive Lou's calm suggestions and Joe's peremptory ones, often less like suggestions than commands. Their favorite day-shift aide used their room as a sanctuary. When events in other rooms that morning or her sons' behavior last night upset or saddened her, she'd come in and talk awhile just to get cheered up. On especially harried evenings, the 3-to-11 charge nurse would spend her coffee break sitting in a chair across from the two men's beds, telling them her troubles. "They have a tendency to calm me down," she said.

On a summer evening Lou and Joe walked together to the nurses' station for their evening pills. They looked like two retired vaudevillians, walking side by side on canes. The nurse on duty, standing behind her pill cart, said she didn't like to see nighttime come. "I like it," Joe said, "because I shack up with nurse's aides."

"What?" said the nurse. She looked confused.

"He's having an hallucination," Lou said.

Then the nurse got it. She smiled. "In your dreams," she said to Joe, handing him his pills.

Joe left chuckling, saying, "In my dreams."

A little later Lou returned to the nurses' station and flicked on the night lights. And then April came in to put lotion on Joe's feet. The other day April brought in her new boyfriend for the two men to examine. Joe had told her he approved of the boy. Now, as she rubbed the lotion onto Joe's right foot, she remarked that she was moving into an apartment.

"How much it cost you?" Joe asked.

"Five hundred, plus phone and utilities."

"You don't make that much," Joe said.

"I take home almost three hundred a week," she said. Then she broke the real news. "I'm moving in with Eric."

"Get married," Joe said.

"I'm waiting for him to ask me."

"You girls —" Joe began.

"Careful," April said. "I've got your foot." She held the foot slightly aloft, the one with the big toe missing.

"No," said Joe. "You girls take too many chances. There's a girl here I won't mention went with a guy and now he's got another girlfriend."

"Do I look worried? I'm not worried at all."

"That's why I don't like the men," Joe said as April pulled off her rubber gloves and tossed them in the trash can. "Eric'll quit you and leave you with the apartment."

"Gosh. Have a little faith."

"I'll have faith when you get married!"

"Don't get snippy with me." April put her hands on her hips.

"I'm not snippy with you," Joe said. "I'm snippy with Eric."

"I'm waiting patiently for him to ask me." April started out of the room. She stopped at the door. "Just because we're living together doesn't mean we're gonna have a sexual relationship."

Joe laughed. "*Good*bye," he called.

"It may be so, but I don't know," sang Lou from his bed, the covers up to his chin.

4

It was either 1915 or 1916. Outside the gate of the factory that had begun to make the first all-steel car bodies stood a long line of men. An old gentleman with a white goatee, wearing a Panama hat — he looked like an old southern colonel to Lou — was walking down the line, conducting job interviews. "What can you do, son?" he asked the man in front of Lou.

"I can do anything, sir."

"Sorry, can't use you," said the colonel, and he moved on to Lou, who now knew what he shouldn't say.

"What can you do?" he asked Lou.

"Well, I'm willing to do anything, sir. But I'd like a job in the electrical plant."

"There's no job in that department," the Colonel said. "But I'll get you another."

Seated by the window, Lou said, "I started in the door department. Twenty-seven cents an hour, ten hours a day, and six hours Saturday. And no coffee break. It hadn't been invented then."

Lou hadn't worked long in that factory before he noticed that the procedure for drilling holes in the car doors could be improved. The men who did that work drilled the holes and then they tapped the threads. Lou went to the foreman and said, "Why can't they put that hole in there and tap it at the same time?"

The boss brushed his suggestion aside. "Oh, that won't work."

"Okay," said Lou from his seat by the window. "I was just a kid. But six months later, when I started working in the electrical department, they were doing it."

Lou still got results. These many months ago, he'd gotten Joe into attending M&M's and into eating prunes, and, more recently, into telling his wife he loved her over the phone, at least once in a while, and maybe Joe was swearing less, but maybe not just now, since this was baseball season. He had gotten results when he'd explained to Dave, the boss of the kitchen, that cabbage should be cut across the grain. And the Forest View night lights always went on at the proper time now.

But Lou didn't know how many times he'd told Bruce, the director of maintenance, that the elevators needed attention, and so did the air-conditioning system, only to hear Bruce politely reassure him that everything was fine. And this business of having residents wait uncomfortably outside the dining room until a nurse's aide arrived — Lou had harped on that at many Resident Council meetings. State law, he was told, required that a nurse's aide be present to supervise before residents entered the dining room. What was the reason? Because, he was told, some residents might choke on their food, and nurse's aides were trained in the Heimlich maneuver. Well, Lou wanted to know, why not train the dietary aides? They *were* trained, he was told. Well, then, why not let the residents sit down at their tables before the nurse's aide arrived? Because regulations required that a nurse's aide be on hand.

"*Meshugge,*" Lou said upon reaching this dead end.

The other day, during this summer's first heat wave, a fire started in one of the motors of the air-conditioning system. All the residents had to eat inside their rooms until the thing was fixed. Lou sought out a supervisor. If the authorities were so afraid of people choking on their food, Lou asked her, then how could they let people eat unsupervised inside their rooms? The supervisor said the aides were on lookout in the halls. "*Meshugge,*" Lou said afterward. He sighed.

"I'm a whistle blower," Lou said. He spoke without obvious pride in the fact, as if it were just a condition that he'd have to put up with. He'd saved up a number of items to talk to Bruce about, so as not to be pestering him constantly. Now Lou went off on his cane, searching the building for Bruce's voice. He heard Bruce talking in a corridor downstairs, and made for him. "Bruce?" said Lou. "Bruce, I don't want to be a trouble-maker, but who's supposed to clean the showers?"

"Housekeeping," Bruce said.

"When?"

"When they can get in," Bruce said.

Lou said he felt the showers should be mopped and sprayed with disinfectant after every use. Bruce said the nurse's aides were supposed to do that.

"Because you hear so much about athlete's foot," Lou went on.

"Okay, Louie. We'll look into it. I'm sure it's supposed to be mopped up every day."

"I've never seen anyone mopping it. And the other thing I talked to you about the other day."

"The handrails," Bruce said.

In various parts of the building Lou found some hand-rails, which he relied on, sticky. Bruce said he was taking care of that.

Lou went on with his list. Bruce always had time for Lou. Working here with only one helper, he didn't always have time to follow up on Lou's suggestions. Lou said he'd noticed that the non-slip strips on the floors of the showers were gone. Bruce said he was working on that. The last strips he used hadn't stuck.

"Who'd ya buy from?"

"Brigham's."

"Why don't you go right to the source? And by that I mean 3M."

Bruce had gone to them, he said, but their stuff was too expensive.

"That reminds me," Lou said. "I still need a little piece of double-faced tape."

"For your soldiers."

They talked a while longer. Bruce and his assistant had erected a couple of forest green, fringed canopies on the grounds outside. Lou had heard about the canopies. He hadn't inspected them, but he had some advice to lend. Bruce might want to consider anchoring the canopies with concrete blocks, just as Lou himself did, a few years back, when he erected a children's swing set for a friend of Ruth's. "The thing held up pretty good," said Lou, hanging his cane on a handrail so he could depict what he had done. "Four concrete blocks."

"Anchored it down," Bruce said. "Well, we'll look into it, Louie." But Bruce was just humoring Lou this time. Bruce had already put up the canopies and he thought them sturdy enough.

Lou headed back upstairs. "I wonder if I should keep stirring the pot. See, when I was working in Burlington, safety was part of my job." Lou nodded to himself. "It's a little late in the game for me to change my ways."

Lou knew Joe's pneumonia hadn't altogether left. Joe still hadn't gone back to the exercise bike. He still felt too short of breath, but hadn't said much about the problem, to Lou or to the staff. Lou wished that Joe would sit up more often, but he didn't feel that he could chide him about that anymore. He listened in silence to Joe cough at night, and he worried. "It scares the *hell* out of me — pardon my French," he said to their favorite aide when Joe was out of the room.

Lou's own health seemed stable, and then one day it didn't. The trouble started over a dinner of beef stew. "I've yet to have a piece of stew meat around here I could chew," Lou explained to the dietary aide. But Lou didn't eat shellfish, so he didn't want the alternate, which was seafood salad. So Lou asked, as had been his custom at these times for more than a year, to be given a plain cheese sandwich. But the waitress returned to say that Dave had left orders not to slice any cheese. Lou ended up with a meager supper — "four crumbly little pieces of toast with a little cream cheese on them" — and he was furious.

Joe told Lou to calm down. He didn't think he'd ever seen Lou get this riled up. It couldn't be good for a man Lou's age to get so angry, Joe thought. Damn that kitchen. If he had two working hands, he'd have gone in there and pushed the cook aside and made the cheese sandwich himself. Even he could make a plain cheese sandwich. It wouldn't cost anyone much to give Lou a plain cheese sandwich.

It might have been coincidence, but all that night Lou's left side ached, and then around midnight he awakened with a pain on the left side of his chest. He recognized it. He'd had severe angina a couple of times, but not since coming to Linda Manor. This felt different, a fluttering feeling and what he thought of as "a little *knip*," like a hand in his chest grasping his heart and giving it a twist. The sensations frightened Lou. They always did. The world shrinks at such moments. It becomes not much larger than one's chest. But the pain wasn't strong enough to justify his calling the nurse. If he called the nurse, he'd wake up Joe, and the nurse wouldn't do anything that Lou couldn't do for himself. He leaned out from his bed, pulled open the dresser drawer, and his hand found the special compartment that held his pills of nitroglycerine. Lou put a pill under his tongue. As it dissolved, so did the pain. He lay awake for a few minutes, to be sure it wasn't coming back, then drifted off to sleep.

Lou reported all this to the nurse the next morning. He figured it was his own fault. He'd gotten too angry over that business with the cheese sandwich. He said to Joe, "I'm foolish for letting myself get so upset. But I just can't help it."

"Well, don't get upset, that's all!" Joe said.

"I can't control myself. When I know I'm right on something, I get upset."

That afternoon while Lou rested upstairs, Joe went to the lobby and, in between his coughing fits, fumed to Art and Bob. "It doesn't do Lou any good," Joe said. And then, as if he'd just realized it, Joe exclaimed, "Jesus Christ, you know that could *kill* him!" His face was suddenly gnarled, as when he was imagining his granddaughter dead from earache. Mouth open, he gave his brief, dry-heaving sob. "Goddamn fools," Joe said. "A *cheese sandwich.*"

That night Lou had another attack. This was unusual. Again, he kept the news from the staff and Joe until morning. Lou took another nitro pill and went back to sleep. But he didn't feel right when he awoke. The pain in his chest wasn't strong — just a pin, not a knitting needle, like something hovering. Lou took yet another nitro pill.

Was he all right? Joe wanted to know. Maybe Lou shouldn't go down to breakfast.

Lou said he felt well enough to make the trip, but afterward, back in the room, Lou sat in his chair with an uncommon stillness, as if listening to distant sounds. He squeezed his eyes shut. Once in a while he seemed to wince. Joe was staring at Lou.

"It still keeps coming and going," Lou said. "It's not what they call a chest pain, just a sticking in one point. It just gets me a little bit scared."

A nurse came in. "How you feeling now, Lou?"

"On and off," Lou said. "This pain keeps coming and going. It's not severe or unbearable."

"Mmmm," said the nurse.

Joe stared on at Lou.

"Are you going to check my vitals?" Lou asked.

"Soon," said the nurse.

"I wonder if Tylenol would do some good," Lou said.

"It wouldn't hurt," said the nurse. She left the room.

Joe lay back and stared at the ceiling. Lou had these spells every so often. Sometimes they would coincide with something that upset Lou, like the time when he dreamed about giving away his woodworking tools and woke up with chest pains. Sometimes the spells seemed to come all on their own. Usually they went away fairly quickly once Lou took his nitro pill. Joe had gotten used to this, in the way soldiers get used to bombardment in their bunkers. He just had to lie here and wait it out. What did the nitroglycerine actually do? Joe wondered. Why hadn't it worked yet? Where was the nurse with that Tylenol? Joe looked across the room. Lou sat very stiffly in his chair. Joe couldn't just lie here. He rose. "I'm gonna go find out about, uh, Tylenol, Lou."

At around ten, Joe's daughter arrived for a visit. She was striking looking, in her thirties. She had dark, curly hair and was about as tall as Joe. Today she wore a gray dress. She came at least once a week to visit. She stopped as usual to kiss Joe, who, as she approached him, seemed at once to put on extra years. Beside his lovely daughter, he looked like an old pensioner.

Then she crossed the room, leaned down, and kissed Lou on the top of his head.

Lou smiled for Joe's daughter, but he continued to sit in that stiff, still way.

"How are you, Lou?" Joe's daughter asked.

This was a dangerous question at Linda Manor. Ask the wrong person and you might get a real answer. But never from Lou. In the time Joe had known him, Lou had always said "fine," even when he wasn't.

"Lousy," Lou replied.

Joe sat up and stared at Lou.

"What's the matter?" asked Joe's daughter.

"Out of breath," Lou said.

"What is it?" Joe demanded.

Lou shrugged.

Joe's face contorted, his mouth open. He looked at his daughter and said, "That's the first time I ever heard him say 'lousy.'"

"I must be getting old." Lou smiled. "Phil said he was watching a cooking show. They put pansies in the salad. I figure I'll go tell Dave."

Lou never said "lousy." Now he was trying to cover up his indiscretion, to put Joe and his daughter at ease. By Jesus, he was tough, Joe thought.

The three of them chatted, Joe sitting up to look at Lou now and then. Finally, sometime after Joe's daughter left, a little before lunch, Lou's stiffness and the wary look he'd worn since breakfast passed. And Joe lay back, relaxed.

"I don't like to say it in front of Ruth," Lou said to Joe, "but, you know, when it happens, I want it to happen quick."

"You die after me," Joe said. "Day after, you can die."

That afternoon, now that Lou was feeling fine again, Joe turned to less important worries. "The Red Sox. They stink. Last night. Three men walked and two guys couldn't bring them in. They leave men on base all the goddamn time." He sat up. "And that's swearing, that's not a prayer, and you can go boo about it."

"Okay, I forgive you for that, Joe."

Joe lay back down. Lou suggested, "It's those prima donna pitchers."

"No! Hitters, too. I'd fire the manager, the general manager, and all the ball club. And I'd bring up, uh, Pawtucket manager and his whole team. Bring the whole team up. Currrist!"

Almost everything was back to normal. A few days later, Lou's doctor visited and deemed Lou's angina "stable." But Joe still had some shortness of breath, and he had that cough. It wasn't a constant thing, but it wouldn't go away. It would start with his laughing, at a Red Sox rally or one of Lou's stories. Once started, the cough went on for minutes, Lou gripping the arms of his chair at the sound, while Joe gasped for air between the spasms, his feet kicking his mattress.

5

Last night Joe told the nurse he needed a wheelchair for today. He knew the routines at the VA hospital. Now he sat in the borrowed wheelchair in front of the Forest View nurses' station, fifteen minutes early, waiting for the driver to arrive. The driver wasn't late, but already Joe had asked the charge nurse to call and make sure he was coming. Joe looked diminished in the chair. He looked up at one of the nursing supervisors, a tall woman anyway and very tall standing beside his wheelchair, and he said to her in a voice that sounded choked, "I'm afraid they're gonna keep me." Joe's eyes studied the nurse's face, to see if she was hiding something, afraid she might be.

"No they're *not*," she said. She leaned down, her face close to his, and rubbed her hand on his bald dome. He did not protest. Held in her embrace, Joe looked away and stared at nothing.

"*Route* Nine," Joe murmured as the car turned onto the two-lane highway. Joe smiled to himself. He didn't say much the rest of the way. He sat in the front seat and looked out the window.

They had to go only about a mile. A golf driving range went by on the right, and then a little bunch of stores, a liquor store among them. And then off to the left appeared the outer grounds of the VA Medical Center — beside the road a pretty pond and a wide, upward-sloping field, as closely mown and verdant as a fairway. The field ends at a stand of tall evergreens, framed against the sky on this blue and green and golden summer morning. Out beside the entrance there is also a garden, meant for the eyes of passersby. The garden is always immaculately tended, no matter what the state of the national economy. In the garden a cluster of pruned shrubbery spells out the initials VAMC, just above which the hospital always plants a sign. The slogan changes periodically. Sometimes the sign reads, TO CARE FOR HIM WHO SHALL HAVE BORNE THE BATTLE. Today it read, PRICE OF FREEDOM VISIBLE HERE.

Sometimes lone figures appear from among the trees at the top of the hill, old men or young, walking across the grassy hillside, down an unofficial path known locally as the Ho Chi Minh Trail. They are heading, it is generally assumed, for the liquor store across Route 9, though actually, most go to the convenience store instead. But the landscape was empty at this morning hour. Nothing besides pond and garden, field and woods, and the top of a smokestack, rising above the trees, was visible. Trees hid all the buildings of the medical center. Perhaps it was that fact, the impression that something was being hidden, which made these outer grounds seem eerie in their emptiness. Their military neatness proclaimed that this VA hospital wasn't like some others — the filthy sties to which some veterans had returned from Vietnam. But the landscape's prettiness and orderly solitude made contemplation of what lay behind the trees all the more appalling, like a flaming shipwreck on a calm and sunny sea. The wards of the hospital proper, the locked psychiatric wards, the drug and alcohol rehabilitation wards, the nursing home wards, in one of which Joe had lived during the longest four months of his life. To Joe, these spruce grounds were not pretty. They were dismal.

The car went up the drive on a winding way all overhung

with trees, past old brick buildings and numbered parking lots, and then into a courtyard, surrounded by more brick buildings coupled together with walkways. It was an angular and complicated-looking place, worn by time and traffic. It was a place of boxes inside boxes. Joe had lived on C Ward, one of the innermost boxes, but today, he hoped, he wouldn't go much farther than the waiting room and a doctor's office. After the usual difficulties — swinging his feet out the door, rising slowly, his good arm quivering as he lifted himself — Joe transferred from car seat to wheelchair, was pushed on a brief passage through the summer morning, up a concrete ramp, and into the outer waiting room in front of the receptionist's window. Joe surrendered his VA identity card. The fact that his eyes never left it would by itself have proved he was a veteran, and remembered all the many ways of getting lost in paperwork. He could hardly have forgotten. From time to time he would receive notices from here canceling cholesterol checkup appointments that he'd already kept. He put the identity card back in his pocket and started waiting.

Half a dozen men sat on vinyl chairs in the center of the room. Most of them were watching a game show, craning their necks as if looking at airplanes. The TV was mounted high up on a wall. On the walls were a few framed photographs of men in suits, depicting, as in an Army orderly room, the chain of command. Joe looked around. It was all the same. The place was clean as always. "And the nurses and aides upstairs, they're wonderful. Just like at Linda Manor. But . . ." Joe's voice trailed off, and in a moment a nurse came up and wheeled him into an office. "My blood pressure will be higher," he told her as she put the cuff around his biceps, "because of the VA and everything."

The nurse smiled.

"I mean it."

But it wasn't much higher than usual, 150 over 88.

"Is he gonna check my lungs?" Joe asked the nurse when she took off her stethoscope.

"I think so."

"I *feel* all right. Except, you know, for my stroke."

The nurse departed. Joe looked around the small gray room. He sat beside a metal desk. "Adjust. Jesus Christ. Adjust," he said. He flexed his left arm. He growled, looking at his biceps. "But. Lou and I have adjusted." Joe sighed. "I don't want booze anymore, but yesterday after supper I'd have given a thousand, no, I'd have paid anything for a cigarette."

The doctor came in a moment later, a trim, dark-haired young man in a white coat, with a pleasant smile. He sat down facing Joe, introduced himself, and asked Joe how he was.

"I feel well," Joe said emphatically. "You know. Stroke, you know. I feel all right. So why the hell did they send me here?"

"So they didn't tell you?" The doctor leaned toward Joe, his elbows on his knees.

"The nurse said it was to check my lungs."

"Yes. The x-rays show an area on the right side that's either pneumonia or a scar. I don't know. It could be a persistent pneumonia. It could be that. Sometimes there's a cancer or a growth. If you asked me do you have lung cancer, no, I don't think so."

"I don't care," said Joe.

The doctor blinked. "Are you coughing a lot?"

"Once in a while I cough at night."

"Any fever or sweats?"

"No."

"Are you losing any weight?"

Joe smiled. "No-oooh."

The doctor leafed through Joe's records, asking questions. Was Joe a smoker? Was he still a smoker? When had he quit? How many packs a day had he smoked? "If you had to average it over fifty years, would you say you were a two-pack-a-day smoker?"

"Yes. But I used to drink, you know."

"But you gave it up," said the doctor, looking at the records. "Says you were in the Navy. Where?"

"South Pacific."

"Says you were a lawyer."

"Uh, probation officer. I practiced law on the side."

Joe's aphasia seemed to strike most often when he wanted most to speak his mind, and also when he was feeling nervous. "Wait a minute now," Joe told the doctor at one point when he couldn't get an answer out. "I got half a brain, you know." The doctor's questioning had turned from medicine to small talk, and Joe was uneasy without knowing exactly why.

In fact, the doctor, expecting Joe's visit, had studied Joe's chest x-rays and had a plan in mind. He'd arrange a battery of tests for Joe and have the resident lung specialist examine the results, all of which would mean that Joe would have to spend a few nights here in the hospital. Getting back to business, the smiling young doctor said that what he was going to do now was formally admit Joe to the hospital.

Joe's face flushed. "Oh, *bullshit!*" he roared. He came halfway out of the borrowed wheelchair. It looked for a moment as if he were going to throw himself onto the doctor.

The doctor stiffened momentarily, rocking back in his chair.

Then, leaning forward again, he explained that he wanted Joe to have a CAT scan and a bronchoscopy. He explained the procedures. A bronchoscopy meant putting a tube down Joe's throat to have a look inside his lung.

Joe waved his good hand at the doctor. "The hell with it!"

"That's up to you," said the doctor. "None of these tests can be done at Linda Manor."

"I don't want to be here anymore," said Joe, his face still flushed.

"A CAT scan test is done as an x-ray test. It's done in Providence, and hear me out before you say 'bullshit.' If you have Medicare —"

"No, I don't have Medicare."

"Or you have a bank account."

"No," Joe said.

"The CAT scan will give the lung specialist an idea," the doctor went on. "But to figure out why an old pneumonia is still there, he needs to look in your lung with the tube."

"All right," said Joe, "I'll get the CAT scan. But I don't want to be in the hospital *any* more."

"You mean never, or any more than is absolutely necessary?"

"Never." Joe's eyes were narrowed. The doctor seemed momentarily lost. Joe, in a gentler tone, said, "Because I'm seventy-two years old, and I, uh, you know."

"You can't die young anymore," said the doctor, and he smiled.

"No! I'm old."

"And whatever happens, happens."

"Right!" Joe said.

"All right. I can accept that."

"I don't want tubes in me," Joe said.

"You want quality of life, not quantity?"

"Yup."

"Okay," said the doctor. "We're on the same wavelength."

"My wife and daughter signed, uh, the paper. At Linda Manor."

"I think I have the beginning of the idea." The doctor leaned again toward Joe. "But you should know some other things. If it's pneumonia or TB, those are potentially very treatable. But there's no way to know how to treat it if we don't know what it is. If it's something more serious like lung cancer, it might also be treatable, but not outside the hospital. You might say you don't want that —"

"That's right," Joe interrupted.

"But I can't know what's there," the doctor continued, "unless you have the CAT scan and bronchoscopy. I'm not saying that to persuade you."

"Okay. But I don't want to spend the night here." Turning his face half away from the young man, Joe waved his hand again. "Lung cancer, forget it."

"Don't give yourself lung cancer."

Joe looked at him and, as if explaining something obvious to a child, said, "I know I don't have lung cancer. I know I don't have TB."

The doctor put on his stethoscope. He listened to Joe's heart and lungs. "When you were in the hospital in Pittsfield, did they check your prostate gland?"

"They took it out." Joe grinned.

"I want you to have a chest x-ray today."

Joe smiled. "That'll give me cancer."

"All the x-rays?" said the doctor. "Hold on a second and I'll address that."

"No. Because I'm kidding." Joe added, "You know, I don't want a CAT scan."

"It's up to you," said the doctor. "But I'd do it if I were you."

"Okay, I'll get the CAT scan, period," said Joe. He looked squarely at the doctor. "But they have to take me back to Linda Manor."

"You drive a hard bargain."

"I'd commit suicide if I have to stay upstairs," Joe said. "Honest to God."

"Fair enough. You like Linda Manor."

Joe stared at him, pausing a moment to assemble the words. "I like it better than here."

So they struck a compromise. The doctor would have Joe x-rayed again right now, to see if anything had changed with the problem in his lung. And while Joe was getting x-rayed, the doctor would see what he could do about getting Joe a CAT scan locally, so that he wouldn't have to spend any nights in the hospital.

Joe rode the wheelchair down several corridors, then up an elevator, down another corridor — a passage of enough turns to make a nervous person worry about ever getting out of there. But he was calm now. He got his lung x-rayed again and was rolled back to the lobby and parked beside the rows of chairs at the center of the room.

There were two rows, placed back to back. Joe sat at the end of the row that faced the television. A couple of children in the row behind him were talking about their pets. Joe listened, smiling, his eyes on the TV. Another game show was in progress. From the cluster of people waiting arose a collective odor of dried sweat. A couple of young men with packs of cigarettes rolled up in the sleeves of their T-shirts sat nearby. A woman was speaking to an unshaven elderly man in ragged-looking clothes. "Can you spare me some money for food and cigarettes?" The old man didn't answer her. Joe had gone to the Linda Manor beauty shop for his bimonthly haircut just the other day. He'd gotten his usual close cropping, so that the haircut would last. The fringes around his bald dome were almost as short as his considerable five o'clock shadow, which appeared within hours after he shaved. All of Joe's head looked like it needed a shave. Joe wore sweat pants and a polo shirt. He looked as if he still belonged here.

Joe stared up at the TV. His thoughts went elsewhere. "Once they get you in this place, they don't like to let you go . . . What the hell. You know you're not gonna live forever. If I were fifty, I'd do it. Most people aren't like Lou. People don't make ninety-two. People don't do that often . . . Upstairs. There were five of us in a room. No TV. And I depend on TV. And I just *lay* there. I can't read. Lou's all right because he's active. People keeping people alive. For God's sake. It's ridiculous." Joe looked around the waiting room. "They might forget me, and I'll sit here till tomorrow. For Christ's sake, what's takin' him so long? That's why I don't like coming to these goddamn places." He made a face and looked back up at the TV. "Room with five guys, and one guy I could talk to, and he used to go away. I was here four or five months . . . I gotta wait for him. Then I gotta wait for transportation."

The doctor, walking briskly, stopped beside Joe and said, "I'll be with you in five minutes."

"Okay," Joe called after him. The doctor disappeared into an office.

"That was nice. That was really nice. He's the only one ever did that."

Joe looked back at the TV. The game show was concluding. "He didn't win the car," Joe murmured. Then the nurse came for him.

Joe was wheeled up to another desk, inside another gray-looking office, but in front of the same young doctor. "You know, I want to thank you," Joe said. "You're the only, uh, physician who ever came out and told me you'd be out in five minutes."

The doctor grimaced. "Well, that's something I did right. Now let me go over something I did wrong."

He said that he'd just studied Joe's latest x-ray, and the picture seemed to show that the irregularity in Joe's lung, whatever it was, had diminished greatly. It wasn't gone, but the problem seemed to have improved enough to make the doctor think that it might clear up altogether by itself. He would put the issue of the CAT scan and bronchoscopy on hold, and have Joe come back in about a month for another x-ray. "So I'll see you in four weeks," the doctor said.

Joe had begun to smile.

"You're happy," said the doctor, "but I feel like an idiot. I never saw a lung problem that went on month after month and then improved like this."

"But I have inner strength."

"I'm sorry to worry you," said the doctor.

"I wasn't worried," said Joe, leaning toward the young man. "Because when you reach your seventies, every day is a good day."

The doctor needed Joe's identity card to fill out some paper-work. Joe handed it to him, saying, "But, uh, give it back." Fifty years had passed since, administratively speaking, Joe's identity had depended on military dog tags, but again Joe's eyes stayed on that card for as long as the doctor had it. Joe returned the card to his pocket, and in a little while he was riding back toward Linda Manor.

"A longer stay than you anticipated, Joe," said the driver.

"Yeah," Joe said. "You wait, you know."

"Well, it's no different in the service," said the driver.

"I know," Joe said.

Joe meant to prevent him, but the driver had to finish the chord and utter the old military saw: "Yeah, just like in the service. Hurry up and wait."

Joe smiled out the windshield as the Grecian portals of Linda Manor hove into sight.

Joe said that he'd been bluffing the doctor about suicide. "I don't have the guts."

The VA doctor had said his lung was on the mend. The doctor ought to know. Joe went back to riding the exercise bike, but he didn't get very far. Five minutes on the bike, which once would have merely warmed him up, left him panting now. "Cripes," he said. "Before, uh, pneumonia, I was doing an hour." He rode the bike only one more time. He got short of breath immediately, and he thought he felt another blister coming on. Afterward he told Lou that he'd never ride the bike again. He rarely made such statements idly.

The bike hadn't flattened his belly, but Joe knew that it had helped to keep his weight down and his diabetes under control. And riding doggedly on his trips to nowhere had sometimes served as an act of sweet memory, in which Joe repossessed his former strength. But riding had become too painful. And perhaps in reminding the doctor that fighting against the tide of age inevitably reaches a point of futility, Joe also reminded himself of the fact. Maybe Joe felt he didn't need the bike anymore. He mourned it just once. "It made my leg feel *strong.*" And he didn't mention it again.

Joe waved away Lou's questions about his shortness of breath, but Lou guessed it was still with Joe, because from time to time Joe skipped M&M's.

At night, the room illumined by the glow of the ball game on TV, Lou lay silently on his side of the curtain, as if he were asleep. But Lou was wakeful, waiting for the sound of Joe's coughing to begin, like a person waiting for an alarm. Lou couldn't talk to Joe about his coughing anymore. Joe made it plain that the subject irritated him. On a morning a week or so after Joe's first visit to the VA, Lou waited until Joe went into their bathroom, and then he whispered, "When he coughs at night, it sounds like it's coming out of a hollow barrel. I don't think he's got that out of his system yet. I can't say anything about it."

6

At midmorning, seated in her rocking chair by her window down on Meadowview, Dora took up her pen and hardbound diary. She leafed to today's page. "Beautiful morning here," Dora wrote.

It was gray outside and too warm for morning. In the lobby, a visitor greeted Bob by saying, "Hot enough out there for ya?"

Those open canopies that Bruce and his assistant had erected, without cement-block anchors, one in front of the building and the other out back, certainly looked pretty through the windows, surrounded by the green grass, like miniature versions of wedding tents. But no one sat beneath them. In this weather, even the residents who liked to go outside now ventured only a step or two beyond the doors and then turned back. Today was hot and humid again. Surrounded by combustible air, under an ominous sky, Linda Manor lay sealed.

By early afternoon every window had a view of rising thunderheads. Lou, in his chair by the window, couldn't see them, of course, and Joe, on his bed, didn't notice. "If you could settle all the problems on the second floor, they'd make you secretary of state," said Joe to Lou. Joe was thinking of the bickering and the yelling they'd heard in the halls last night. Fleur and Phil, among others, still mixed it up. At the nurses' station, Fleur had said to Phil, "You don't like me talking loud, but I don't pay it any mind." And Phil had yelled at her, "I don't like you talking, period, sweetheart." Phil had added, more calmly, "At least I'm not a policeman anymore."

The first thunderclap seemed to shake the floor. The glass in their window rattled, and Lou and Joe both flinched, turning toward the window.

In suddenly gloomy light, Joe got up, put on his shoes, and limped across the room. By the time he got to the window, the rain was coming down in sheets. It streaked the glass in front of him. The window rattled steadily in the wind. Staring down, through the streaks of driving rain, Joe looked at the canopy in the grassy yard below. It was lurching on its four steel legs, its once rectangular shape distorted to a series of parallelograms. Joe lifted his eyes to the tree line. Tall pines and maples tossed from side to side. Leaning on his cane, standing at the window, Joe saw ocean waves he hadn't seen in fifty years.

He was grinning. "Head into the wind!" he cried at the glass. He was quoting the captain of one of the ships on which he'd served, a man of Swedish blood, the model of seamanship to Joe, who had never been to sea when he came aboard that ship as a brand-new ensign. The captain had promoted him almost at once, explaining simply that Italians made good sailors. Joe wasn't so sure about that. Off the Philippines, in the midst of a typhoon that sank several American ships, Joe stood on the bridge and watched with rising panic as the gauge that measured the ship's roll plunged past what he thought was the point of no return. They were going to capsize, he said aloud, and the captain, as Joe sometimes told the story, growled at him, "No we're not, you goddamn fool," and banished him from the bridge.

"Head into the wind!" said Joe toward the window again, lifting his cane and shaking it, and grinning.

"Tie yourself to the mizzenmast," said Lou, still sitting in his chair. Lou chuckled. Then he asked in a serious voice, "What does that mean?"

Joe laughed. "By God, that's a real storm, you know it?"

"They said it wouldn't last long."

"How'd you like to be out now?" Joe said. "If I were well, I'd be out now." Rain drummed on the roof right overhead. Lightning flickered. "I gotta go to the bathroom, darn it."

"Well, don't do it on the floor!" Lou said, and again he chuckled.

"I *know* that," Joe said. "I hope it stops before the game tonight." He gazed out for a moment longer, looking down at the canopy. Two of its supporting legs had lost their footings. It stood all twisted out of shape, the canvas top shuddering in the wind like an animal in its death throes. Joe described what had happened to the little tent. "I think it's torn."

Lou shook his head over this news, but didn't comment. Then he murmured, "I hope Ruth and Bob are home."

Joe turned from the storm-tossed landscape and limped to the bathroom. When he returned to the window, the storm had become just a soaking rain in gloomy light.

Lou asked Joe what he saw now.

"Person getting out of their car."

"He'll get a wet tushie."

"Ah, dear," Joe said.

"Yup," Lou said. "That's nature."

Watching the rain, Joe spoke to Lou about a woman whose obituary notice had been posted just this morning. "I knew her when I was downstairs. Very nice woman," Joe said.

"She used to greet us all by name," Lou said.

"Nice woman," Joe said.

"She was all those weeks in the hospital, and what did they do for her?" Lou asked. Distant thunder made Lou turn his head toward the window for a moment.

"The Sox are tied for first," said Joe, pensive at the window.

The canopy lay on the grass below, a heap of green cloth and twisted metal legs, abject in the rain.

❖   ❖   ❖

A resident could go on living a long time at Linda Manor. Bodies were well cared for here. In some cases, doctors spared Medicare no expense in order to keep people alive. The woman in her nineties whose surgeon had amputated her gangrenous arm, for instance. She had died anyway within a month or so. Some residents were kept alive with feeding tubes inserted in their stomachs, just as at the VA. Not a pretty sight, but then again the alternative was not attractive either. One nurse still remembered vividly the frightened eyes of an all but comatose resident whose next of kin had forbidden the feeding tube.

That friend of Joe's whose obituary he read the other day had been a painful case, a case to give Joe pause as he looked out the window at the summer thunderstorm. One day she had awakened with pain in her hip. The pain increased. She was sent to the hospital to treat her aseptic hip displacement. At the hospital, however, other problems suddenly developed. She languished there three weeks, at a cost to taxpayers of about $50,000, her general condition rapidly deteriorating. Then she was shipped back to Linda Manor, to die in her husband's company. Her last weeks would have been much happier if she'd never gone to the hospital. But no one could have known that beforehand.

When you put yourself in the hands of doctors, you assumed that they knew what was best for you. But you couldn't know before they went to work on you whether they did or not. It was easy to imagine a dreadful chain of events. Joe could go back to the VA for his next lung examination and end up being hospitalized to death, like that friend of his. Anything was preferable to dying that way, Joe thought. He'd seen enough of hospitals, especially the VA. "Jesus Christ, you can't think you're going to live forever." Joe didn't know what he would do this next trip back to the VA. Probably everything would turn out all right. If it didn't, he'd have to decide when the moment came. Or maybe he'd already decided. It was hard to be sure until the time.

Joe's coming appointment hung over him as August wore on. But the Red Sox did not stay tied for first place long, and their uneven performance gave Joe a surrogate for his worry. He donned a pair of multicolored surfer's shorts and turned on the TV, singing along to the national anthem. "He's out of tune with me," Joe said of the organist. An enemy batter singled in a run. Joe shouted instructions at the Red Sox manager. "I said he should walk him! For Christ's sake, *walk* him." The Red Sox shortstop let a ball go through his legs. "See?" he said to the manager. "See?" he said to Lou. Joe's appointment at the VA receded before the ecstasies and yearnings and bitter disappointments that the Sox engendered through a lot of August.

"They'll still make it," Joe said to a fellow resident, talking baseball down in the lobby on a hot afternoon.

"Oh ho ho."

"I got faith," said Joe, shaking his fist in the air. "I don't have faith in anything else, but I have faith in the Red Sox."

7

"I used to love to travel, you know that? 'I want to go down to the sea again, bum-baba, bum-baba, bum. And all I ask is a tall ship and a star to steer me by.' " Joe lay on his bed. He began describing a sunrise he once saw in the South Pacific — remembering himself vow never to forget the sun coming up over that island — when the door to the room slowly opened. The bald head of Norman, the Alzheimer's victim who searched the halls for exits and his wife, peered in around the edge of the door.

Lou rose and made his way to the door. "This isn't your room," Lou said softly. Placing a hand on Norman's shoulder, Lou steered him out. "Good fella." Lou returned to his chair, leaving the door ajar.

"All-timer's, that's all," said Joe.

Joe turned to baseball. "Six and a half games out. They won't win."

They'd had their breakfast. Joe lay on his bed, killing the time before he had to leave for the VA. Over the intercom in the ceiling just outside came Sue's voice, delivering the usual morning announcement. "Have a *good* day, everyone."

Joe bared his gums and growled. "*Rrrrr.*"

"That's universal anymore," Lou said. "Have a good day. You go to a store" — Lou made his voice nasal — " 'Have a good day.' "

Joe was gazing at the ceiling. "If they find something wrong with me, I say, 'Bullshit. Send me back to Linda Manor.' "

"I don't know why you want to come back to Linda Manor after what you heard this morning," Lou said. Down at breakfast the fifth Nudnik, Ted, had said that the people around here didn't know what they were doing.

"Orange juice, eggs," Joe said.

"Blueberry muffins."

"Prune juice, milk, bananas."

"Grapefruit, both whole and in segments," Lou said.

"Waffles," Joe said. "Where do you get that? You don't get that at home. And Art insists on three-minute eggs."

"Bob gets poached eggs," Lou said, "and spills half on his napkin and picks it up again."

"And Ted said, 'They don't know what the hell they're doin'.' Jesus Christ!"

"I told you, Joe, he's been pushing Phil around too long. Phil said the other day, 'Nobody knows what the hell they're doin' around here.'" Lou sighed. "Ahh, dear." He lay awake last night wondering about the old firehouses that, when he'd left Philadelphia, had become social clubs. "I'll have to try to remember to ask my brother about them," Lou said aloud, but to himself. Then he was back in Philadelphia again, taking Joe around old neighborhoods. He wound up at the parlors where the sailors got tattooed. "We used to call them moving pictures. I was never tempted."

"I wasn't either," said Joe. He said he wished he could just stay here today. Right now he could have wished for nothing more than to be allowed to lie listening to Lou all day. But it was time to leave. An empty wheelchair sat waiting for Joe when he limped to the nurses' station and signed out.

"I hate to do this, makes me nervous," Joe murmured as he was wheeled down the central corridor, heading for the lobby.

The dietary aide High-Five Mary, the one who always slapped fives with the Nudniks before meals, was coming down the corridor in her apron. "Where you going, Joe?"

"VA hospital," said Joe, looking up at her.

"That's nice," Mary said.

"Nice?" Joe said.

"Different faces," Mary said.

"I don't want to see any different faces."

"You like ours?"

"Well, I like *yours*."

"Aren't you sweet," said Mary.

"I'm an anxious person," Joe explained as he was pushed into the lobby. Besides, he said, the VA carried unpleasant associations for him.

The man pushing Joe's wheelchair said, "It must have been lonely for you there."

"It's lonely anywhere," Joe said. "But I have Lou. He keeps me sane."

❖　❖　❖

"Beautiful morning here," Dora had written quite accurately today. Joe got only tastes of the weather, transferring in and out of the car. He handed over his identity card to the receptionist, saying again, "Make sure you give it back," and then was wheeled upstairs for yet another chest x-ray, from which he soon returned, to sit again in the borrowed wheelchair in the waiting room.

The other people in the room might have been the same who'd sat here last time. They weren't, of course, but that was how it seemed, as if they'd been sitting here a month. An old man near Joe stared at a photograph of the President on the wall, reading the President's name aloud — "George Bush" — as if aware of it for the first time. The room was full of men today. They seemed resigned to waiting, more resigned than Joe at least. An unshaven man with a couple of inky tattoos on his bare arms — he might have been forty or he might have been sixty — his pants sagging for lack of a belt, wandered past Joe, muttering. Joe glanced at him and nodded significantly. On the TV high up on the wall, a game show was again in progress. Joe glanced up at it from time to time.

He wore a white polo shirt. It had a few small reddish stains on the front. It was a tricky business, eating left-handed with a brain organized for right-handedness. "Diet Jell-O. I spilled it." Joe looked down at himself. "I'll change it tomorrow." He laughed a little and looked around the room. Nurses and orderlies and white-coated doctors passed by now and then. Joe was looking for the young, black-haired doctor who had received him here last time. "He's making me wait." He wondered if he'd ever been to a doctor who hadn't made him wait. "Jesus Christ, why don't they space the time?"

Joe kept glancing around, rather like Bob at this moment. "*Come* on. All right. Here." The young doctor was walking down the hall, but he didn't seem to see Joe. Half turned in his wheelchair, Joe expelled a breath through narrowed lips. It didn't make much sound. "Oh, Christ, I used to be able to whistle." Joe couldn't remember the young doctor's name. Hurriedly, he turned his wheelchair around. He beckoned to the doctor.

The doctor spotted him and lifted a finger. "Momentarily," he called to Joe, and walked swiftly into one of the offices off the waiting room.

Another patient, another old veteran with tattoos, limping on a cane toward a chair, stopped in front of Joe and pointed down at Joe's shoes. "I need a pair of those."

Joe didn't answer. He was muttering to himself. " 'Momentarily.' *Eeeeee.*" He bared his gums and lifted his cane from his lap as if to strike downward with it. Then he smiled. In a moment a nurse came out to fetch him. He had not, in fact, been kept waiting long. After all, the technicians had to develop today's chest x-ray before he and the doctor could have anything to discuss.

Joe was wheeled into an office of two rooms. He sat in one room beside the doctor's desk while the doctor studied x-rays in the adjoining room. Joe looked at a photograph on the doctor's desk. There were children in the picture. "Nice-looking kids." He thought about his first son. *He'd be about forty-five now.* Then he turned his head toward a sound that came from the other room, a metallic snapping like the sound of a handsaw blade being bent, the sound of the doctor looking through Joe's x-rays.

Joe frowned. "I don't care what the —"

From the adjoining room came the doctor's voice. He was talking on the phone. "Is there a radiologist there today?"

"What?" said Joe under his breath, his face reddening. "Jesus Christ, get out of here. I don't want —"

"There's a gentleman, Joseph Torchio," said the doctor's voice. "I'm trying to find old films."

Joe muttered imprecations. "Oh, goddamn, come on. Cut the shit. And I don't use that word." Joe glowered. "I feel all right."

"Those have to be kept," said the doctor's voice from the other room.

"*Rrrrrr.*"

And then at last the doctor appeared in the doorway, dressed in his white coat. He smiled down at Joe.

"What," Joe demanded.

The doctor sat down. "The x-ray doctor, who wasn't here, now is. He's sending his secretary down to get the x-rays."

"Well, you told me last time it was clear," Joe said.

"Clear in comparison," said the doctor. "It looked like a pneumonia. Nothing serious. But not clear absolutely. How are you?"

"I'm *very* well."

They sat talking for a while, awaiting the radiologist's secretary. Joe, by his own account, hadn't always been polite in his former life, but everyone who'd known him remarked on his ability to charm strangers when he chose. Besides, Joe liked the looks of this doctor's children. They chatted pleasantly. Then the young doctor said to Joe, "Well, it's like Groucho Marx says: 'You're in trouble. Not only are you sick, but you've got *me* for a doctor.' "

Joe let out a truly big laugh. The doctor left the room, to confer with the radiologist. "You know, I'm missing my lunch," Joe said, but he didn't curse. He repeated the Groucho Marx line and chuckled. Then he waited in silence, watching the door for the doctor's return.

"All right?" Joe asked.

The doctor sat down, leaning toward Joe. He looked serious. "Well, not exactly. The problem is not cleared. Let me go over it. In January you had an x-ray and the lung was clear. In June the x-ray showed a probable pneumonia. In July the x-ray showed significant improvement from June. But this x-ray is unchanged since the last one. The lung's not clear, especially compared to January. So that leaves the question unresolved of what's going on."

"Well, I lay in bed a great deal," Joe said. "That may have something to do with it."

"It may," said the doctor. "The lung tissue is a little collapsed on itself. By now it should have opened up again, and it almost always does." The doctor wet his lips, as if getting himself ready. "The last time you said you'd agree to a CAT scan, but you didn't want to be in the hospital and you didn't want tubes down your throat."

"That's right," said Joe, his face coloring.

"And that if it was cancer, you wouldn't want —"

"That's right," Joe said, more loudly.

"The other choice is to have a CAT scan and the lung doctor examine you."

Joe waved his left hand at the doctor. "The hell with it."

"When you say the hell with it —"

"I'll write it down," Joe said, more loudly still, his eyes fixed on the doctor.

The doctor blinked. He spoke softly. "I have to assure myself that it's not because you're real down or blue."

"No. Because I'm seventy-two." Joe had no trouble saying the number.

The doctor smiled. Youth repeats sayings, too. "You can't die young anymore."

Then Joe laughed. He leaned toward the doctor. "That's right. I'm seventy-two. I eat well. I sleep well."

"You're happy as you are. But I have to think you could end up leaving here worried."

"No, no." Joe waved a hand at him.

"It's probably not a cancer," said the doctor. "The overwhelming likelihood is that it's a pneumonia." He looked Joe in the eyes. "There *is* a possibility that it's very bad."

Joe nodded.

The doctor wondered about Joe's wife. How would she feel about all this?

"Well, she has cancer," Joe began. Joe listed his wife's medical troubles for the doctor, as he often did in his room at Linda Manor when the subject of other people's ailments came up — when, perhaps, Joe felt tempted to talk about his own. Finishing the list, Joe went on to say again that he'd executed a Health Proxy. His family knew he didn't want to be kept alive on machines, Joe said.

The doctor began again to speak.

Joe interrupted him. "Wait a minute. I want *pills*. I don't want to suffer when the time comes." Joe smiled, then thunderously concluded, "But, Jesus Christ, I don't want anything done to me!"

"Makes sense to me. My eighty-year-old grandfather was just visiting, and he feels the same."

"No," Joe said. "You make seventy, you did okay. You make eighty, good for him."

"Do you notice any change?" the doctor asked.

"Short of breath, that's all."

The doctor took Joe's blood pressure. Joe predicted that it would be high, but the doctor said that it was fine. "How long have you been married?" he asked Joe.

"Forty-eight years," Joe said.

"Sounds like you cared about each other quite a lot," said the doctor.

Joe's face contorted. His shoulders heaved.

The doctor bit his lip. He looked away. "Really loved each other," he murmured.

But, as usual, the spasm of soundless crying passed quickly.

Joe was smiling now, reaching for a tissue on the doctor's desk. "My stroke, you know." Joe laughed. "You shouldn't have said that."

The doctor made one last pitch for medicine. "Normally, even if you didn't want a CAT scan, we'd —"

"No!" Joe said.

"Even if you didn't have a CAT scan," the doctor continued, "I'd do an x-ray in two months."

"No," Joe said. "No more x-rays. Please."

The young doctor smiled wistfully. "All right. You'll let someone know if you're having trouble with your breathing, all right?"

"All right." Joe smiled, too. "You know, my wife. Forty-seven, forty-eight years, we fought every day. You know that? Friday she comes to see me, and we'll still fight. Stubborn woman."

Joe delivered that last line with obvious irony. The doctor laughed. He offered Joe his hand, and after a moment of difficulty — the doctor reversing his right hand so that it could meet Joe's left, meet it palm to palm — they shook.

8

Joe stood in the doorway. Sounds of old-time radio, of *Amos 'n' Andy*, reverberated through the room. Lou sat in his chair by the window with his eyes closed and a smile curling his mustache.

"*Hell*-oh," said Joe.

Lou turned his head toward the doorway. His fingers groped for his tape machine beside him, found the machine, found the right button, and pressed down. The show stopped. "Hi. Well, how'd it go?"

"Okay," said Joe, limping toward his bed.

"So what did the doctor say?" Lou asked.

"I don't know. He said, 'You're really sick and you got me as a doctor.' That's a joke. Groucho Marx said that."

Joe lay down. Neither man spoke for a while. Finally Lou said, "Fleur was out there giving the nurse a hard time. She sounds like a broken record. Every day after lunch it's 'Can you get in touch with whoever.' " Lou went on through the scant local news, and then wondered aloud when working-men's lunches had first begun to be wrapped in waxed paper instead of paper bags. Joe and Lou were once again at home.

The next day Ruth, her stockinged feet up on the footboard of Lou's bed, asked Joe what the VA doctor had told him.

Joe was wearing his surfer's shorts, which made his pale legs paler. He looked like a tourist fresh to the beach. He didn't answer right away, but it would have been hard for Joe to refuse the request of such a pretty woman. And Ruth was his good friend. Joe turned his head on his pillow and, facing Ruth, said, "Don't tell my wife. Don't tell my daughter."

"I'm going to call them right away," Ruth said.

So Joe told her. "He says my right lobe, my shortness of breath, you know. There's a thing on my right lobe. When I got over walking pneumonia it didn't go away and it should have. He said it could be, it probably wasn't, uh, cancer. I said, 'Well, *good* bye.' " Joe smiled at the ceiling.

"Well, that's ridiculous." Ruth's face had darkened. "If it is, you probably can have it treated."

"The hell with it. I'm seventy-two."

"I think seventy-two is very young!" Ruth said. She went on more softly, "Since I'm only six years away from it."

"You come from good genes," Joe said.

"That's beside the point," Ruth said. "Seventy-two is very young."

"It depends upon your genes," Joe said.

"Oh." Ruth clamped her mouth shut. She eyed Joe severely.

In his chair by the window, Lou smiled. "I never wore jeans," he said, "and *you* wear shorts, Joe."

Ruth laughed, eyeing Lou. She might have silver hair, but she was still a child, and he was still her father. Gently admonished, Ruth and Joe desisted. Ruth changed the subject, and Joe would not let it be reopened.

Bob was sitting in the lobby when a gurney passed, a couple of ambulance attendants on either end, a resident strapped to the cart. Failing residents were often taken out on gurneys to the hospital. Bob's mustache twitched with consternation. He said with feeling, "Adios, amigo." He added, "It's a bitch."

There was, of course, some winnowing on Forest View. Joe was limping toward the elevator downstairs when from around the corner came a couple of uniformed paramedics pushing a gurney. Hazel was strapped to it, the woman who lived next door to Lou and Joe, who gave Joe the sports and comics sections of her paper every day. She didn't seem to see Joe. She looked as if she held her breath. Joe watched the gurney pass. "Good God. Good God." He boarded the elevator along with a woman in a wheelchair. "They just took Hazel to the hospital. Gollee, huh? Christ."

The woman in the wheelchair didn't answer.

Joe limped into his room. Ruth was there with Lou.

"They just took Hazel," Joe said.

"I know it," Ruth said.

"Holy mackerel, huh?"

"She has a heart condition. Probably she'll be all right," Ruth said. "She's a nice lady."

"Yes, she is," Joe said.

Lou sipped at his morning brandy and didn't comment. Joe lay down and wiped his good hand downward over his face.

Some days later, as Lou and Joe sat in the chairs outside the Forest View elevator station, Ted swayed into view and took a chair opposite them. He crossed his legs slowly, wincing.

"How do you feel, Ted?" said Joe.

"I feel okay, I guess. Everybody else okay?"

Lou leaned toward Joe and whispered, "Andrea told me he blacked out today."

"Time for supper, is it, Joe?" asked Ted. It was about 2:30 in the afternoon, in fact.

"Nope," said Joe. "We're just going for a walk."

"I blacked out," said Ted. "Somebody told me I did."

Ted got up. For a moment it seemed he might fall over. He walked slowly back toward the nurses' station. There was a dark patch on the back of his pants. Joe looked away. A nurse, passing by, caught sight of the chair that Ted had sat in. The seat was glistening wet.

"When Ted gets down to the dining room, I'm afraid he's

gonna fall over," said Lou. "It's a shame. He's gone downhill a lot in the short time he's been here."

Joe watched as the nurse, returning, bent down and wiped clean the seat of Ted's chair, and for a few minutes no one spoke. The time was approaching for Ted to be sent downstairs.

Joe's cough lingered. Lou overheard a nurse say that Joe lay down too much for the good of his lungs, and Lou began a new campaign. "Joe, as soon as you come up here, you take your shoes off and lie down. You should sit up more."

But Joe said all he needed was cough syrup.

Then Lou again suffered Joe's coughing fits in silence, and merely asked from time to time if Joe had enough tissues.

"I gotta get some Robitussin," Joe answered. "That makes you pregnant, you know."

"You're thinking of estrogen, aren't you, Joe?" Lou asked.

"No, no," Joe said. "Robitussin makes you, uh." He coughed a little. "It makes you, uh. You get the sperm from, ah, the hell with it."

"The hell with it, Joe."

Joe tried again. "Robitussin, if you take it, the sperm goes in the egg much faster. I don't know where I heard it, but I heard it."

"Well, you got enough tissues, Joe?"

"Yeah."

Later on, when Joe was out of the room, Lou said, "I told him a couple times already he should sit up more. He's not a little boy. I told him a couple times. I can't tell him anymore. I told the nurse, too."

But then Joe got a cold, and Lou reopened his campaign.

"I'm through with Robitussin." Joe lay on his bed. "My

daughter told me — not suggested, *told* — to take antibiotics, and I said I would. But I won't. Because then I'd have to see, uh, the doctor, and he might send me to the VA." Joe laughed. "So I'll die."

"Don't say that. The best medicine is that chair in the corner, Joe."

At Lou's bidding, an aide had placed an armchair beside Joe's bed. A few days later, when Lou and Joe came up from the dining room, Joe sat down in it.

"He's been sitting up quite a bit," Lou reported a few days after that. "Last night he had me get on the phone and tell his wife he was sitting up. I said, 'If he doesn't, I crack the whip.' She said, 'Good. Keep it up.' "

Joe had made his decision about medicine and he was sticking by it. He'd let nature deal with whatever was wrong in his chest, and refuse all drastic measures. In the meantime, he'd take care of himself — go to M&M's, keep on trying to diet, and even sit up more often, if only because, with Lou around, it was easier to do so than not. This regimen seemed to work. As summer wore on toward a close, Joe's cough gradually abated.

One morning while getting dressed, Joe said to Lou, "I had a dream last night. You told me a man had a stroke, and then he had another stroke, and it, uh, cured him." Joe laughed.

At times, Joe seemed more calmly philosophical than ever before, and more inclined toward wistful reminiscence. Lying on his bed — he wouldn't sit up all the time — he recalled for Lou his boyhood days on Dewey Avenue, when he raised racing pigeons behind his grandfather's house, in a stable down the hillside, in a gully beside the Housatonic. "I used to get egg boxes and cut 'em in half. Raise my pigeons in the egg boxes. I was never handy with hammer and nails. I bent the nails for my friends. I would run down the hill and feed my pigeons."

Joe laughed backward at those memories. He went on: "I went with Italian boys and Jewish boys. Sal Bernardo. Boomie Green. He went to Albany and he disappeared. He loved to gamble. The other craps shooters became lawyers and doctors. But I never was interested in craps because I used to go look at my pigeons. Most of the guys I remember are dead now. Dwyer, George O'Brien, Eddie Radkey, me. Holy mackerel, everybody's dead." Joe paused. "Except me."

Lou stirred. On a TV news show last night, Lou reminded Joe, they'd heard an expert predict that the United States might be a second-rate economic power in ten years. "But I don't think I'll be around."

"What do you mean?" Joe pulled back the curtain. "I might die and you might live. Who's being pessimistic now?"

"I just don't think I'll be around in ten years."

"Why not?" Joe said. "A hundred, a hundred and two."

"They'll show my picture. Look at this handsome man. Has all his teeth."

Joe lay back and laughed.

As always, they had many visitors. One curious visitor asked them if time did not go very slowly for them here.

"Time doesn't hang too heavy on me," Lou replied. "I can't seem to remember the date when Jennie passed away. I can't remember the date exactly when we came out here. Because from the time we came out here to the time she passed away I was occupied with her." He paused, then said once more again, "I thank the Lord I didn't have to leave her alone."

One of Joe's favorite jokes, told by Ruth, was of the ninety-year-old who, when asked how he was, replied, "Fine, but I don't buy green bananas anymore." To the visitor, Joe explained that for him time didn't go slowly at all. "Time is very short. For me. And Lou, too."

9

When Joe returned to Pittsfield after the war, after three years at sea, he thought he'd like to stay attached to water. He and his friend Ray bought a boat, and Ray tried to teach Joe how to sail, out on one of the lakes near town. Joe kept trying to sail the boat directly into the wind. Ray explained that this was impossible. But Joe never really accepted the fact. Rather than bow to physics, he quit sailing.

Ray remembered an earlier time, when he and Joe were just twenty years old and had both read most of Shakespeare and Joe was in the midst of reading Dante in Italian. They shared their passion for literature and philosophy freely, as only the young can. They'd talk about Eugene O'Neill and other favorite writers as if the writers were close friends. They'd swap quotations. One would quote, the other would name the poet or philosopher. They'd pose theoretical conundrums to each other: If you had a choice between saving your mother or your wife, which would you choose? Both had grown up devout Catholics, and it was through their relentless, questing conversations, Ray believed, that both had shed their faith. Ray remembered, from this time, climbing with Joe on a starlit night to a hilltop near Pittsfield. Joe looked up at the sky and said to the God he no longer believed in, "If you want to prove you're there, strike me dead." The memory of that evening had given Ray pause from time to time over the years, as he'd watched Joe's life unfold.

It wasn't possible to capture Joe's life through anecdotes, Ray believed. But the life, as he now saw it, could be divided, roughly, into three parts. There was the young Joe, a youth of great intellect and promise and fierce determination, the Joe whose high school classmates declared him "Future Dictator" in their yearbook. And there was the tragic figure, stuck in the wrong job — in Ray's opinion — dealing daily with the dregs of Pittsfield society, who saw his first-born son taken by leukemia and his first daughter born retarded, who drank too much, and was himself struck down, by stroke, in what should have been his prime. The third was the invalid Joe. One day in Linda Manor's lobby, thinking back to that starry night on the hilltop when Joe challenged God to prove His existence, Ray said, "If I were God, I'd prove it this way. Bit by bit, not in one big blast."

Ray believed that Joe had far more talent as a violinist than Joe would himself acknowledge now. In his late teens, however, while putting up storm windows, Joe fell off the roof of his parents' house and put his hand through a windowpane. The broken glass severed tendons in his wrist. After that, he quit the violin. Visiting one afternoon at Linda Manor, Ray recalled that accident. Lou had mentioned *Fiddler on the Roof*— recently he and Joe had listened and watched, respectively, to the movie version again. Ray remarked to Joe, "*You* were the original fiddler on the roof. You fell off and wrecked your tendons, and couldn't play anymore."

Joe made a face. "Yeah, well, the hell with it." And Ray changed the subject.

After Joe's stroke, Ray struggled mightily with Joe's rehabilitation, trying among other things to help Joe read again. After a while, Joe gave up on reading. It was just too frustrating. But Ray didn't give up, not until just recently. Some months back he brought Joe a couple of new books. The next time he visited, Ray asked Joe how he liked them, and Joe replied, "Jesus Christ! Why do you do that to me?" Ray knew he couldn't read. Joe seemed very angry. In that moment, Ray thought he saw a glimpse of Joe as he used to be, the man of violent passions. It was the last such glimpse he'd seen, and Ray could have wished for others.

They had been great friends, friends through almost all the stages of their lives, friends for life. "If Joe were to go, I lose one third of myself," Ray said. And yet he found himself making up excuses now to stretch out the time between visits to Joe. When people told him they wanted to live to a great old age, Ray would say ironically, "May the view from your nursing home window be beautiful." The first time he visited this room, Ray looked out the window and said, "Well, Joe, the view from your window is beautiful." That time he did not speak ironically. It was a fine view, Ray thought. And Linda Manor was spectacular, as nursing homes went. But after every visit Ray would go home and mix himself a stiff martini. Visiting Linda Manor distressed him, partly because he would imagine himself there and also because he had imagined a rich old age for Joe, filled with literature, and he thought of Joe's life and of its ending here as a tragedy — "a tragedy of all that talent gone to waste."

During one of Ray's visits, he and Lou and Joe were chatting amiably in the room upstairs, Ray in his street clothes, Lou and Joe in their usual outfits of indoor living, the three men discussing medicine. Joe asked Ray, "You had your prostate out?"

"No," Ray said. "Why should I? I treated mine with respect. I didn't try to drown mine."

From his bed, Joe pointed a finger at Ray. "All right."

Lou smiled. "Don't pick on my friend Joe."

Ray changed the subject. "Giuseppe," he said to Joe, "when you coming home again?"

"I *don't* know. I'm getting institutionalized now. I like it here." Joe grimaced and said, "No." But perhaps Joe disavowed the statement partly for Ray's comfort, and in order to save face in front of him.

Ray could by now predict that when he walked into the room for a visit, Joe would ask at once about Ray's family. "He asks about my son. He doesn't talk about himself. He immediately connects himself to me. He goes right to the center of my interests," Ray said. This was in part, Ray felt, Joe's way of trying to re-establish their old relationship. Ever since their early school days, Joe had exerted a power over him that he couldn't fully account for.

Many people said that Joe had adjusted admirably, without complaint, even calmly, to life inside a nursing home. Of course, Ray understood that for Joe there hadn't been much choice. But it did a disservice to his vision of Joe to find him well adjusted to this life. "What irritates me," Ray said, "he's capable of doing this here. Can you imagine what he could have done in another setting?"

In Pittsfield, in the morgue of the *Berkshire Eagle*, there was an obituary, written many years ago:

Joseph A. Torchio, the chief probation officer of the Central Berkshire District Court, died at the age of 54.

In 23 years as a probation officer in Pittsfield, Mr. Torchio and the judges he assisted made the local court a leader throughout the Commonwealth in using probation instead of jail sentences in the correction of offenders.

Recent statewide plans to assure every youthful offender either a probationary period or a rehabilitative program before his misdeeds warrant a jail sentence were anticipated on an informal basis by many years in the Pittsfield District Court.

Mr. Torchio envisioned in his role as probation officer a responsibility to speak out on public issues in the community which affected rehabilitation. He was a vocal supporter of low income housing, more facilities to handle family problems, recreational facilities for youngsters, an enlightened parole policy, and an alcoholism clinic. He served as chairman of the city's Advisory Council on Public Welfare and also helped advise the Boys Club.

Mr. Torchio began his career as probation officer in July, 1950. . . . His appointment represented a return to his native city, which he left in 1942 to join the Navy. He was discharged from the Navy in 1945 as a lieutenant after service that included 3 years in the South Pacific.

From 1946 to 1949, Mr. Torchio was employed as a vocational rehabilitation training specialist for the VA in the Worcester area. In June of 1949 he joined the Youth Services Board for work with juvenile delinquents. For a brief period before the war Mr. Torchio worked in prisoner rehabilitation with the U.S. Prison Association of Massachusetts.

A graduate of Pittsfield High School, Mr. Torchio earned a BA in sociology at the University of Pennsylvania. He earned an MA in sociology at Boston University and received his law degree from Boston College Law School.

Joe lay on his bed laughing, bouncing up and down on his back and clutching his belly, when he heard about this document.

Lou was smiling.

Joe's laughter subsided. "I'll be . . ." he said.

Joe figured an old friend, Bill Tague, had probably written the obituary. It was strange to think of Bill's writing it, imagining Joe dead nineteen years ago. And now Bill himself was dead. "I'll be . . ." said Joe. "Goddamn fool." He smiled and chuckled.

"Mark Twain," Joe said. "Obituary. What'd he say?"

"The report of his death has been grossly exaggerated," Lou said. He raised his index finger. "And another one. 'How come you haven't spoken to your wife in fifteen years?' 'I didn't want to interrupt her.' "

"Winiferd," said Joe.

"You said it, Joe, not me."

The obituary, typed on copy paper with handwritten corrections in the margins, was two and a half pages long. Joe laughed again. "Christ. I wasn't that important."

"I never knew I had such a nice roommate," Lou said. Then Lou's face assumed its solemn, its rabbinical look. "You're all right, Joe. Seriously."

"Yeah. Wait a minute. They didn't put in there that I was a teacher four years, at Berkshire Community College, uh, at night. I could call Bill Tague. But I need a séance to do it." Joe smiled. "They didn't put in I was chairman of a committee for the Salvation Army."

"Now's your chance to get 'em to rewrite it, Joe."

"Yes!"

Even with those omissions, the obituary was the record of a creditable public life, which had ended long ago. The paper would surely shorten it when Joe actually died. His public accomplishments would count for less than they had nineteen years ago. The things he'd done that were bold and innovative then had become commonplace. Fewer people knew him now in his hometown. Certainly, there'd be nothing to add to the obituary. These days Joe lived a life that was reduced in most respects — reduced, it might be said, to awaiting death. One time, speaking of Ray, Joe said, "He was with me in the beginning. He was with me in the end." What remained, Joe himself sometimes seemed to say, was only epilogue. But another time, thinking back to the part he played in Eleanor's cabaret, Joe remarked, "Some people think I *am* Simon Legree. They don't know how I am in here."

Joe had been a big man in his town, but not as big as others wanted him to be, and it wasn't that big a town. Of course, even the great and powerful, if they live long enough, live to retire, and they make sad figures if they retire only with their medals. Private life goes on for everyone. A moral life doesn't have to end with youth or public life, or even with confinement in a nursing home.

Joe's obituary would be shorter than the prematurely written one, but his life had expanded. That was the remarkable fact. Strangely, he had changed himself in here, inside a nursing home, of all places. He'd done the opposite of what might have been predicted. One might have thought such a fiery temperament would expend itself in fury at the irritations and confinements of this place. But when his powers to act had greatly diminished, Joe had taken control of his life. He'd done so by gaining a greater control of himself. Passions still lurked in him, but they didn't rule him anymore. He still possessed his great sympathetic capacity, and through it he'd connected with many fellow residents and with almost all of the staff. He'd made himself as useful as he could. He had entered a little society founded merely on illness, and, accepting it for what it was, realizing it was all there was for him, he had joined it and improved it. He had made a lot of friends in here, and one friend for life.

10

Dan had not gotten his breakfast eggs runny, in spite of his calls to the senator's office. Now, in the fall, he was in trouble with the state, and his emphysema had worsened.

When Dan moved into Linda Manor over a year ago, Medicaid assumed his cost — about $45,000 a year. In principle, people moving into nursing homes must pay their own way, until they've used up all but their last $2,000. But the law exempts some kinds of property, and it also allows people to reduce their assets, to "spend down," in various ways *before* they enter nursing homes and go on Medicaid. Spending down had become a way, notoriously, for people both of modest and substantial means to avoid paying their own nursing home bills. Dan had spent down, quite legally, the little he had before he went on Medicaid. But he continued to receive Social Security and a tidy veteran's pension. The checks kept swelling his bank account above the spend-down limit. By law, Dan should have paid the excess to Medicaid, but Medicaid sent Dan incorrect bills — bills that were much too small. Dan also got some wrong information about the rules of spending down. Either that, or he misinterpreted what he heard. Dan, in relative innocence, worked hard to keep his bank account below $2,000 by buying things.

Almost no one from the world outside came in to visit Dan. He had no siblings. His parents were dead. He'd been married for only about a year back when he was twenty-one. He had no children. He had no pictures of family or friends on his walls, only a porcelain kitten on top of his TV to remind him of Pepe, the cat he lived with before he entered the nursing home. "I'd give a lot to have little Pepe back," Dan would say, glancing at the figurine on top of his gigantic TV. "Why, we had more fun than a barrel of monkeys." When he used to go downstairs for meals, Dan sometimes brought along one of the items he had purchased during his long spend-down. Other residents avoided Dan, by and large. He brought the gadgets for conversation starters.

He had bought the television set, with its twenty-seven-inch screen and internal VCR, as well as a fine pair of binoculars for watching birds and airplanes out his window, two radio scanners — he still hadn't figured out how to program the more powerful one — and an electronic amplifying antenna, his programmable phone, an electronic device called an entertainment center, and an electronic dictionary. "You can spell and get it corrected," he'd said, showing it off. "And that was fifty-nine dollars, on sale from a hundred and eighty-nine, because them are expensive. There are some wonderful bargains out there today, if you're fortunate enough to have a little extra cash." He had bought his own bedside table and a $1,000 wheelchair, both of much higher quality than the institution's, and a gadget that kept track of appointments and told the time in twenty-two of the world's cities, the best stereo Walkman money could buy, a very good watch, a fine German clock, a nifty machine that would have stamped his return address on letters if he'd had anyone to write to, a pair of down sleeping bags, a huge $100 Swiss Army knife fit for a wilderness expedition, and a top-of-the-line camcorder, which he hadn't found a use for yet. He had not prepaid his funeral expenses. "That's too far down the road," Dan had said. "I don't want to be rushed into it."

Recently, he had bought another, more powerful pair of binoculars, with electric-powered zoom lenses, for viewing the moon out his window. But that was going to be his last purchase. Medicaid had finally found the error in their books, and said he owed them thousands. On top of that, Dan had now been sent downstairs. "Sent downstairs" — a grim, bell-tolling term among the able-minded residents of Forest View.

When Lou heard the news, he began to visit Dan in his new room on Meadowview. After one of those trips, Lou reported to Joe, "Dan had trouble with his legal whatever. And the weather's been bad for his breathing. Poor Dan. Problems, problems, problems."

"Why do you go in there?" Joe asked.

"I don't go in there. I stand in the doorway, and I get the same story every time. And I always say, 'Joe says hello.'" Lou looked upward and said, "For telling a lie, forgive me."

"Why do you go in there?" Joe asked again. "You feel obligated?"

"No," Lou said. "Disinfected."

Lou made visiting Dan a regular practice. Every few days he went. The visits all resembled one another. Lou would stand, leaning on his cane, near the foot of the bed and listen as Dan rattled on about his legal problems, his loss of appetite, the incompetence of the staff. He didn't seem exactly morose. He seemed to take some pleasure in moroseness. Lou would try to kid him out of it once in a while. Dan said that the other night the nurses let him go to sleep without his sleeping pill, and he didn't even realize it until he woke up. And Lou chuckled and said, "You mean they didn't wake you up to give you your sleeping pill?" And without so much as a chuckle in return — come to think of it, Lou had never heard him chuckle, let alone laugh — Dan said no, they hadn't. "I wouldn't go as far as to say there's a vendetta against me," he said.

One day Joe decided to visit Dan himself. He went down alone, to do his own *mitzvah*. But it didn't work out.

"What a pain in the ass," Joe said to Lou.

"Joe, don't say that. Just say P I A."

"Camcorder!" Joe said. "What does he need a camcorder for?"

"So he can record little green people running around."

"What you go camping with," Joe said. "Down, uh, sleeping bag! He's got *two* sleeping bags. I don't know if they're electronic or not. And when I visited him, I said, 'How the hell are you gonna sleep in a sleeping bag if you need oxygen?' "

"What'd he say?" Lou asked.

"Well, I was walking away when he answered," Joe said.

Actually, Joe didn't object to Dan's equipment. He objected to the fact that he'd never heard Dan talk about anyone except himself, or about much of anything except his own problems. Joe didn't think Dan deserved to be visited. Joe suspected that Dan would not do the same for another person. Lou suspected so, too, which was why, at bottom, Lou did visit him.

Once, in deep rumination in his chair by the window, Lou said of one of his great-granddaughters, "She's kind and considerate. I guess she takes after me that way." Then, as if awakening, Lou shifted in his chair and smiled. "I am kind and considerate, aren't I?" Dan was just a lonely guy who needed company, Lou thought. He was also a test for Lou. In the privacy of the room, Lou and Joe had made Dan the butt of many jokes. Lou still could not resist from time to time. And so, a few days before the Day of Atonement, when one is supposed to seek forgiveness from people one has wronged, Lou went down to Meadowview, and, pausing in the doorway to Dan's room, Lou said beneath his breath, "I'm sorry." Then Lou went in and listened to Dan for about twenty minutes, which was itself also an act of atonement.

A roommate so given to *mitzvahs* could put a strain on anyone's conscience. But at Linda Manor there was never a lack of opportunity for *mitzvahs*. Lou returned to the room on a day in early fall and told Joe that he'd heard Winifred weeping in her room. Joe thought about this news. Then he put on his shoes and limped downstairs. "She said, 'I lost my courage,'" Joe reported back to Lou. "I said cliché things, you know. 'Keep up your courage. Smile.' She was depressed. Awful depressed and I sat and said clichés. I brought her out of it a quarter, uh, a quarter better."

Joe's friend Hazel came back from the hospital and was restored to Forest View. She told Joe her heart problems came from stress. She said she got upset when her bed wasn't made promptly. "Go make Hazel's bed now," Joe said after breakfast to one of the aides that day.

Bruce and his assistant had started building screens for the south Forest View porch. Lou checked on their progress regularly. He didn't think it fast enough. "I wish I could see a little bit. I'd make those screens for them." The porch opened off the Forest View living room. Lou went in there to check once again on the project. Looking through the glass door, he could make out the shapes of Bruce and his assistant. They were working on their hands and knees, it seemed. No wonder they were taking so long, Lou thought. He knew from long experience that you save a lot of time and do a better job if you spend a little time to set up a job properly. Lou tapped on the glass.

Bruce opened the door. "Hi, Lou."

"Why don't you get a couple tables and work off them?" said Lou.

Bruce laughed. "Too easy."

Lou walked away shaking his head. "*Meshugge.*" Later Lou told Joe he figured that they'd finish up the screens just in time for winter.

Meanwhile, one of the elevators had broken down again. Lou saw the familiar shape of one of the housekeepers getting into the one still-functioning elevator and said, "Take a lunchbox with ya." Lou knew what was wrong and he knew the cause. "It needs a new motor now. I said at the beginning — and I wasn't just talking through my hat, because I had experience — that they needed maintenance. And I don't think Bruce understands these elevators. I don't think he called for maintenance until it broke down."

After the elevator broke, Lou made a special trip downstairs to the administrator's office. He reported back to Joe: "I says, 'Something should be done about that.' I says, 'First of all, God forbid someone gets stuck inside and has a heart attack.' She said, 'Don't even mention it! If someone gets stuck, we'll call on Bruce or Mike.'" Lou replied, "But they might not be here when it happens!" Lou told her that there should be a key that would unlock the elevator in case of emergency, and the administrator promised Lou she'd find out where that key was kept and make sure all the nursing supervisors also knew where it was. A few days later, Lou went out again, looking for nursing supervisors. "I want to follow up on this key business. I've been told they know where it is. I'm not gonna let it ride until I know for sure." He visited every unit and questioned the charge nurses. They all knew where the key was, and Lou was satisfied.

Lou allowed that the kitchen was making progress. They put the beef stew in a bowl now, for instance. "Progress," he said. "But it's awful slow. I'll be an old man before it's all straightened out."

On the "Today's Events" bulletin board downstairs, a new message read, "Let's Take One Day at a Time. Have a Great Day Everyone." But it wasn't easy to distinguish one day from another here, or even this year from the last. Lou and Joe's days ran along mainly as they had last year, with small variations.

On the elevator back from breakfast, Lou took the controls. Pleasant, confused Clara came along. "Call out your floors, please," said Lou. It was one of his old elevator jokes, but Clara had slipped some.

"Second," she said. "I'm not sure."

Lou was quick to save her. "You're not sure? If you're not sure, we can't let you out."

Clara laughed.

M&M's was more crowded than previously, but the routines were the same. On non-M&M's mornings before Ruth arrived, Joe had taken to watching on TV the real-life courtroom arguments presided over by Judge Wapner. Joe liked to argue with the disputants and sometimes with the judge himself.

He was watching, and Lou was listening, to an especially good show one fall morning when a new aide — there seemed to be quite a few new aides lately — came to the door and called in, "Did either of you have a bowel movement today?"

Joe turned from the TV. "No. Hey, wait a minute!" Joe glanced at the puzzled-looking aide. He looked at the TV. "Oh, all right. Yes. And so did he." Joe gestured toward Lou. He waved at the aide as if throwing something at her, and turned back to the show. He and Lou would break her in later.

Lou's wristwatch stopped keeping proper time. He tried wearing it upside down, and for a while it worked better. Then it functioned only after dark. "It's gotten to the point where it only wants to work nights," Lou said. Then the watch seemed to work only when Lou placed it on his bedside table. Lou told Joe he had a plan. He'd get a leash and tie it to his table and drag his watch around that way. Finally Lou gave up on his watch. He wouldn't go to the expense of buying a new one. "There's no place that I'm goin' that's that important that I have to have the time," he said. When he wanted to know the time, he asked Joe. Joe had to count up both to the hour and the minute, and sometimes got balled up.

"That's all right," Lou would say. "I'm in no hurry."

Lou still went faithfully to all meetings, and Joe never did,

but he might have now begun working his way toward atten-
dance. At the September Food Committee meeting Joe got as
far as the doorway to the activity room. He stood there, leaning
on his cane, listening in. Elgie spotted him and said in her
high, cheery voice, "Come on in!"

"Come on in!" Winifred called.

"No," Joe said. "I'm just looking."

One evening, Joe hung up his phone just as Lou was coming
from the bathroom. "Well, if it makes you feel any better, I told
her I loved her," Joe said grumpily.

When Joe was out, Lou shook his head and recited the
catalogue of things in Joe that still did not add up: Joe's continuing weight-loss program, now minus the bike; Joe's pessimistic, superstitious utterances; Joe's movies; Joe's interroga-
tions of the staff. On the other hand, Lou thought Joe was
swearing less, in spite of the Red Sox.

"With all his faults, I like Joe," Lou said. "I think I pretty
much know how to handle him. When to say yes and when to
say no. When to kibitz and when not." But Lou didn't always
know. One autumn morning, as they were heading out of the
room together, Lou said, "Joe, close the door."

And Joe exploded. "Jesus Christ! You say that every goddamn time!"

Lou's head rocked back a little in surprise. "I just say that as
a joke."

"Well, you say it every goddamn time, that's all."

Lou smiled and headed on toward the elevators.

Then they agreed, tacitly, to make the business of closing the
door into a joke. Joe began to move more quickly when it was
time to leave the room for meals or M&M's or the lobby. He

often managed to precede Lou out of the room. "Don't forget to close the door," Joe called back to Lou.

"What'd you say, Joe?" Lou cupped a hand to his ear.

"Don't forget to close the door."

"I can't hear ya, Joe." Lou pulled the door shut.

When Joe seemed to be getting riled up in an argument, Lou still silenced him by saying, "Behave yourself. I'm old enough to be your father." And Joe laughed and said, "I *know* it." Speaking of Lou, Joe said, "I got three degrees, but I don't know as much as he does."

Lou reminisced again about the time, back when he was in his mid-fifties, when the company he'd worked for in Burlington, New Jersey, had gone out of business and he'd had to look for a new job. "I spent a few months searching for work. They kept saying no, even though I knew darn well I was qualified," Lou said.

"Because your hair was white," Joe said, finishing Lou's story for him.

"Burlington," said Joe later on that day while out for a walk around Forest View. "Every day Lou mentions Burlington. I don't mind. Good God." It was a sentiment that Joe repeated nearly as often as Lou repeated stories. "You know," Joe went on, "I get along better with Lou than I ever did with anyone in my life. He never fought with his wife. I said, 'For Christ's sake, that's impossible!' He's amazing. He likes all his grandchildren. He likes all his great-grandchildren . . ."

On a day early in fall, both men bound for lunch, Joe again preceded Lou out of the room. Joe reached up and touched the *mezuzah*. He'd been doing this fairly regularly for nearly two years now, imitating Lou, saying out of Lou's earshot, "Why take chances? You never know who's right, you know."

Following Joe out, Lou said to him, "You're still touching the mezuzah. In fact, you knocked it off the wall the other day."

Joe stopped and turned to face Lou. "I didn't know you knew I touched it."

"Can't hoit," said Lou, putting on a Brooklyn accent. "I touch it, too."

"I didn't know you knew I touched it," said Joe. He blushed.

As September wore on, the Red Sox again climbed back into contention. Joe cheered them on from his bed while Lou lay in his, rooting silently, saying to himself, "I wish they'd get a hit." The Sox might have played better in the last days of the season if they'd known how ardently Joe, in his nursing home bed, yearned for their success. He mourned the season decorously. Down in the lobby, he said to Art, "You and I should be sad. The Red Sox lost."

"Boo-hoo," Art said. "Did you have a bundle on them?"

"No."

"That'd be a reason to be sad," Art said.

"They haven't won the, uh, World Series, since you were twelve," said Joe. "They won the year I was born." He laughed a short laugh. "Well, wait until next year, that's all."

From their window upstairs the maples in the woods looked unreal, bright green and red. They were colors of insanity and exaltation. Paper maple leaves, more sedately colored than the real things, adorned the activity room's windows, as in elementary schools elsewhere.

Lou asked Joe if he saw any change in the colors in the woods. Joe said yes, he certainly did. So it was time, Lou thought, to go to the graveyard, before the weather turned cold. He figured this would be his last trip there until next spring.

"This morning I pulled the drape around six o'clock, and the sky was the most beauty-ful rose color," Lou said as he prepared to leave the room. Lou put on a cardigan sweater, got his striped cane with its handle of "gen-u-ine plastic" from his wife's walker, and groped around inside his closet for his blue windbreaker. He made sure, of course, to pull the door fully closed. Joe was elsewhere.

Lou signed out at the nurses' station. Every resident who was, in the local idiom, "going out on pass," had to sign out. Then it was down to the lobby, a memorized passage strewn with the same memorized dangers — the Hoyer Lift outside Winifred's door, the copying machine in the front hall. Lou was a little preoccupied this morning, with two issues. First, the ointment he used for his hemmorhoids. Medicaid wouldn't pay for the brand he used to use. "So they got a different one. Okay. It did the job. It ran out this week. I got a new one. It was supposed to be in my drawer. I searched high and low. Then I found a package, a fancy package. I haven't opened it yet. You need an engineering degree to open it. It's an engineered package. Now, what I want to know, why did they substitute a more expensive package for a less expensive tube?"

Lou sat down near the lobby door to await Ruth. The second issue on his mind was a story he'd heard on the news. "About a nursing home in Indiana where cleaning agents were mixed together wrong and produced hydrochloric acid, which got into their ventilation system. I wonder if they clean the filters as often as necessary on their air conditioning here. I asked Bruce, but he didn't really give me an answer."

The question took Lou back to the day the pen factory in Burlington burned, to one of his fights with his cruel boss Whitehouse, to the many old records of his days in fountain pen manufacturing. He'd thrown those records away. "I keep thinking about a lot of things I should have done. I should've kept all those recipes and formulas and the pen sizes. After a while I got tired of looking at them. I don't know what I'd do with them now. But I could look back at them," he said.

Then Ruth arrived. "Put your jacket on, Dad, because it'll be chilly."

She held his left hand, and Lou used his cane as an antenna, walking very slowly down the sloping concrete apron to the car. Out in California, back when Lou was in his late eighties, he'd been helping Jennie, as Ruth was now helping him, out of a doctor's office and down a sloping concrete apron just like this one. Jennie had lost her balance, and Lou couldn't hold her up. He managed to get his hand around her head so that, falling with her, he kept it from hitting the pavement. The memory was fresh. It might have happened just the other day.

Ruth guided Lou to the passenger seat. He placed his cane snugly in the angle between the open door and the car frame while he climbed in. Not that he thought Ruth would close the door on his hand or leg, but accidents happen. When Lou was all settled, he removed the cane.

"So anyway, Fleur was on a rampage yesterday," Lou said as Ruth turned the car onto Route 9.

"Again?" Ruth said.

"Yeah, she got hold of Norman and tried to choke him," Lou said. "And Linda Manor now has a cat for a mascot. Joe said,

'Why do we need a cat?' And I said, 'It'll save money. We can use it for CAT scans.' "

Ruth smiled. She told Lou she had a new friend who wanted to come to the nursing home and meet him.

"Did you check my schedule?" Lou asked.

"Not yet."

"I'll cancel my tennis date," Lou said. He squinted his eyes. Lou looked very small in the passenger seat. He also looked fully composed. "Penney's is having a sale on shoes," he said after a while. "What's Sugar Babies?"

"Ya got me, kid."

"Well, the sale's over."

"Thanks a lot for telling me," Ruth said.

"Well, anyway," Lou said. "Dave is in today. He came over to say hello, and I said, 'What day is this?' 'Sunday,' he said. 'Can't be,' I said. 'Why?' 'Because you're here,' I told him."

"Oh, that's mean. He was in yesterday."

"He *had* to be," Lou said. "There was no one else to do the work." Lou still periodically gave Dave what Lou called "ear jobs." The other day he heard Dave's voice in the lobby, and he called to him, "Hey, Dave. Goin' out to get something good to eat?" And another time: "Seriously, Dave, you know what I'd like to know? What do you do with the flavor you take out of the chicken?" Lou hadn't even considered apologizing to Dave before the Day of Atonement. Dave was still Lou's weakness.

The small city of Northampton has two Jewish cemeteries, situated side by side on the outskirts of town. The area's earliest Jewish settlers established the first one. They came from Germany, became fairly prominent, and were embarrassed by the Eastern European Jews who arrived later. Hence the two graveyards. The gate to the first was locked. It contained only a smattering of headstones. Ruth parked the car beside the gate to the second, newer one, which was much fuller. For a time on his visits here, Lou used to walk in from the gate, but the ground is uneven and Jennie's grave is at the far end of the lot. So Ruth opened the gate and drove in, down a corridor between headstones. Ruth helped Lou out of the car.

Tall oaks surround the cemetery. It is a pretty spot, but it was noisy at this hour. A superhighway passes nearby, running north toward Vermont and Canada. The sound of cars mingled with birdsong. Acorn shells crunched under their shoes as Ruth, holding fast to her father's arm, led him toward a block of polished brown granite. "It's a little bumpy," Ruth said to Lou. He didn't speak. He had not spoken since climbing out of the car. There was a Star of David at the top of the stone's bright face, and under it the inscription FREED. In a column running down the left-hand side of the stone were these words:

JENNIE
BELOVED WIFE
MOTHER
GRANDMOTHER
GREAT-GRANDMOTHER
JAN. 9, 1898
MAR. 8, 1990

The right-hand side was blank.

Ruth looked uncharacteristically solemn now, and one could see her father's face in hers. She stared at him. She looked a little tense. Lou shifted his cane to his left hand. He placed his right hand on the rough top edge of the headstone, leaning on it, and looked toward the ground, at nothing it seemed, a slight frown turning down the corners of his mustache, deepening the lines that framed his chin. They didn't speak or move at all from their positions for several long minutes. Then Lou shifted his cane to his right hand and turned toward the car. Ruth took his hand, squeezing it, and they walked slowly back, acorn shells crunching under their feet.

They drove out of the graveyard in silence. Ruth had to close the gate, so she parked on the other side of the street, beside a mailbox, the shape of which Lou could evidently make out, because when Ruth got back in the car, he said to her, "Want me to check the mail?"

These were the first words he'd spoken since they'd arrived. Ruth laughed. Lou smiled. The car ride back to Linda Manor reminded Lou, as car rides often did, of that one time in his life when he'd sat behind the wheel of an automobile and nearly crashed it into the prison gate back in Philadelphia — of that time when, as Lou would say, he didn't learn to drive. "It almost ruined my life," said Ruth, glancing over at Lou in the passenger seat. "To have a father who didn't drive and who almost banged into the gates of —"

"Eastern Penitentiary," Lou said.

"That's another reason I don't run for public office," Ruth said.

That evening, after Ruth had left, Lou went outside to take the air. He went no farther than the aluminum-clad Doric column to the left of the front door. He held his cane in his right hand, its tip planted on the concrete. He leaned his back against the column. "Holding up the building," he said.

Lou's mind was back at the cemetery. "The reason I go there,

I just feel that she woulda wanted me to do that. I just can't help feeling that there is a hereafter," Lou was saying, when the front door flew open.

Bob stood in the doorway. His wings of gray hair seemed swept back by fury. His mouth was working, as if he meant to chew his mustache. Holding the door open with his body, Bob jabbed his cane in Lou's direction. "Can't see! Can't see!" Bob shook all over.

Lou began to chuckle. He recognized the voice, and understood the problem. He'd been standing in Bob's view of the parking lot.

"Can't see!"

Lou chuckled again. Slowly, feeling his way with his cane, Lou walked to the column on the opposite side of the front door.

"Beautiful! Excellent! Thank you kindly."

The front door closed.

Lou leaned his back against the column. From the south came a whacking sound. "That's a helicopter," he said. He smiled. The day had warmed up. The evening autumn breeze ruffled Lou's white hair.

"In the Rosh Hashanah prayers, the way I remember, it's predicted who shall live and who shall die, who shall pass away peacefully and who shall — well, I forget the words. But it goes on that penitence, hope, and charity can avert a severe decree." All that, to Lou, implied an afterlife. "I can't conceive of anything like this." He raised his cane and swept it in an arc before him, as if from a promontory and toward a vast landscape. The gesture took in the parking lots, just a gray expanse to Lou, like all the world that lay beyond about five feet. "The universe or whatever. I can't conceive of it being in existence without at some point something being there to create it. There had to be some supreme being. That's just my theory. As a kid I could never fathom that the universe was so big."

When Lou talked about death, he still expressed some trepidation about the event itself but none about its consequences. There was, after all, a chance that death might mean a reunion with Jennie. One could always hope. In the meantime, he didn't usually mind the waiting. This life still had some things for him to do and to discover.

Lou sighed, and smiled again. "What's that song? Don't step on that ant, it might be your grandmother." He chuckled, squinting his eyes tight, and said, his voice serious again, "It's a mystery."

II

The first snow fell the second week of November. Joe went to the window. "It's snowing, Lou. Can you see it?"

"Honestly, no."

Later that week, half a dozen residents trooped into the activity room to meet some new friends, a group of children from a local junior high. Ruth had made the arrangements, and the teachers had prepared the children.

In her room, Winifred was being made ready for lifting. She said she did not mourn the passing of autumn. "So many people have a misconception about winter. They think everything is dead and so forlorn. But it's not. It's just resting." She was out and around in her wheelchair less often recently. "To get jostled and pinched and turned and bent in places that don't bend anymore just isn't worth it." But she would have undergone worse torments than the Hoyer Lift for the sake of a get-together. And so today again, Winifred submitted as the aides trussed her up in the sling. One aide attached the buckles to the gallows-like device and turned the crank, a ratchety sound. And Winifred ascended, like an engine block being hoisted for repair. The aides rolled the contraption toward her wheelchair. Furled in the Hoyer sling, swaying gently in the air, the dangling Winifred rolled on toward another day.

Most of the residents arrived early to the activity room for Ruth's party. Excessive punctuality, it is sometimes imagined, comes naturally with age, like white hair and bifocals. But usually residents had nothing better to do. Ruth directed traffic. "Hi, Arthur!"

"*Bonjour, mes amis,*" said Art, wading into the room and taking a seat at a table.

"Dad," Ruth said to Lou, "why don't you sit down here."

Joe limped in. He said to Art, "I was looking for the right chair."

"I thought you were looking me over," Art said.

Joe began to sing, "Hey, look me over . . ."

Art tapped out the rhythm with his cane on the floor.

Winifred, now positioned in her wheelchair at a table nearby, was saying to another resident, "I'm not sure what these kids will want to know about."

"Did she say she didn't know if she'd have enough to say to the kids?" Art said to Joe. "That'd be the first time she was ever in that predicament."

In came Dora on her walker, small and wide and beaming.

341

"Dora, how *are* ya?" Joe said from his chair.

"I couldn't be better," Dora said.

"Doctor been in to see you?" Joe asked.

"Hasn't been in this month," Dora said.

"Get your sleep?" Joe asked.

"*Every* night. I sleep good." Dora was ready to go on, but just then the children arrived, a shy-looking group, all wearing name tags. Ruth took over. "Okay, Kathy, come here. This is your friend Hazel. Okay, Kim, this is your friend Elgie. Eileen, this is your friend Winifred."

Joe offered his left hand to the boy assigned to him, saying, "I can't shake hands with the other hand."

Lou's boy wasn't shy. He sat down on the edge of his chair next to Lou and said, "You mind if I ask you a few questions? If they're too personal, just tell me."

Lou smiled.

"It was rough!" Joe was saying, the next table over. "Sure. A Navy ship in the South Pacific."

"How young are you?" asked Lou's new friend. The boy had black hair. He'd have to start shaving soon.

"Ninety-two," Lou said.

"To me, old is dead," said the boy.

Lou smiled.

"Do you play cards?"

"When I could see."

"Do you like animals?"

"Dogs," said Lou. "I don't like cats."

"Do you collect anything?"

"Woodworking tools," Lou replied.

He scarcely had time to answer one question before the boy asked another. He had a list of questions. "Did you have any childhood heroes? Did you use any slang when you were a kid? Strange words to your parents and not for you? Like 'cool' or 'awesome'?"

Lou smiled on. Winifred had spread old photographs across her table. Joe was asking his boy more questions than the boy was asking him. All around the room, in every little huddle, the residents were smiling. They were bathing in the kinds of looks that children give. Not that children don't judge adults, but they do it differently. They don't judge the pretty and the ugly, only the mean and the gentle. These children hadn't really needed coaching. Sitting a foot away from a ninety-two-year-old clearly didn't make Lou's new friend uncomfortable.

He had put away his list of prepared questions. "Any questions for me?" he asked.

Lou started to speak. His voice broke, then reassembled. For a moment he'd seemed on the verge of tears. "Stay away from —"

"Drugs?" said the boy.

"Yeah," Lou said. Then he smiled again. "And stay away from wild women." To tout the virtues of not smoking, Lou bared his teeth. "They're my own."

The boy leaned forward and peered into Lou's mouth. "Oh, cool."

"Do you have any brothers?" he asked Lou.

"I have two brothers." Lou didn't say that only one was living.

"Who's the boss, them or you?" asked the boy.

Lou was smiling, the kind of smile that seems to want to become more. "I was the oldest of seven," Lou said.

"Do you like art? What kind?"

"No special kind."

Behind Lou, Joe was giving his young friend some boxing instructions, demonstrating left-handed the proper way to jab. "So, uh, you box with sixteen-ounce gloves?" Joe was saying.

"So you don't like horror books?" Lou's friend said.

Lou bent close to him. "No."

"That's good. Because I don't either."

Joe was talking about Joe Louis now.

"I was just wondering what kind of toys did you used to have," said the boy assigned to Lou.

"I didn't have toys."

"No time, huh. Always working."

"One thing I always wanted was a kite," Lou said. "I made one, but I couldn't make it work."

"Oh, yeah, I have that trouble," said the boy.

"I sold newspapers when I was ten," Lou said.

"I do yard work," said the boy.

"Well, in my city, we didn't have any yards."

"Where'd you grow up?"

"Philadelphia. The city of brotherly love, they call it." Lou told him about his schooling.

"I'm gonna be goin' to Smith School to be a cook," said the boy. "Is there anything else you want to know about me?"

"I'm trying to think." Lou told him about the time when his mother brought him home by the ear from "the hotties," the warm spot in the Delaware River where boys used to swim. "I remember, vaguely, they used to have horse-drawn trolleys," Lou went on.

"Oh, that must've been cool. I like old pictures. If I go to college, I'll major in cooking, electronics, or . . ."

"Better make up your mind," Lou said. "Learn to cook."

Then the boy looked furtively around the room and leaned a little closer to Lou. "Are you guys allowed to drink what you want?"

Lou cupped his ear. His hearing had faded some in the past year, and the boy had asked the question in a low voice.

"Do you like soda?" the boy asked.

"No." Lou shook his head.

The boy looked around again, leaned toward Lou, and said, "If you wanted, I could probably sneak something in for you."

Lou beamed. He patted the boy's arm. "No, that's all right. We get everything we need here."

Everyone agreed. The visit was a great success. They'd do it again soon. Lou left smiling. He was in such a good mood he decided to visit Dan.

12

The trouble with visitors is that they have to be thanked for coming, and forgiven for going away. They are always welcome, but their usefulness is circumscribed.

The central problem of life at Linda Manor is, after all, only the universal problem of separateness: the original punishment, the ultimate vulnerability, the enemy of meaning. Lou keeps an old appointment calendar in which are recorded the birthdays and anniversaries of all his relatives. He keeps it so he won't forget to offer congratulations, over the phone, at the proper times. All of Lou's solutions come in such simple clothes. At another time, in another place, Joe might not have understood. But he has lived in a little room with Lou for going on two years, and he understands now. Joe points toward the chair by the window and says, "There are no smart guys. The only smart guy *I* know sits over there."

Late on a frigid November afternoon, Joe's friend Ray, tall and thin and fit looking, arrives for a visit. After some small talk, Lou excuses himself, to give Joe and Ray privacy. Lou is expecting company, too. He's gotten word that a friend is in town and plans to stop by this afternoon, a man who had recently spent a couple of months convalescing at Linda Manor. He and Lou used to speak Yiddish together. Since then, Lou's friend has moved to California. Lou heads down to the lobby to wait for him.

Lou hears voices around him. There are a lot of visitors today. Feeling his way with his cane, he skirts the piano and sits down on the sofa by the front door. He crosses his legs, leans his cane against them, and waits.

In a few minutes he sees the movement and brightening that mean the front door is opening. Shapes appear, and from them come voices. He recognizes the voice of his friend. Lou smiles, the smile drawing intricate connections among the furrows of his face.

Age, it seems, tends to cull evenly among groups of friends, so that very few groups survive intact. This fellow lived in the area for years, but most of his old crowd have died. Coming back with his daughter to take care of some business, he felt impelled to make contact with the people he'd met in his time at Linda Manor. His walker rattles. Lou moves aside. His friend parks his walker and sits next to him. In the window behind them, a pale sun hangs just below the state flag.

"I've been looking forward to your visit," says Lou, his voice gravelly yet smooth, like pebbles in a river. "I got advance notice."

"How's your friend? Joe."

"Fine," Lou says. "He just had someone visit from his hometown. So what have you been doing with yourself?"

"Living in California off the fat of the land. Does your daughter still come every day?"

"Yeah." Lou mentions the kids from the junior high. "One wanted to know if he could sneak in any soda for me." Lou's smile makes webs of his face's wrinkles again, as intricate as memory. He musters his news. "My sister was up here a few weeks ago, and my son was here. And Thursday we're all going up to my daughter's. The *mishpocheh*." Lou lists all the members of his family who are coming. And then he runs out of news. There's a long pause.

"So."

"So what's happening with your house down here?" Lou asks. "Selling it?"

No. He hasn't tried to sell it yet.

"I guess I'm gonna stay put here," Lou says.

Has Lou considered moving to one of the local retirement homes?

"I don't want a change. I know most of the people here, and Ruthie comes down most every day." Then Lou laughs. "And I know my way around! I follow the white line in the carpet."

"So what else is new? What's the color of the scrambled eggs today?"

Lou looks away. "I never ate eggs for breakfast."

Again, they fall silent. It's that time of winter afternoon when the world pauses, and they pause with it, two old men in reunion on a sofa, in slanted light. From across the lobby come other voices. And then Martha appears, carrying her pocketbook, dressed in her winter coat. She laughs merrily. "Well, folksies, goodbye." She goes out, heading home again, and in about a minute returns. "It *is* cold," she says.

The lobby is quite full. Voices from the separate conversations blend into an intermission-like buzz around Lou, in the midst of which Joe's voice can now be heard. Joe limps into the lobby, the much taller Ray, dressed in his overcoat, walking slowly beside him. The little group of men coalesces near the front door, but Ray's overcoat marks him as not really one of them, and in a moment the group begins disbanding. Ray has to be going.

"Okay, I'll see ya," Joe says.

The door closes and Joe sits down in the festive lobby. Visitors do leaven life's routines. They bring news of other worlds — the family news, the meteorological news, the hometown news. It is always nice to have visitors, especially when winter is closing in around the building and it feels more than ever like an outpost.

But it is getting late. Those stirrings begin, and sighs, and the long, drawn-out "Well," which everywhere signify the beginning of a day's partings. Well, Joe says finally, it's time to go upstairs and get some pills.

Joe shakes hands with Lou's friend. "I'll see ya." Joe turns and limps past the potted plant and around the piano, which catches his reflection and overstates his roundness. He heads slowly toward the wide doorway, back toward the inside of Linda Manor.

Lou's friend will be leaving soon. He isn't a part of this place anymore. Lou probably won't see him again. But his ninety-two years afford a lot of experience with partings. Lou gets up. "Well, *zei gezunt, fohr gezunt.*" This is Yiddish for "Be well, travel well." Lou extends his hand. He's glad that he still has the strength to deliver a firm handshake. He clasps his friend's hand and holds it for an extra moment.

Then Lou starts after Joe, in his well-braced walking stance, a sturdy old sailor at sea in a storm.

Joe looks back over his shoulder. "Come on, Lu-Lu," Joe calls.

ACKNOWLEDGMENTS

Seth Goldsmith of the University of Massachusetts found Linda Manor for me and helped immeasurably throughout, lending me counsel as well as many books and articles. Ann Hallock performed a variety of difficult tasks ingeniously and thoroughly. Elizabeth Coughlan helped to organize my notes. My thanks to Larry Cooper, the estimable manuscript editor. I got help and comfort from all of the following: Jerry Avorn, Robert Bagg, Madeleine Blais, Georges Borchardt, William Cooley, Blanche Cooney, Stuart Dybek, Ed Etheredge, Elise Feeley, Warren Fisher, Sandy Goroff-Mailly, Jonathan Harr, Joe Kanon, John Katzenbach, Jamie Kilbreth, Cindy Klein, Mark Kramer, John O'Brien, Barnaby Porter, Susan Porter, Tim Rivinus, Mike Rosenthal, Allison Ryan, Norman Spencer, John Sterling — and also from Alice, Fran, and Nat. I wish to thank the *Berkshire Eagle* for allowing me the freedom of their files, and the Cooley Dickinson Hospital for allowing me to observe a cataract operation. I also wish to thank the many people who submitted to interviews. I am grateful to all of the staff and management of Linda Manor, to relatives and friends of residents, and, above all, to those dozens of residents with whom I spent a year indoors. I am greatly indebted, once again, to Richard Todd.

I cite only two published works in the text: Thomas R. Cole, *The Journey of Life: A Cultural History of Aging in America*, Cambridge University Press, Cambridge, 1992; and Eleanor L. Niedeck, *W. B. and the Big Black Trunk*, printing by Boonville Graphics, Inc., Boonville, New York, 1980.